WINSTON CHURCHILL AND THE
DARDANELLES

TRUMBULL HIGGINS

Winston Churchill and the
Dardanelles

HEINEMANN : LONDON

William Heinemann Ltd

LONDON MELBOURNE TORONTO

CAPE TOWN AUCKLAND

Printed in Great Britain by

WESTERN PRINTING SERVICES LTD, BRISTOL

Acknowledgments

THE AUTHOR wishes to thank the following for permission to quote passages contained in this book:

The Executors of Admiral Sir Reginald Bacon and Hodder & Stoughton Ltd for material quoted from Admiral Bacon's *Life of Lord Fisher of Kilverstone*. Owners of the Copyright, Charles Scribner's Sons, and Cassell and Company for material quoted from Sir Charles Callwell's *The Life and Diaries of Sir Henry Wilson*. Rear-Admiral W. S. Chalmers and Hodder & Stoughton Ltd for material quoted from Admiral Chalmers' *Life of Lord Beatty*. Faber and Faber Ltd to quote from Sir F. Maurice's *Life of Lord Haldane of Cloan*. The Army Quarterly for quotation from "Policy and Strategy" by General Sir W. Robertson, in the October 1921 issue. Wm. Collins Sons & Co. Ltd for quotation from Arthur Bryant's *Biography of Lord Alanbrooke*. Cassell and Company Ltd for passages from Admiral Bacon's *Life of Earl Jellicoe*. Macmillan & Company Ltd to quote from Sir George Arthur's *The Life of Lord Kitchener*; and from Antony Brett-James's *Wellington at War*. Hodder & Stoughton Ltd for passages from Admiral Fisher's *Memories*.

For quotes from Winston S. Churchill's *World Crisis*, Volume II, we would like to thank Odhams Press Ltd. Edward Arnold Ltd for passages from General Sir Ian Hamilton's *Gallipoli Diary*. Longmans, Green & Company Ltd for quotations from P. Mackesy's *War in the Mediterranean*. Hutchinson & Company Ltd and Curtis Brown Ltd for material quoted from Sir John Kennedy's *The Business of War*. William Heinemann Ltd for quotations from *The Memoirs of General Lord Ismay* Copyright © 1960. John Murray for material quoted from Sir Philip Magnus' *Kitchener: Portrait of an Imperialist*. Curtis Brown Ltd for quotations from Admiral Wester-Wemyss' *The Navy in the Dardanelles Campaign*. Columbia University Press for passages from C. Herold's *The Mind of Napoleon*. Lord Esher, G.B.E., for the quotations from his father's book, *The Journals and Letters of Reginald Viscount Esher*. Alfred A. Knopf, Inc. for reprints from Arthur Marder's *Anatomy of British*

Sea Power, Copyright 1940 by Alfred A. Knopf, Inc. David McKay Company, Inc. for permission to reprint from *Time Unguarded,* by Sir Edmund Ironside, originally published under the title *The Ironside Diaries. The Economist* of London for permission to quote from their Book Review on Suez. Constable & Company Ltd for quotations from Sir Harold Nicolson's *Curzon, The Last Phase.* The Oxford University Press, for quotations from Arthur J. Marder's *From the Dreadnought to Scapa Flow,* Volume I. Martin Secker & Warburg Ltd for material quoted from W. S. Blunt's *My Diaries.* Ivor Nicholson & Watson Ltd for quotations from Lord Riddell's *War Diary.* Constable and Company Ltd for quotations from Sir Charles Callwell's *Experiences of a Dug-Out.* George Allen & Unwin Ltd to quote from Lord Hankey's *The Supreme Command.* Controller of Her Britannic Majesty's Stationery Office to quote from General Aspinall-Oglander's *Military Operations: Gallipoli.* Jonathan Cape Ltd to quote from Arthur Marder's *Portrait of an Admiral;* and Mr Marder's *Fear God and Dread Nought.* Cassell and Company Ltd to quote from Sir William Robertson's *Soldiers and Statesman;* and Lord Asquith's *Memories and Reflections.* The Earl of Balfour and The Beaverbrook Foundations for permission to quote Lord Balfour's words from David Lloyd George's *War Memoirs.*

IN MEMORY OF
LORD RIDDELL

Preface

Why, my dear Hankey, do we worry about history? Julian Corbett writes one of the best books[1] in our language upon political and military strategy. All sorts of lessons, some of inestimable value, may be gleaned from it. No one, except perhaps Winston, who matters just now, has ever read it. . . . Obviously history is written for schoolmasters and arm-chair strategists. Statesmen and warriors pick their way through the dusk.[2]

LORD ESHER, MARCH 15, 1915

In case of unlimited war your main strategical offensive must be directed against the armed forces of the enemy; in case of a limited war, even where its object was positive, it need not be.[3]

JULIAN CORBETT IN 1911

Man is a mad creature who is afraid of his madness. He does not embark upon adventures, even the most extravagant ones, unless he believes them to be reasonable, and he succeeds in making them appear so, not by the light of experience and reason, but by superimposing delusions and visions upon the reality and so covering everything . . . with a reassuring and fascinating mask.[4]

GUGLIELMO FERRERO

He is an artist, and will provide what is suitable for his audience.[5]

DAVID LLOYD GEORGE
ON WINSTON CHURCHILL, IN 1913

I T is both astonishing and significant that the famous Dardanelles-Gallipoli expedition of 1915 has not yet really been considered from, presumably, its most important facet, that is, as a failure in the higher direction of war in Great Britain. Until recently the source material for such an account was inadequate, but the gradual relaxation of the restrictions on the papers of the

Committee of Imperial Defence, especially those of Herbert Asquith, Lloyd George and Bonar Law, supplemented by the memoirs of Lord Hankey and the studies of Franklyn Johnson, have made new insight possible in this essential domain. The fundamental research on the Royal Navy by Arthur Marder, likewise, has been of the utmost value for understanding the positions of Admiral Fisher and of the Admiralty War Staff in this great campaign.

A series of brilliant apologists, notably Sir Winston Churchill and General Sir Ian Hamilton, have loaded the odds on the side of one interpretation of this campaign, an imbalance in no way redressed by the official British historians, Brigadier-General C. F. Aspinall-Oglander and Sir Julian Corbett. It is a small reflection upon such distinguished military historians to point out that they, too, were involved in the planning for the expedition which they describe and defend with such skill. C. E. W. Bean, the official Australian historian of the campaign, represents a somewhat different outlook. An Easterner in strategic sentiments, nevertheless, he did not think much of Churchill's contribution to the expedition, although like most early critics he tended to overestimate the role of the First Lord of the Admiralty.

For this last reason the author has been particularly concerned with the influence of the Prime Minister, Herbert Asquith, of the Secretary of State for War, Lord Kitchener, of the Chancellor of the Exchequer, David Lloyd George, and to a lesser extent with Bonar Law and Colonel Hankey, as well as the constant pressure upon events in the East of the main British Front in the West. To the military historian, campaigns which fail are far more illuminating than those which succeed, and the inherent conflict of policy with strategy, especially within a context of coalition and amphibious warfare, is still very much with us today.

In this connection the author can do no better than to quote another preface written by another student of war, Field Marshal Sir William Robertson. Wrote Sir William following the First World War: "Finally, I may remind the reader that the inner history of any war is seldom to be found complete in the official account of it. Parts of the story are, for one reason or another, not allowed to be published, and while the operations themselves are usually described at great, and sometimes wearisome, length, not much is said—especially in cases where failure occurs—about questions of high policy, upon the decision of which the operations ought to be founded. We are told what was done, but not always why it was done, or who was responsible for causing it to be done."[6]

The author wishes to express his indebtedness for assistance to the Admiralty, the Bodleian and the Bonar Law-Bennett Libraries, the British Museum, the Imperial Defence College, the Imperial War Museum, the United Service Institution, and the War Office Libraries, as well as to the Cabinet Office and the Public Record Office. The aid of many officers, critics, and members of the faculty at Oxford University has also been of great value. The devotion to scholarship manifested by the opening of the papers held by Lord Beaverbrook and Mr Mark Bonham Carter must be especially acknowledged.

T.H.

LONDON, JUNE 1, 1963

Contents

CONTENTS

I

The Kingfisher

(to 1910)

*You are naturally sarcastic about my Dardanelles, and I hope the matter
will not come up in our time. . . . I consider the loss of Constantinople would
be the ruin of our party and a heavy blow to the country.*[1]

LORD SALISBURY
TO LORD RANDOLPH CHURCHILL IN 1886

*Cease your preaching! Load your guns!
Their roar our mission tells,
The day is come for Britain's sons
To seize the Dardanelles.*[2]

MUSIC HALL HIT IN 1896

Anxiety, not a sense of security, lies at the root of readiness for war.[3]

LORD ESHER IN 1907

So Jacky [Fisher] *is growing roses, is he? Well, all I've got to say is that
those roses will damned well have to grow.*[4]

A FISHER COLLEAGUE IN 1912

IN the autumn of 1806, during the great struggle of the third
coalition against Napoleon, the Russian government appealed
to Great Britain to relieve Russian troops for use in Germany by
means of a British naval demonstration against the Turks. The
aggressive British Admiral, Sir Sidney Smith, who fancied himself something of an expert on matters Levantine, informed the
Cabinet in London that a "line of battleships alone [will] have
weight in the minds of the inhabitants of the Seraglio, and the

nearest will ever be obeyed", an opinion reinforced by that of the British Ambassador at the Porte.[5]

On November 22, 1806, the Admiralty ordered Nelson's successor in the Mediterranean, Lord Collingwood, "to detach a force to the Dardanelles, to be ready in case of necessity to act offensively against the Turks". Since, in the opinion of the Admiralty such a task would "require much ability and firmness in the officer who is to command it", Collingwood was ordered to entrust its execution to Vice-Admiral Sir John Duckworth.[6] Haste was essential for, aided by French engineers, the Turkish batteries would soon render the passage of the Dardanelles Straits impossible.

Bad weather, however, delayed the assembly of Duckworth's ships long enough to allow doubts to grow in the mind of the new commander regarding the chances of forcing the Straits. Duckworth, it now appeared, was no Sir Sidney Smith and he expressed his hesitations in language which would be heard again in the future of the Dardanelles. Wrote Duckworth: "For though I consider it the duty of an Admiral to fight, it is a much more essential and bounden part of his duty to have mind enough not chimerically to sacrifice the force entrusted to his charge."[7]

Unhappily for Duckworth, British prestige had become so publicly committed by British diplomacy to this questionable nautical enterprise that the reluctant Admiral was eventually impelled to take the plunge. With negligible losses, on February 19, 1807, Duckworth's squadron broke through the Straits and entered the Sea of Marmara. Contrary, however, to the anticipation of His Majesty's Ambassador at the Porte, instead of being seized with panic, the Turks in Constantinople redoubled their energies in building new batteries to protect their capital. A dispute between Admiral Duckworth and his more daring subordinate, Sir Sidney Smith, now broke out, with the result that after eleven days the British warships returned down the Dardanelles Straits, enduring, as Duckworth had feared, rather more casualties from the ever stronger Turkish batteries on their departure than on their entry. In the conclusion of a recent critic: "Only the poor practice of the

Turkish gunners [had] saved the squadron from extensive damage: another week might have made the Straits impassable."[8]

In the ensuing storm of criticism in Great Britain regarding this inconclusive and humiliating episode, the opinion was generally expressed that had Duckworth's squadron been accompanied by a sufficient body of troops with which to occupy the Gallipoli Peninsula and its persistent batteries, the Turks would have been overawed by the arrival of his ships-of-the-line before their very capital. But, in order to intimidate instead of being intimidated, Duckworth's ships had to be sustained by secure lines of communication through the Dardanelles. Certainly Admiral Duckworth himself came to this consoling opinion when asked why he had not renewed his naval assault. Within three weeks of his ignominious retreat he affirmed: "I must, as an officer, declare it to be my decided opinion that, without the co-operation of a body of land forces, it would be a wanton sacrifice of the squadrons . . . to attempt to force the passage."[9]

Again foreshadowing the future, a body of troops adequate to occupy the Dardanelles was available at that time in the Mediterranean, but in the judgment of one embittered general officer: "Instead of acting vigorously in either one or the other direction, our Cabinet comes to the miserable determination of sending 5 or 6 men-of-war, without soldiers, to the Dardanelles, and 5,000 soldiers, without a fleet, to Alexandria."[10] Apart from the inclination of most statesmen toward compromise, even within so unyielding a dominion as war, the Ministry of All the Talents had erred in another matter, one of more moment in conflict than in peace. This was in having ordered, or in condoning, the appointment of inferior commanders in the Mediterranean. Such commanders were to find themselves closely associated with diplomats and were to be confused by the association.[11]

On the level of policy Duckworth's failure was also unfortunate since, among other factors, a loss of faith in British support caused the Russians to sign the Peace of Tilsit with Napoleon. Nevertheless, as the official British Army historian of Gallipoli has sharply observed, the lesson, "for that time, was learned". Another expedition on the part of the Royal Navy to Copenhagen later in 1807 included some 27,000 troops. This conjunct, or combined, operation, was so completely successful in achieving its objectives that it established the basis thereafter for Wellington's classic exploitation of the more agreeable potentialities of peninsular warfare.[12]

Some seventy years later, during the Russo-Turkish war of 1877–8, the British Cabinet ordered another reluctant admiral to pass the Straits for the sake of aiding Turkey against Russia. Notwithstanding the fact that the Turks were now allied to Great Britain, Admiral Sir Geoffrey Hornby wrote to the Foreign Secretary, Lord Derby, that he would be unable to keep the Straits open for transports and colliers if the Russians occupied the Gallipoli Peninsula with mobile guns. Fortunately, Disraeli agreed with the considered conclusion of Lord Aberdeen's Government during the Crimean War that Gallipoli in British possession was an essential pre-condition for a British fleet movement through the Straits. But the next year Admiral Hornby again reminded the Admiralty that "not all the fleets in the world" could by themselves keep the Dardanelles open for unarmoured ships.[13]

Technological changes as well as a strengthening of the land defences of the Dardanelles with Krupp guns in the 1880s caused the Admiralty to doubt whether a combined assault itself on the Straits might be practical. A memorandum of June 10, 1890, from the First Lord of the Admiralty to Sir Anthony Hoskins, the British Naval Commander-in-Chief in the Mediterranean, warned that British naval supremacy in the Channel might be endangered by large-scale operations at the extreme end of the Levant. Hoskins' unyielding reply is worth citing in detail as an example of the shift in professional British naval opinion on the question of forcing the Dardanelles over the course of the nineteenth century. Hoskins wrote to the Admiralty:

If, as I presume is the case, the Turkish batteries and gunners are fairly efficient, such an attempt would in all probability end in disaster,

4

and even if by a rush past at night the squadron succeeded in reaching the Sea of Marmara without serious injury, its position will be hazardous in the extreme.

We cannot in these days expect to repeat the experiences of Sir John Duckworth in 1808 or even of Sir G. Phipps Hornby in 1878, and the loss of some of our ships would be for a time irremediable. The defences of the Dardanelles are now extremely strong, armed with modern heavy B.L. guns, and the nature of the Channel gives them every advantage against ships. They have generally availed themselves of these advantages and especially to establish high commanding batteries which our fire could not reach, and torpedo defences which must be a subject of grave consideration in such an operation. Modern battleships, strong as they are against each other, are less suited even than their predecessors to engage well-placed and well-armed forts successfully, for even one well-placed shell from a modern gun of heavy calibre would in all probability suffice to put a ship out of action.

If the operation is to be attempted under the conditions named, the advantage to be gained being considered to be worth the risk to be incurred, it should in my opinion be undertaken with the whole strength of the Mediterranean Fleet.[14]

In 1895, when in order to intimidate the Turkish Sultan a large British squadron was collected at the Aegean island of Lemnos off the mouth of the Dardanelles, the First Lord of the Admiralty explained to the Prime Minister, Lord Salisbury, that should the British push through the Straits a superior French fleet could easily trap them within its seductive portals. Salisbury thereupon lost his temper and declared that if British warships were made of porcelain he would, of course, pursue a different policy.[15]

During this crisis the Directors of Military and Naval Intelligence of the British Army and Navy drew up a good many plans for the seizure of the Gallipoli Peninsula. Regretting the inadequacy of Lemnos as a naval base, the D.M.I. and D.N.I. estimates of British troops required for such an operation varied between 1892 and 1896 from 10,000 to 25,000 men. Since this last figure was impossible to obtain without prolonged preparations in England, and thus without adequate warning for the Turks, to the

5

keen disappointment of Lord Salisbury the project was condemned as quite impracticable by officers of both the British Army and Navy who were consulted.[16]

In October 1896, at the request of Lord Salisbury, the War Office and Admiralty were again asked for appreciations on the Dardanelles. The Director of Naval Intelligence submitted a memorandum which stressed that the seizure of the Gallipoli Peninsula was not possible since the Royal Navy could no longer pass the Dardanelles and cover a landing by the Army. The development of mines and torpedoes, in addition to the lack of a proper naval base in the Aegean, were cited as causes for these developments.[17] A more serious criticism of Lord Salisbury's hopes appeared in a long memorandum of the Director of Military Intelligence. Dated October 13, 1896, a somewhat condensed version of this striking document reads as follows:

The popular idea of coercion was that the British Fleet should force the Dardanelles and dictate terms to the Sultan at Constantinople. This would be a risky enterprise. The Dardanelles batteries and defences were quite strong. And in what a dangerous position they would be: in front, the Bosphorus defences and the Black Sea Fleet; in the rear, the but half crippled works of the Dardanelles and the whole naval power of France. Even if France and Russia remained in an attitude of observation the fleet could do nothing to coerce the Sultan. It could not occupy Constantinople, and there was no desire to bombard it. No transports, store vessels, or colliers could pass the Dardanelles.

The next plan was to occupy the Gallipoli peninsula at the lines of Bulair, and take the batteries on the north bank of the Dardanelles in the rear. To effect this operation by surprise would require at least 10,000 troops; and to occupy the peninsula in face of energetic opposition would need an Army Corps. Even the former number could not, even temporarily, be withdrawn from the Mediterranean garrisons, already very weak; the larger force would tax the resources at home; and the time requisite for mobilization and transport [of such a force] would enable full preparations to be made for resistance. The position, if attained, would be a commanding one, enabling the fleet to enjoy free passage of the Dardanelles, and adding weight to British views in the eventual settlement. But the possibility of very serious opposition was so great that the operation should not be attempted without the co-operation of other powers.

A minor operation—that of seizing the extremity of the Gallipoli peninsula at Cape Helles, and there commanding to a certain extent the outer entrance of the Dardanelles at the fort of Seddul Bahr—might be effected by a small force of about 5,000 men supported by the fleet, whose presence would be necessary to enable it to hold the position; but the small advantage to be gained was incommensurate with the immobility imposed upon the fleet—unless they were in a position immediately to dispatch large reinforcements.

With the exception of Italy, whose position had been seriously weakened by the Abyssinian campaign, England had no friend in the councils of Europe. Under such circumstances a policy of knight errantry or adventure was entirely out of the question. The D.M.I. also added:

Even if Italy co-operated navally to coerce the Sultan, and there was no action apprehended by other powers, the best course would be not to force the Dardanelles, but, as a preliminary step, to occupy the Gallipoli peninsula and take the batteries in the rear. Though this operation was quite within their power, it would be inadvisable, even with the support of Italy, to engage English forces in an enterprise from which they might find it extremely difficult to withdraw.[18]

Following the Dogger Bank incident with the Russian Navy in October 1904, Sir John Fisher, now First Sea Lord, once again was asked to look into the problem of forcing the Dardanelles. Fisher knew the Straits intimately from many visits to Turkey and only three years before had offended the First Lord of the Admiralty with his suggestion for an alliance with Turkey as the best means of protecting the "Dardanelles Key" against Russia.[19] In 1904 Fisher expressed the usual professional opinion that "even with military co-operation", forcing the Straits would be "mightily hazardous", a view which he reiterated in July 1906, to the new Liberal Cabinet of Sir Henry Campbell-Bannerman.[20]

On December 19, 1906, the freshly organized General Staff of the British Army, in a detailed memorandum of particular significance for the future, agreed with the Naval Intelligence Department "that unaided action by the Fleet, bearing in mind the risks

7

involved, [was] much to be deprecated". Even should a squadron of His Majesty's "least valuable ships" reach Constantinople, there was nothing to prevent the Turkish Government from retiring to the interior, while the British squadron would face high losses on its return through the Straits.[21]

The General Staff memorandum next examined the chances of seizing the Gallipoli Peninsula by surprise with a small force. This was considered possible, but left in abeyance the question of reinforcement or alternatively of evacuation. Finally, the possibility of a large-scale combined assault by the British Army and Navy was considered. With the ample warning for the enemy inherent in such an operation, the General Staff doubted whether the Fleet could guarantee an effective landing by the Army at all in the face of an anticipated force of at least 100,000 Turkish troops. The General Staff memorandum concluded: "However brilliant as a combination of war, and however fruitful in its consequences . . . the General Staff, in view of the risks involved, are not prepared to recommend its being attempted." Although more optimistic regarding the effect of naval artillery than was the General Staff, the Department of Naval Intelligence conceded that heavy casualties, evidently for the Army, were probable.[22]

With further consideration of the problem in 1908 and 1911, the General Staff of the Army summed up its conclusions for the pre-war period that "without surprise any attempt to land an Army on the Gallipoli peninsula would be too hazardous".[23] As an epilogue to this whole debate, during the Italo-Turkish War in 1912 five Italian torpedo boats attempted to penetrate the Straits but soon retired, following a fierce reception by the Turks.[24]

Parallel to the development of tactical planning for the Dardanelles, throughout the half century before the First World War organizational methods in Great Britain for higher strategic thought were improved. If events between the Crimean and the Franco–Prussian Wars marked the transition of the British Army from aristocratic to somewhat more middle-class values, only under the impetus of Disraeli's new imperialism was an attempt made to integrate the activities of the Admiralty and the War

Office with each other, as well as with those of other departments of the government. Disraeli's Colonial Defence Committee, emerging between 1878 and 1885, directly anticipated some of the functions of the subsequent Committee of Imperial Defence. The significant recommendations of the Hartington Commission (one of whose members was Lord Randolph Churchill) in 1889–90 emphasized the role of the First Sea Lord as the Cabinet's only adviser on "all great questions of naval policy", such as the distribution of the Fleet.[25] The Commission also proposed that the Army set up a General Staff as a "thinking department" for long-range strategic planning. The Hartington Commission noted that no combined plan of operation for the defence of the Empire in any contingency had ever been worked out by the Admiralty and the War Office. To overcome this dangerous fragmentation of power the Commission recommended the creation of a Naval and Military Council headed by the Prime Minister.[26]

Notwithstanding the efforts of several influential publicists, such as Sir Charles Dilke or Spenser Wilkinson, it took the embarrassments of the South African War to realize the recommendations of the Hartington Commission.[27] In the first report of the Esher Committee in January 1904, a committee of three members of which Admiral Fisher was one, it was stated: "The British Empire is pre-eminently a great Naval, Indian and Colonial Power. There are, nevertheless, no means for co-ordinating defence problems, for dealing with them as a whole, for defining the proper functions of the various elements; and for ensuring that on the one hand, peace preparations are carried out upon a consistent plan, and, on the other hand, that, in times of emergency, a definite war policy, based upon solid data, can be formulated".

The Esher Committee laid the utmost stress upon having the Prime Minister as the invariable President of the Committee of Imperial Defence. He was to have "absolute discretion" in the selection of its membership and the aid of a small but permanent secretariat. Initiated with the strong support of its first chairman,

Arthur Balfour, the Committee of Imperial Defence survived the subsequent distrust of Sir Henry Campbell-Bannerman, the hostility of Admiral Fisher to a true joint planning body, and, to a degree, even Herbert Asquith's tendency to pack it with important, but not strictly essential statesmen.[28] As a result, although in theory only a consultative body, in practice it became the centre of what authoritative political-military and inter-service planning and decision-making there existed in Great Britain in the period up to the First World War. Nevertheless, throughout Fisher's tenure as First Sea Lord, and indeed until the great strategic decisions reached under its auspices in 1911–12, the deliberations of the Committee of Imperial Defence were usually treated as "the amiable aberrations of a few well-meaning, but harmless amateur strategists".[29]

Almost concomitant with the establishment of the Committee of Imperial Defence was another recommendation of the Hartington Commission, made possible as a result of the invaluable humiliations of the Boer War. At the Army Staff College at Camberley and elsewhere, Colonel G. F. R. Henderson had long advocated a scientific General Staff for the British Army on the standard Prussian model. Now, in 1905, General Neville Lyttelton, Chief of Staff, wrote to the Secretary of State for War to explain that a General Staff must be "a collective body of experts" which could arrive at "a carefully balanced opinion . . . after mature thought and deliberation". As the Americans had similarly discovered in 1898, the Anglo-Saxon tradition of amateur land warfare was becoming less and less tenable under conditions of modern technology. In 1906, the new Liberal Secretary of State for War, Richard Burdon Haldane, was shrewd enough to accept and constitute a General Staff for the Army and thus gain credit for this long overdue innovation. The subtle Haldane was characteristically preparing by German methods to wage effective war with Germany, should this prove necessary.[30]

An immediate consequence of the establishment of a thinking department for the Army was the formulation of serious military plans and preparations to aid France in a war against Germany, a war which during the Moroccan crisis of 1905–6 had begun to seem quite possible. Such planning, in turn, led to a sharp and, indeed, fundamental, strategic conflict with the Royal Navy, then in the throes of equally urgent reforms under the driving impulsion of the First Sea Lord, Admiral Sir John Fisher.

Although in 1905–6 the subsequent Secretary to the Committee of Imperial Defence, Captain Charles Ottley, had successfully advocated the setting up of a sub-committee on Oversea Expeditions in the C.I.D. to co-ordinate Army and Navy planning in combined operations, Jacky Fisher soon made clear that he would have nothing to do with the heresy of joint inter-service planning. He boycotted and thereby aborted Ottley's promising start towards the organization of effective amphibious warfare. In common with most of the Royal Navy, Fisher profoundly distrusted the potentiality of an alliance with France as leading to a large-scale Continental strategy on the part of the British Army and he preferred to undertake what planning the Navy did in the strictest secrecy and isolation from the Army.[31]

Fisher's own plans for a war amenable to the interests and outlook of the Navy involved the amphibious conveyance of 60,000 British troops through the shoals and sandbanks shielding the North German coast of Schleswig-Holstein. It contrasted sharply with what the Admiral considered the "nuisance" of ferrying the 100,000 men of the Army and C.I.D. plan merely across the Channel to France.[32] Conversely, in formulating the basic Army plan, the newly constituted General Staff had assumed that it was upon major land operations in Europe that "the successful issue of the war as a whole will mainly depend".[33] In the stern language of Lt.-Col. Charles Repington, the Army believed that "nothing counted in comparison with weight at the decisive point, and that fooling in the Baltic was the sort of stuff amateurs were teaching the Navy, whose leaders seemed to be completely ignorant of strategy". The General Staff was also inclined to distrust the impact of a naval blockade upon Germany and with good reason felt that Fisher had vastly underestimated the impact which

Moltke's efficient railway system, coupled with a modern military organization, would have upon an isolated British Army operating according to the dictates of what the General Staff considered an obsolete maritime strategy.[34]

A good deal of the remarkable personality of Jacky Fisher is reflected at a joint meeting of a Cabinet and Committee of Imperial Defence sub-committee in December 1908, when, under the chairmanship of the Prime Minister, Herbert Asquith, the question of British grand strategy was again considered. After General Sir William Nicholson had explained the General Staff plan for the prompt dispatch of 120,000 men to France in the event of war, the Prime Minister pressed the silent First Sea Lord to put forth his own views. So far neither the Prime Minister nor the C.I.D. had been privileged to learn of the basic naval plan of 1907, a secret apparently shared by Fisher only with Admiral Sir Arthur Wilson.

At last induced to speak by Mr Asquith's repeated request, Fisher roundly described the Army's strategy as " an act of suicidal idiocy" and maintained that the Germans would drop all their other projects for the sake of destroying the small British Army in France. Therefore Fisher asserted that the Army should be restricted to the recovery of Heligoland, the garrisoning of Antwerp, and to sudden descents upon enemy coasts, such as that of Pomerania, only ninety miles from Berlin. Indeed, this particular stretch of Baltic strand would become something of an obsession with Fisher, however incredible a location for even a raid it might appear to the Army. Fisher followed this up with an impassioned tirade "against the War Office and all its ways, including conceit, waste of money, and ignorance of war. He claimed that the British Army should be administered as an annex to the Navy and that the present [Continental] follies should be abandoned." At this point Mr Asquith abruptly adjourned the meeting of the C.I.D., an action which Fisher's biographer and intimate, Admiral Sir Reginald Bacon, has deemed significant for a future and more momentous encounter between the Prime Minister and Admiral Fisher.[35]

The notably strenuous personality of the Kingfisher—among the gentler appellations by which he was known in the Navy—combined with his far-reaching and vital reforms, eventually brought Fisher into a collision course with another admiral whose ego, if not intelligence, matched his own, namely Lord Charles Beresford. As on the more famous occasion of Fisher's clash with Winston Churchill in 1915, in this earlier period each admiral successfully torpedoed the reputation of the other and with it his own career, although in Fisher's instance, not irrevocably.

Having been retired a year earlier than was customary in April 1909, as a result of none-too-discreet pressure on the part of Fisher, Beresford addressed the Prime Minister with charges to the effect that the Admiralty was mustering too few auxiliary ships, and that it had no war plans and no staff worthy of the name to create such plans. As a result of prolonged investigation under the personal supervision of the Prime Minister himself, the C.I.D. concluded that the only Beresford charge with much validity was the lack of more than the rudiments of a naval general staff. To be sure, in order to head off Beresford's criticism, in October 1909, the Admiralty had announced the creation of a Navy War Council for the consideration of strategic problems and war plans, but in the opinion of one authority this Council did not constitute a true naval staff, since its function was merely advisory and it met only on the invitation of the First Sea Lord. In fact, so sympathetic an observer as Arthur Marder has concluded of Fisher that his concepts of command were absolutely incompatible with either a true naval war staff or with an effective agreement with the War Office on any major strategic plans.[36]

In these circumstances it is not surprising the easy-going Asquith found it simpler to retire Fisher into the peerage with full honours in January 1910. Nevertheless, as Winston Churchill has written generously: "There is no doubt whatever that Fisher was right in nine-tenths of what he fought for. His great reforms sustained the power of the Royal Navy at the next critical period in its history. He gave the Navy the kind of shock which the British Army received at the time of the South Africa War."[37] The more is the pity that the matter could not have rested there and that the ruthless demands of war dragged forth the grand old sea dog from his unsought but well-deserved repose.

2

Lord of the Ascendant
(1908—1913)

The more he scents frustration, the more he has to fight for; the greater the obstacles, the greater the triumph.[1]

DESCRIPTION
OF WINSTON CHURCHILL, IN 1899

Winston is the cleverest of all the young men, and the mistake Arthur [Balfour] made was letting him go.[2]

JOSEPH CHAMBERLAIN

My young friend yonder thinks himself Othello, and blacks himself all over to play the part.[3]

HERBERT ASQUITH
ON WINSTON CHURCHILL, IN 1912

Well, if you can show me an Englishman that's tougher than you are, Winston, I'll eat my hat.[4]

AMBASSADOR JOSEPH KENNEDY IN 1940

DURING his anxious search for allies among the statesmen to assist him in his ever-sharpening battle with Beresford, Fisher, as a guest of King Edward at Biarritz in April 1907, became well acquainted with a new luminary of the political firmament, Winston Churchill. In his own graphic phrase the First Sea Lord "fell desperately in love" with the new Under-Secretary of State for the Colonies, and felt Churchill "quite the nicest fellow I ever met and such a quick brain that it's a delight to talk to him". The king found the two "chatterers" most amusing and Churchill left Biarritz primed to do battle for Fisher's cause, already imbued

15

with the rather florid *Weltanschauung*, not to mention dialogue, of the old Admiral. Some months earlier Churchill had manifested a similar regard for Fisher when he remarked that in contrast to Arthur Balfour, who saw too much of both sides of most issues, he liked Fisher because the latter always painted violently with a big brush.[5]

In this period Lord Randolph's son was making an impression upon others less emotional than Jacky Fisher. Figures so penetrating and diverse as the *éminence grise* of the C.I.D., Lord Esher, and among Churchill's then Radical colleagues, John Morley, John Dillon, Beatrice Webb, or Wilfred Blunt, have testified in vivid language to the brilliant facets and exuberant charm of the ambitious young statesman. The prescient Esher, for example, who described Churchill, in July 1908, as "clever and ingenious, but wild and unpractical" and a Napoleon who "wanted to push to the front of the Cabinet", had by September of that same year decided that Churchill's "faults and mistakes will be forgotten in his achievements" and that Lord Randolph's son had "real political fire". The new Liberal Foreign Secretary, Sir Edward Grey, was less restrained; for him Churchill was already nothing less than a genius,[6] and half-seriously Grey recognized that "Winston, very soon, will become incapable from sheer activity of mind, of being anything in a cabinet but Prime Minister".[7] Beatrice Webb, on the other hand, remarked on Churchill's "capacity for quick appreciation and rapid execution of new ideas, whilst hardly comprehending the philosophy beneath them".[8]

But the greatest of all Winston Churchill's conquests, and in many respects his closest political friend, was the most spectacular political phenomenon of the Edwardian era, David Lloyd George. Dubbed the Heavenly Twins from their intimacy, as would be seen in Fisher's rapport with Churchill, there remained more than a suspicion of mutual jealousy between them.[9] And, as with Fisher, long after his intimacy with Churchill had faded, the Welsh Wizard left an incalculable spell behind him. Fisher's legacy to Churchill was his amphibious conception of strategy;

Lloyd George's, his opportunist policy, and on occasion his notoriously flexible politics.

In April 1908, when Henry Herbert Asquith took over as Prime Minister from the dying Sir Henry Campbell-Bannerman, he offered Winston Churchill the Cabinet post then held by Churchill's uncle, Lord Tweedmouth, the First Lord of the Admiralty. Despite an augmenting interest in all matters military, at this juncture the Admiralty did not attract the ambitious young statesman as a role with which he could "do" anything. So early as 1902, essentially still a brash young journalist in Parliament, Churchill had deprecated the power of Admiralty as a "poor ambition" to an astonished Austen Chamberlain, and in 1908 even Fisher's advocacy of his acceptance of the post did not shake Churchill's preference for the Board of Trade.[10]

It must be recalled that at this time Winston Churchill was a radical among Radicals and that he still conceived of his task with respect to the armed forces as one designed to vindicate his father's reputation as an economizer, hostile to any growth in the military estimates. In his speech to the House of Commons in May 1901, attacking the plans of St John Brodrick, the Conservative Secretary of State for War, to raise three Army Corps for future overseas expeditionary forces, Churchill had maintained that one corps was "quite good enough to fight savages", while three were not enough "to begin to fight Europeans". A European war, Churchill went on in 1901, "must demand, perhaps for several years, the whole manhood of the nation, the entire suspension of peaceful industries and the concentration to one end of every vital energy of the community. In former days," lamented the young M.P., "it was possible to limit the liabilities of the combatants. But now . . . a European War can only end in the ruin of the vanquished and the scarcely less fatal commercial dislocation and exhaustion of the conquerors."

Almost as palatable to ears of the Radicals and economizers were Churchill's remarks on the Army. Declaring that "the honour and security of the British Empire did not depend, and could never depend, on the British Army", Churchill concluded that "the only weapon with which we can expect to cope with great nations is the Navy. Why," he demanded, "should we sacrifice a [naval] game in which we are sure to win, to play a [land] game in which we are bound to lose?"[11] Jacky Fisher would have approved of that particular sentiment, if by 1908–9 he had come to distrust Churchill's flirtation with the Radicals, economizers and, above all, with the friends of Lord Charles Beresford in the Navy.[12]

In short, given the arguments he had expressed so early as 1901, Churchill's economizing tended to be more at the expense of the Army than of the Navy. Thus when, in June 1908, while struggling to find funds for the new Liberal social services, Lloyd George proclaimed that no reduction in Army estimates in the next year meant no new Dreadnoughts, he could easily employ Churchill as his stalking horse against Haldane's War Office.

Churchill's attempt, however, to demonstrate that the British Army staffs and its supporting services were unnecessarily large, although it was to be a perennial theme of his memoranda to the War Office in future decades, met with "Pussy" Haldane's rebuttal to the effect that the British staffs and supporting services were proportionately lower than those of any other leading power. Haldane also referred somewhat obliquely to the British General Staff and Foreign Office disposition to aid France in time of war. Ultimately, on this last and vital issue, still concealed from the more Radical members of the Cabinet, Asquith had to support his War Minister. Lloyd George, perforce, was compelled to await a more favourable day and cause with which to topple what may possibly have been his real target all along: the Prime Minister himself.[13]

Following the great naval scare of 1909 in England over the German Navy, and the resulting rapid growth of Churchill's interest in military problems, in the spring of 1910 Churchill attempted to renew friendly relations with Jacky Fisher, now in retirement. Although at Lord Esher's suggestion Fisher had given Churchill an opening by writing to him after a long silence, the old Admiral rebuffed Churchill's "most affectionate" reply, notwithstanding the assurances that he remained the one man Churchill really loved.[14] By summer Churchill was again asking Fisher to dine; enjoying the courtship to the utmost, Fisher replied that he was currently "engaged to McKenna",[15] Tweedmouth's successor as First Lord of the Admiralty.

Within another fifteen months Fisher was confessing somewhat shamefacedly: "I was up till 2 a.m. with Winston. *He is a genius without doubt.* He was very affectionate, and so was Lloyd George. But ON THE WHOLE I'm sorry I went! I rather feel as if I have condoned the damned dirty trick played McKenna. Winston agreed with my view that I stated as regards the Navy. WILL HE ACT THEREON? He says he'll make a great public show of being cordial with Beresford and his clique! and hoped I wouldn't mind. Of course it's all a slap at McKenna. Winston takes his oath to me that he was guiltless as regards to replacing McKenna."[16] For, recognizing the way the international winds blew, in 1911 the two most brilliant opportunists in the Cabinet, Lloyd George and Churchill, were to abandon the Radicals and join the Liberal Imperialists on matters of defence and foreign policy, and with this shift in position would come new opportunities for each statesman.

As early as the autumn of 1910 Churchill's restlessness in the Radical camp had been discerned by Lloyd George, and in the harshest language the statesman whom Churchill considered the greatest political genius of the day had to remind his younger colleague of the dangers of what he termed ratting twice on his political colleagues and supporters. A trip up the Dardanelles to Constantinople that same season also taught Churchill much about the successes of German, and difficulties of British, diplomacy at the Porte. Admiring the Young Turks, he told Wilfred Blunt that he would advise Turkey to stay out of all wars for the next five years, while improving her army and finances. In his turn on a later occasion, the Young Turk leader, Enver Pasha, would suggest to Churchill that no great empire, such as Britain's, could survive without both an army and navy.[17]

If the second Moroccan crisis was about to entangle Winston Churchill in its coils at the War Office, in whose affairs he now became fascinated, the cautious Haldane far from repulsing him as a busybody from another ministry had long since given Churchill *carte blanche* to see whom and what he wished. There old friends from South Africa, such as Lieutenant-General Ian Hamilton, and new acquaintances, most notably Brigadier-General Henry Wilson, the Director of Military Operations, took Churchill in hand and, as it turned out, also took him into what had previously been a distinctly Tory or, at best, a Liberal Imperialist camp.

Churchill has described Henry Wilson as an officer of "extraordinary vision and faith" with unequalled knowledge of the Continent. An eloquent and a passionate Irish Francophile who, according to a recent biographer, actually knew no more of the secrets of the French Army General Staff than the latter thought good for him, Wilson promptly made a profound impression upon both Winston Churchill and most of the other members of a Cabinet better acquainted with warriors of a more stolid and inarticulate cast.[18]

As so often happens with the more brilliant soldier, the statesmen on their part failed to pass muster in Wilson's opinion. When, during the final hurried conferences on the Moroccan crisis in August 1911, meeting with Haldane and Wilson, Sir Edward Grey inquired of the General whether he thought Germany would go to war with France or Great Britain, the logical reaction of the Director of Military Operations was that this was a question he should be asking the Foreign Secretary. Grey then advanced the theory that Russia was a decisive factor, a notion which according to his own account Wilson shattered rudely by emphasizing that instant and whole-hearted British action was required to save France, regardless of Russian pressure. The statesmen agreed without heartiness, and Wilson was left profoundly dissatisfied with the grasp of the situation possessed by Grey and Haldane. Grey not only had no idea of what war meant, but struck Wilson as "not wanting to know", although he considered that an imminent war was perfectly possible. Not surprisingly, Wilson concluded that the Foreign Secretary "knew nothing of policy or strategy going hand in hand".[19] Few statesmen do at any time—and still fewer soldiers.

A week later Haldane had dinner with Asquith, McKenna, Grey and Churchill and, in the words of the Director of Military Operations, told "those ignorant men something of war". As a result, the Prime Minister scheduled for August 23 a special meeting of the Committee of Imperial Defence to face for the first time the co-ordination of the detailed Army General Staff strategic plans with such Navy strategic plans as existed.[20]

Prior to this famous conclave, Henry Wilson took time out "to demolish" what he termed "a ridiculous and fantastic paper" on the opening stages of a proposed Franco-German war presented by Churchill to the Prime Minister on August 13 for consideration by the C.I.D. Wilson was under the impression that Churchill had been assisted in this initial venture into grand strategy by Lord Kitchener and General Sir John French, "neither of whom know anything about the subject". At this juncture Churchill was probably still Kitchener's bitter enemy, but the implications of his remarkable memorandum do move along the lines of Sir John French's subsequent strategic thought.[21]

In essence Churchill's memorandum had infuriated Henry Wilson, not so much because of its well-justified pessimism regarding the chances of a French offensive in Lorraine, concerning which Wilson himself knew too little, but far more in view of the memorandum's implication that instead of operating as an integral component of the French left flank, the whole British Expeditionary Force should be employed as an independent force by sea against the vulnerable outside right flank of the ever-lengthening and ever more strained German lines of communication through Belgium and France.

At the end of August, in a letter to Sir Edward Grey, Churchill was more explicit. Adhering to Major-General James Grierson's conception between 1906 and 1908 of a British continental strategy, Churchill wrote: "We should, if necessary, aid Belgium to defend Antwerp and to feed that fortress and any army based on it." If the seduction of the B.E.F. into Antwerp had been one of Schlieffen's fondest hopes from the moment of the conception of his great plan in 1905-6, an uncommitted British Army on their maritime flank constituted an infinitely more incalculable and thus greater threat to the Germans. Churchill also dwelt on the benefits of blockading the Rhine, another expression of his already distinctly maritime rather than continental conception of strategy. As he would subsequently say in his own defence, his interest in Antwerp was no "foolish impulse" of a frantic moment in 1914, but expressed a long standing "pursuance of convictions reached by pondering and study".[22]

In 1908 the plan of the former Director of Military Operations, General Grierson, for an Antwerp and Belgium emphasis in British strategy had been knocked out by the Royal Navy's refusal to transport the Army north of the Channel; here the Navy had played into the hands of Francophiles such as Colonel Repington or General Wilson, who preferred in any event a British commitment to the left flank of the French Army.[23] Thus isolated from any service support in August 1911, Churchill's plan would be simply ignored by the Committee of Imperial Defence.

The great C.I.D. meeting of August 1911 was convened in the utmost secrecy on the morning of the twenty-third. Chaired as usual, by the Prime Minister, the customary membership of the Committee of Imperial Defence included the Foreign Secretary, the civil and military heads of the two services, the Director of Naval Intelligence, the Inspector-General of the Army, Sir John French, and Rear-Admiral Ottley and Captain Maurice Hankey of the C.I.D. secretariat. In addition, two significant new ministers were invited: David Lloyd George and Winston Churchill.[24] In theory the group was balanced, if anything, on the side of a maritime strategy; yet its conclusions were to be overwhelmingly in favour of pushing matters to a conclusion on the Continent.

The tone of the meeting was set by the address of the Director of Military Operations, Brigadier-General Henry Wilson. Speaking brilliantly for almost two hours with a dazzling mastery of detail, Wilson's critique of the still largely unknown plans of Count von Schlieffen was based upon the firm conclusions of the Army General Staff stemming from a war game in the spring of 1905. The gist of this somewhat overestimated exercise at Camberley was that, failing British aid, the French Army almost infallibly would be defeated in rather short order by a German envelopment through Belgium; hence as large and rapid as possible a British intervention on the French left flank was essential.[25]

Notwithstanding close questioning by Lloyd George, who already was much in favour of relying upon the Russians, Wilson assured the Committee that, owing to the Russian slowness in mobilization and their inadequacy of communications, only about half of their Army could play a role in the supposedly decisive opening stages of a war. A more penetrating question, regarding the chances of the French Field Army surviving its proposed offensive in Lorraine in sufficiently good shape to retreat south of Paris, left Wilson's interlocutors uneasy on the chances of a British Army evacuation from France. But, as an unsympathetic member of the C.I.D. secretariat, Captain Hankey of the Royal Marines, has recalled, Henry Wilson's case made a profound impression upon an audience not easily converted by mere displays of forensic versatility.[26]

The Director of Military Operations had left a pointed question for consideration by the afternoon session of the August 23 meeting: was the Admiralty now prepared to transport all six divisions of the B.E.F. on the tight schedule prepared by the General Staff for their conveyance to France? Fisher's own choice for his successor as First Sea Lord, Sir Arthur Wilson, was selected to present the Admiralty arguments against a contintental commitment. Although in agreement with Fisher's views on grand strategy, Sir Arthur had come to disappoint even the Kingfisher in his new post ashore, let alone Haldane and other more critical civilians. At best Sir Arthur Wilson could not present a case well and, although an able tactician, he could never pass as a strategic dialectician in such company. Furthermore, as his sympathizer, Hankey, has observed, on this occasion the First Sea Lord's presentation savoured of having been cooked up in the dinner hour.[27] The Navy would now pay for an excess of secrecy and a paucity of planning staff.

The First Sea Lord's argument opened with the frank admission that the Navy opposed a full-fledged continental commitment *per se*. For this rather than for technical reasons he wished to retain as many troops in Britain as possible in order to mount raids and to occupy German naval bases to be seized in the Baltic. The Admiralty anticipated that the threat of British landings would be more effective than their actual appearance, an argument with some validity in the anxieties of the German Army. To conclude its case, the Admiralty refused to guarantee the passage of the Army to France within the rigid schedule specified by General Henry Wilson, although no longer denying the practicality of doing so.

Haldane and the soldiers promptly replied that the modern German railway system could move five to ten times as many troops to any Baltic point attacked by the Royal Navy as might be carried by sea. To the disgust of the soldiers, the First Sea Lord confessed to not having studied the potentialities of the German railway system. More astonishingly, Sir Arthur Wilson had no effective answer to the charges of Churchill and the Chief of the Imperial General Staff, Sir William Nicolson, that an amphibious attempt to seize the German naval base of Wilhelmshaven would be madness in view of the risks to the British ships from the superior gunfire of the German forts. In his advocacy of a close blockade and of amphibious operations in the Baltic, Sir Arthur also reflected little awareness of the new danger from minefields in shallow waters.

Not surprisingly, the Foreign Secretary, Sir Edward Grey, already committed to the French Entente, now came over decisively to the side of the soldiers. Moreover, to the humiliation of McKenna, under these auspicious circumstances Haldane leapt into the fray to affirm once again that the Navy should have a proper staff to plan large-scale amphibious operations effectively with the Army. In conclusion, the Prime Minister declared that the War Office plan must be carried out by the Navy, although the Admirals appeared quite unconvinced.[28]

Fisher might carp hereafter about the cheap triumph of the soldiers but, given the obvious naval incompetence on the one hand and the French alliance on the other, the fact of the matter was that the Prime Minister had little choice in backing the War Office. In any event, Richard Haldane gave the great procrastinator no time to dawdle. He took Asquith aside and threatened resignation unless sweeping reforms were made at the Admiralty. In a written reply to Haldane, Asquith conceded: "Sir Arthur Wilson's plan can only be classified as puerile and I have dismissed it at once as wholly impracticable. The impression left on me after consideration of the whole discussion is (1) that in principle the General Staff scheme is the only alternative; (2) that it should be limited in the first instance to the dispatch of four divisions. Grey agrees with me and so I think does Winston."

From long observation of Asquith's undoubted talents as a conciliator, Haldane took no chances. A few days later he dispatched a letter to the Prime Minister which read as follows: "Had war come upon us last month . . . the grave divergence of policy between the admirals and the generals might well have involved us in disaster. The fact is that the admirals live in a world of their own. The Fisher method, which Wilson appears to follow, that war plans should be locked in the brain of the First Sea Lord, is out of date and impracticable. Our problems of defence are far too numerous and complex to be treated in this way. They can only be solved correctly by a properly organized and scientifically trained War Staff, working with the closest co-operation with the military General Staff under the general direction of the War Office. Wilson's so-called plan disclosed an ignorance of elementary military principles which is startling. . . . Unless it [this situation] is tackled resolutely I cannot remain in office." Recalling his five years' experience in handling the generals, Haldane offered to go to the Admiralty to rule the admirals as Jacky Fisher's McKenna never would.[29]

During these days of hot and heavy anxiety over war, Winston Churchill was coming to please others beside the Prime Minister with his seeming desire to reform the Navy and to accept, at least overtly, a continental strategy. Henry Wilson for one, whom Churchill was constantly seeing throughout the crisis, believed in early September that not merely Churchill but also Lloyd George had come over to his views. In reality, it would appear that the Director of Military Operations was so relieved at not having to combat these powerful members of a Cabinet still half pacifist in disposition that at this juncture he preferred to gloss over the continued Antwerp emphasis of the Churchill-Lloyd George arguments.

The position of the Heavenly Twins essentially remained that of the British Army in its original staff conversations with France between 1906 and 1908, at a time when the support of Belgian neutrality rather than of French security had still been the fundamental aim of British policy. For example, on August 27, 1911, Lloyd George wrote Churchill a letter rather more in accord with Fisher's outlook than that of the land-bound Henry Wilson. "150,000 British troops," affirmed Lloyd George, "supporting the Belgian Army on the German flank would be a much more formidable proposition than the same number of troops extending the French line. It would force the Germans to detail at least 500,000 men to protect their lines of communications. . . . The command of the sea would make that position impregnable."[30]

The figures, as well as the aims, of the Chancellor of the Exchequer might be open to charges of wishful thinking; yet there can be little doubt that the Antwerp compromise represented the best chance of thwarting the eventual split between the so-called Easterners and Westerners of the subsequent great strategic debate in Britain during the First World War. Furthermore, in the Antwerp compromise British, if not Entente, policy and strategy, in reality, could go hand in hand, since an Antwerp strategy would uphold the eventual decision of a great majority of the Cabinet to fight to protect the independence of Belgium. On the other hand, neither in 1911 nor in 1914 did a majority of the

Cabinet consciously favour a policy of going to war to save the Dual Entente, let alone fully accept the strategic corollary of such a policy: the dispatch of the entire B.E.F. to the left wing of the French Army immediately upon German mobilization.

What, in fact, happened in the fundamental decision of August 23, 1911, on the part of the Committee of Imperial Defence to support the General Staff strategy, was the normal military inversion of the proper relation of policy to strategy. In practice, as Lord Esher's lambent insight almost alone seems to have revealed,[31] the General Staff strategy had now determined the Cabinet's policy: that is, the General Staff had actually determined for what, let alone how, Britain would fight. Of course, the same inversion of policy and strategy was occurring everywhere on the Continent, and thus a means of war was becoming another cause of war. In exactly the same way, everywhere on the Continent, voluntary alliances for the sake of defensive security were being rapidly transformed into inescapable obligations to go to war on any terms and in the interests of other nations.

It was greatly to the credit of such rank amateurs in strategy as Lloyd George and Churchill that they sensed these developments so early, although neither with Antwerp nor any other position would either statesman ever discover any method of breaking off the shackles of the French alliance without facing the probable defeat of France as a result. In short, Lloyd George could not remark of Henry Wilson (as he would of so many other generals)[32] that he was far too relevant to be formidable.

Having failed to revive the Antwerp alternative to the far more finished product of the General Staff, and appreciating the Prime Minister's need to rid himself of that contented captive of the admirals, Reginald McKenna, Lloyd George visited Asquith in Scotland in mid-September. There he proposed Churchill for the Admiralty post, stressing the political advantages of a reputed Radical and forceful speaker in the House of Commons in serving to assuage the anxieties of the left wing of the Cabinet, then in a furore over the recently disclosed continental commitments of Great Britain.

In comparison with the political potential of keeping such popular and thus powerful figures as the Heavenly Twins on his side, the mounting eagerness of Haldane for the Admiralty necessarily assumed less importance in the eyes of the Prime Minister. Officially, of course, the deciding factor to Asquith was the need to retain the First Lord of the Admiralty in the Commons, and Haldane had already been elevated to the peerage. A more realistic consideration may have been that Churchill was supposed to be more acceptable to the Admiralty than Haldane, although the latter took pains to explain to both the dubious Prime Minister and to Churchill that he was not merely more experienced than the latter in the building up of a war staff, but also that his temperament was better adapted to the "gentle leading" of admirals than that of his ebullient rival for the Admiralty.[33]

For whatever Churchill might subsequently tell the shame-faced Fisher or his adoring private secretary, Eddie Marsh, to Haldane the truth was manifest that Churchill was now pressing Asquith hard for the post which he had turned down three years earlier. In a desperate bid to gain a foothold in the Admiralty, Haldane offered Churchill the War Office for a year with the promise to switch positions again when he had completed the establishment of an effective war staff for the Navy. Too shrewd to fall for this bait on the part of a man whom Fisher enjoyed terming, among other epithets, an "oily old Jesuit",[34] Churchill rejoined that at the Admiralty he would "work closely" with Haldane at the War Office "in the spirit of his father who had always said that there ought to be a common administration" for both services. Eventually Haldane had to agree to this as the best he could get under the circumstances but, as he later wrote to Sir Edward Grey, he remained convinced that "full of energy and imagination" as Churchill was, he did not know the problem to be faced at the Admiralty. Moreover, Haldane considered that his impetuous young rival was "too apt to act first and think afterwards".[35]

Much of what Haldane said and feared on this occasion may have been true, but political conditions were too opposed to the great War Minister. As a consequence, the naval staff established by Churchill in the Admiralty developed less effectively than it might otherwise have done and, unlike Haldane, neither Churchill nor Colonel Jack Seely, Haldane's successor at the War Office, was particularly interested in promoting the growth of joint inter-service war planning either within or without the matrix of the C.I.D. At least, in January 1912, Haldane and Prince Louis of Battenberg were successful in placing the new naval War Staff under the authority of the First Sea Lord rather than under that of the First Lord, as Mr Churchill had proposed.[36] But the full price for Haldane's failure to effect at the Admiralty between 1911 and 1914 what he had realized in the War Office during the previous five years would become manifest only in 1915.

McKenna took hard what he justifiably deemed his ejection from the Admiralty; and in the opinion of Arthur Marder, he could not be blamed for assuming that he was being dismissed because of the disagreement on grand strategy between the two services. As for Churchill, Wilfred Blunt wrote: "Winston goes to the Admiralty, which will be an advantage to him as helping him out of infinite hot water he is in at the Home Office. I am writing to congratulate him, and have expressed a hope that if he bombards a town it will be Naples or Messina rather than Constantinople or Jeddah. The Turks . . . have been fighting the Italians well . . . and at Tripoli the Turkish Army . . . has retired out of reach of the ship's guns and is harassing the Italians on shore."[37] Austen Chamberlain agreed with Blunt that the Home Office was becoming too hot for Churchill and concluded that the latter, having decided that he could not rival Lloyd George "as a demagogue", was now pleased to "cultivate the role of statesman and strong man instead".[38]

Before the new First Lord could create the naval War Staff, which he had been specifically sent to the Admiralty to establish, he faced the painful task of replacing the First Sea Lord, Sir Arthur Wilson, the first of several such replacements on the part of Mr Churchill during the course of the next few years. In 1912 Wilson's dismissal was facilitated by the discovery by the Prime

Minister and the Cabinet of the Admiral's intellectual disabilities, in addition to his continued opposition to the institution of a naval War Staff and to the conveyance of the Army to France. Not daring to recall Fisher and thus to renew the feud with Beresford, and lacking good commanders as grievously as a good staff, Churchill was finally forced to settle for the somewhat weak and colourless Sir Francis Bridgeman as First Sea Lord. On this occasion Asquith would have preferred Prince Louis of Battenberg for the post, but Lloyd George had knocked out Battenberg's appointment on the grounds that the public would object to a man of German background as First Sea Lord. The Prime Minister already had a high opinion of Lloyd George's sensitivity as a barometer of public opinion in irrational affairs.[39]

Before the year was out, alleging over Bridgeman's protest that his health was the cause, Churchill had insisted upon the former's replacement by Battenberg. Lord Charles Beresford and Bonar Law, Leader of the Conservative Opposition, seized upon the issue to precipitate a parliamentary storm, putting Churchill on the defensive and seriously embarrassing the Navy. Bonar Law declared that Bridgeman had been "brutally ill-used" and Bridgeman himself asserted that he had been "fired without warning", not because he was "too weak, but . . . too strong".[40] In any event, with Battenberg's assistance Churchill imposed a naval War Staff upon the reluctant Admiralty to work on war plans and to evaluate all future candidates for higher naval commands. The role of this staff, however, remained purely advisory and subordinate in comparison with that of the British Army or the German Navy. As Churchill has truly remarked, the formation of an effective General Staff for the Navy was a task for a generation, and Churchill's Naval Secretary at this time, the future Admiral David Beatty, has testified that it took the First World War to make the Navy appreciate rather than resent the necessity for such a change.[41]

Another of Haldane's predictions bore some bitter fruit in 1912–13, when Churchill's already manifest tendency to exercise the more generous prerogatives of the long defunct post of Lord

LORD OF THE ASCENDANT

High Admiral, rather than those of a mere First Lord of the Admiralty, brought him into constant conflict with the Second Sea Lord, Admiral Sir John Jellicoe. In a refrain to be echoed by so many of Churchill's professional military advisers in the future, Jellicoe complained that the more Elizabethan than Edwardian civilian above him did not understand his limitations as a member of the laity "quite ignorant of naval affairs".

Defining very well the attitude of the Board of Admiralty towards Churchill in this period, Jellicoe went on to explain in his memoirs: "I admired very much his wonderful argumentative powers when putting a case before the Cabinet or the Committee of Imperial Defence. He surpassed in this direction the ablest of lawyers and would make a weak case appear exceptionally strong. While this gift was of great use to the Board when we wanted the naval case well put to the Government, it became a positive danger when the First Lord started to exercise his powers of argument on his colleagues on the Board. Naval officers are not brought up to argue a case, and but few of them can make a good show in this direction. Moreover, if one is apt to be over-ridden in argument, as was certainly the case with one of the Sea Lords on the Board at the time, it made the position very difficult for the remainder of the Board."[42]

On the touchy question of the disposition of the Mediterranean fleet in 1912, the well-informed Esher would write in a similar vein: "Winston," noted Esher, "brilliant as he is, does not listen to the opposite side, and is impatient of opinions that do not coincide with his own. This is a fatal defect in a civilian minister who has to consider the initial moves in a great war. If Winston is going to wield the armed force of the Empire, he should cure himself of this grave fault."[43]

In fact, at one point at the end of 1913, it seems that all four Sea Lords had contemplated resignation over relatively trivial issues, issues which had been much aggravated by the tactlessness of the First Lord. Churchill had also not endeared himself to his distrustful monarch in this period, with his Radical suggestion that one of His Majesty's new Dreadnoughts should be entitled *Oliver*

Cromwell on the grounds that few men had done more for the Navy than had the Lord Protector. On the other hand, the constant interference of the First Lord, even in technical matters, had already won the hearts of two of the keenest and most intrepid among the younger officers of the Navy, Roger Keyes and David Beatty.[44]

In future years Churchill himself made no bones regarding the prerogatives of politicians in technical matters. With respect to the problem of submarine warfare, he would write in 1932:

The astonishing fact is that the politicians were right, and that the Admiralty authorities were wrong. The politicians were right upon a technical, professional question ostensibly quite outside their sphere, and the Admiralty authorities were wrong upon what was, after all, the heart and centre of their own peculiar job. . . .

But the British politicians—we apologize for their existence—were powerful people, feeling they owed their positions to no man's favour. They asked all kinds of questions. They did not always take "No" for an answer. They did not accept the facts and figures put before them by their experts as necessarily unshakable. They were not under moral awe of professional authority, if it did not seem reasonable to the lay mind. They were not above obtaining secretly the opinions of the junior naval officers concerned with the problem, and of using these views to cross-examine and confute the naval chiefs.[45]

Given his difficulties at the Admiralty, Churchill took good care not to antagonize Admiral Fisher, now in a Nelson-like retirement at Naples. In an eloquent letter in June 1912, the First Lord had written: "I recognize it is little enough I can offer you. But your gifts, your force, your hopes, belong to the Navy, with or without return; and as your most sincere admirer, and as head of the Naval Service, I claim them now, knowing well you will not grudge them. You need a plough to draw. Your propellers are racing in air."[46]

Although gratified by Churchill's continued courtship, the old Admiral was not entirely taken in by his unremitting flattery. In May 1912, he wrote to his beloved Esher to express his fears that Bridgeman and Battenberg were "powerless against Winston" and warned Esher that Lloyd George, in his turn, "absolutely controls Winston".[47] If ever true, this last was no longer so, for in 1912–13, simultaneous with his new role as a strong Liberal Imperialist, Churchill's relations with Lloyd George were undergoing a slump. None the less, as usual, Fisher had grasped the main point in a letter to Esher in April 1912, in which he declared how much he owed Churchill for scrapping a dozen admirals "without fear". Under the shadow of Vesuvius, the far-from-extinct old volcano rumbled happily: "I know of no other First Lord in history who would have done it."[48]

The energetic new broom at the Admiralty had belied Haldane's warnings in at least one respect. Since he was an intimate friend of Haldane's successor as Secretary of State for War, Colonel Jack Seely, it was not difficult for Churchill and Seely to set up a joint Committee of the Admiralty and War Office, entitled the "High Level Bridge", to consider together problems of mutual concern to each service. Henry Wilson prevented the new Committee Secretary, Captain Maurice Hankey, from working out joint plans for the capture of German colonies, because the suspicious Director of Military Operations foresaw in such operations the danger of colonial "side-shows" to the detriment of the great, if brief, continental campaign upon which his heart was set. As Fisher's man in the C.I.D., Hankey had to rest content with a relatively modest improvement in the joint scrutiny of war plans so vital to success in combined operations.[49]

Since one of the avowed reasons for Churchill's appointment to the Admiralty had been his greater acceptability to the Radicals and economizers in the Cabinet than Haldane, in January 1912, the First Lord was the recipient of a hopeful German bid for negotiations in Berlin over the sharpening Anglo-German naval rivalry. Shrewder than the Hegelian metaphysician whom he had beaten to the Admiralty, and still more pessimistic than Haldane concerning the chances of bargaining Germany away from her ultimately hopeless attempt to browbeat Great Britain at sea, Churchill turned down the bid to visit Germany himself, leaving this potentially invidious task to Haldane. At the same time, to

D   33

the chagrin of his former allies among the Radicals and to the delight of the Conservative press, Churchill publicly described the German Navy as a luxury fleet. Lloyd George considered this unauthorized speech calculated to mar Haldane's mission to Germany, a mission which the still fairly radical Chancellor of the Exchequer enjoyed thinking would otherwise have been on a fair way to success.[50]

Haldane's return from Berlin in February 1912, with the text of the proposed new German naval construction plan, precipitated a further concentration of the Royal Navy in the North Sea. This concentration, long before initiated under Fisher and his predecessor, had resulted in the gradual withdrawal of Britain's overseas fleets to face the greater threat at home. Now in Churchill's first naval estimate to Parliament in March 1912, the very centre of gravity of traditional British imperial power, the Mediterranean, was to be sacrificed for the sake of gaining six more battleships with which to resist Germany in the North Sea.

Fisher's direct influence on Churchill over this decision is very apparent. Writing from Naples on March 5, 1912, in characteristically vigorous language, the Kingfisher had advised the First Lord: "Your new scheme of Fleet organization is admirable.... Let the French take care of the Mediterranean, and a hot time they'll have of it with submarines poking about in that lake! We are well out of it." In another memorandum to Churchill two months later Fisher clarified still further his subsequent attitude towards the Mediterranean. He wrote: "The margin of [British] power in the North Sea is irreducible and requires this addition of the Mediterranean battleships.... *We cannot have everything or be strong everywhere.* It is futile to be strong in the subsidiary theatre of war and not overwhelmingly supreme in the decisive theatre."[51]

It is a pity that this truism of all naval or military thought did not sink into Mr Churchill's consciousness more deeply in 1912 or many of his arguments with the Admiralty during each of the World Wars might have been forgone. But, as in the Second World War in Great Britain, both the Conservative press and Conservative soldiers and statesmen were shocked at what one

Tory journal in 1912 termed the abandonment of "the carotid artery of Empire", the calling home of the nautical legions of the British Empire.[52]

The quietly influential Esher led the fight against scuttling the Mediterranean fleet, arguing that any attempt to rely upon the French Navy for the defence of British imperial interests in the Mediterranean was "bound to prove illusory". Whether or not Churchill and the Admiralty had come to such a decision without discussion by the Committee of Imperial Defence, as was alleged by Henry Wilson, the Foreign and War Offices were up in arms against the Admiralty, if for different reasons. At first the General Staff feared that, in the absence of the Royal Navy and with the aid of Turkey, the Triple Alliance would be able to capture Malta, Egypt and Cyprus within a few weeks, an Army mis-estimate regarding the possibilities of seapower almost as extraordinary as any submitted by Admiral Sir Arthur Wilson on the subject of continental logistics. More reasonably, the Foreign Office anticipated the probable or possible defection of Italy, Spain and Turkey into the ranks of Britain's enemies, should the capital ships of the British Mediterranean fleet be removed.[53]

A general conclave of the soldiers and the statesmen finally assembled at Malta at the end of May 1912 to debate the strategic issue in waters which, as Esher took pains to remind Fisher, his hero Nelson had loved only less than Emma, Lady Hamilton. The classically-minded Herbert Asquith regaled his companions on the Admiralty yacht *Enchantress* with the vicissitudes of the great Athenian amphibious expedition to Sicily. There would come a day when the denouement of this Athenian tragedy would seem less amusing to the erudite Prime Minister, and when the young First Lord, who so eagerly strode the *Enchantress'* deck, would resemble an earlier Circe.

At Malta, Churchill's old enemy, Field-Marshal Lord Kitchener, having previously turned down the post of Mediterranean Commander-in-Chief on the grounds of its uselessness, now fought to protect the essentially similar strategic interests of his current Egyptian proconsulate. In deference to the opinions of so formidable a combination as Kitchener, the War Office and the Foreign Office, the Admiralty was compelled to compromise, not only in the direction of stationing two or three battlecruisers at Malta to replace the departed battleships, but also to strengthen the squadron at Gibraltar for employment in either the Mediterranean or Atlantic.[54]

Nevertheless, at a meeting of the Committee of Imperial Defence in London on July 4, Churchill won at least a good compromise, according to Henry Wilson chiefly through a threat otherwise to take the issue to the public. With Fisher present, Churchill argued the former's case against the strenuous opposition of McKenna. He insisted that the Royal Navy must keep a margin of eight capital ships over the Germans in the North Sea and that "all other objects, however precious, must, if necessary, be sacrificed to secure this end". The C.I.D. agreed to this first requirement, but added in a customary concession on the part of the Prime Minister that, subject to this first requirement, Great Britain should maintain a Malta-based battlefleet superior to both the Austrian and Italian navies.[55]

Asquith's evasive language worked, as it usually did in time of peace; Churchill remained silent and Esher recorded cheerfully: "Anyway we can now hold up our heads once more in the Mediterranean—and beyond."[56] A few weeks later, in a memorandum to the Prime Minister and Sir Edward Grey, Churchill asserted that it was untrue that Great Britain was relying upon France to maintain her position in the Mediterranean. More candidly, the First Lord alluded to the price for this unadmitted French protection, the implicit British obligation to guard the coast of northern France against the German Navy.[57]

Like the other members of the Committee of Imperial Defence, Winston Churchill might be learning the methods of strategic compromise as a necessary ingredient to his rising political career. And, like Edmund Burke after 1793, he was about to discover that the methods which were making him so notably the Lord of the Ascendant in 1912, would prove woefully unreal amid the more compelling truths of a prolonged and desperate war.

3

Knavish Tricks

(1913—September 8, 1914)

I hate your pen and ink men; a fleet of British ships of war are the best negotiators in Europe. . . . I now only long to be gone; time is precious, and every hour makes more resistance; strike quick and home.[1]

HORATIO NELSON

The Turkish Army, the very finest fighting army in the world, was ours for the asking . . . but we've chucked it all away because we had damned fools as our Ambassadors.[2]

ADMIRAL FISHER, IN 1911

He [Churchill] is always unconsciously playing a part—an heroic part. And he is himself his most astonished spectator. He sees himself moving through the smoke of battle—triumphant, terrible, his brow clothed with thunder, his legions looking to him for victory, and not looking in vain. . . . In the theatre of his mind it is always the hour of fate and the crack of doom.[3]

A. G. GARDINER, IN 1912

Really, some of these Western Powers should be compelled to pass an examination before they are allowed to begin a campaign against Mohammedan peoples.[4]

LORD KITCHENER, IN 1912

REGARDLESS of Conservative criticism of the growing British dependence upon the French fleet in the Mediterranean, circumstances continued to accentuate this trend. The Italian victory over the Turks in the autumn of 1912 resulted in friction between Great Britain and Italy when the Foreign Office protested against the attempted Italian annexation of certain of the

Dodecanese Islands in the Aegean. Hoping to exploit this friction, Italy's nominal ally in the Triple Alliance, Germany, established a squadron in the Mediterranean consisting of the fast new battlecruiser, *Goeben*, and several smaller ships.

To counter this additional threat the British offered to help the Turks to reorganize their hopelessly obsolete navy. Orders had already been placed in Britain for two Dreadnoughts to be completed for Turkey by the autumn of 1914 and these were now supplemented by a large new British naval mission to the Porte headed by an officer of flag rank. One of the most important tasks in 1913–14 of the last Briton to head this mission, Rear-Admiral A. H. Limpus, was to lay mines and torpedoes in the Dardanelles against another Italian naval penetration of the Straits, such as had been undertaken in 1912.[5]

The Turkish defeat in the First Balkan War resulted in the rise of the Germanophile Young Turk leader, Enver Pasha, to authority in Constantinople. Enver became particularly powerful in the Turkish Army and took over the portfolio of the War Ministry for himself. With the Turkish Army unpaid, demoralized and in rags, Enver appealed for a German Army mission to reinvigorate and, indeed, to recreate his army. The stated requirements for the chief of this German mission specified an officer of "strong character who knows how to gain his point".[6]

Building upon the foundations of his German predecessors, from the date of his arrival in Turkey in December 1913, General Liman von Sanders would not merely fill the specifications for this job, but in the process would become the *de facto* commander of the Turkish Army at the Dardanelles throughout the next two years.

This Anglo-German rivalry was further complicated by the decision, in February 1914, of the traditional claimant to Constantinople, Tsarist Russia, to demand both the city and the Dardanelles in the event of a general war. This Russian decision, coupled with a strong movement within the British Foreign Office in favour of backing Greece rather than Turkey as a more probable and valuable ally in the Balkans, so inhibited Entente diplomacy in Constantinople that, visiting Turkey in the spring of 1914, Lord Kitchener was inclined to consider Turkey lost to the Germans. With Churchill, Fisher and the Admiralty (excluding Battenberg), the Tory Kitchener, as an old Turkish hand and admirer of the potentialities of the Turkish fighting man, intensely regretted this more or less automatic consequence of the British relationship with Russia since 1907.[7]

However, Hellenophile British Liberals and Turkophile Conservatives, soldiers and sailors alike, and that relentless retailer of bazaar gossip, the United States Ambassador to Turkey, Henry Morgenthau Senior, agreed that the Foreign Office, and particularly its successive representatives in Turkey, should qualify as the scapegoat for the frustrations of Entente coalition policy in the Straits.[8] In the classic analysis of Sir Harold Nicolson, such an "error of diagnosis is a common feature in all democratic diplomacy. The central and original cause of illness is too painful to admit or even to contemplate. The manifestations and symptoms of that illness are thus dealt with as if they were the illness itself. And great indignation is expressed when the patient refuses to respond to treatment."[9]

In the planning within the Committee of Imperial Defence for actions to be taken in the event of hostilities, the seizure of the Turkish battleships building in Britain had been long anticipated, both to increase the perilous margin of the Grand Fleet over the German Navy and to keep such invaluable vessels from the hands of a probable enemy in the Mediterranean. For this reason, as well as for the still more urgent need to move the Grand Fleet into the North Sea before a surprise German attack might materialize, the First Lord of the Admiralty was under strong pressure to act rapidly when faced with the likelihood of war. Thus, to the astonishment and gratification of General Henry Wilson, if not to that of the less bellicose Herbert Asquith, warnings of a precautionary period were sent from the War Office and Admiralty as early as July 28, 1914, a full week before the actual outbreak of hostilities between Great Britain and Germany.

Churchill's credit for these early actions was very great; even on July 27 he had instantly approved of Battenberg's refusal to disperse the fleet then assembled in the Channel for a test mobilization, and on the twenty-eighth, as a result of prompting by Lieutenant-Colonel Hankey of the C.I.D., the First Lord had taken the initiative in approving these early warnings in a notably reluctant Cabinet. Among the many consequences of the precautionary period warnings was the seizure of the two almost completed Turkish battleships on Tyneside. The ensuing fury and chagrin in Turkey are often cited as if this British action had been the cause of Turkey's subsequent hostility to the Entente rather than its result, but, as we have seen, Churchill had no choice in, and responsibility only for the timing of, this necessary action.[10]

A more difficult problem, which was facing John Morley's "splendid condottiere"[11] at the Admiralty, in this period lay in the Mediterranean. Here, in Asquith's phrase, "Winston, who has got on all his warpaint", was "longing for a sea fight" to sink the German battlecruiser *Goeben*.[12] But before the elusive *Goeben* could be sunk it had first to be pinned down by the slower British battlecruisers based upon Malta. Still more important to a Cabinet headed by a pacific, if not pacifist, member of the Bar, war between Germany and Great Britain must actually have been declared before action was initiated by the Royal Navy.

Incomplete arrangements for co-ordination with the French Fleet and a primary mission of covering the movement of the French African Army to France had further distracted the British naval command in the Mediterranean, when more by accident than design British battlecruisers blundered into the *Goeben* and an accompanying cruiser which, unknown to the Admiralty, were already moving toward an eventual refuge up the Dardanelles. Thereafter, the British admirals on the spot were bedevilled with Cabinet orders not to violate the touchy neutrality of Italy, a restraint which troubled the Germans not at all. And, as usual, the embryonic staff organization of the Admiralty totally failed to cope with the urgent need to forward all available information to the Mediterranean Fleet or even to bring the primary mission of the Mediterranean Fleet up to date: that is to order the destruction of the two German warships at all costs.[13]

Given such advantages, the German ships got away to the Aegean. There the Royal Navy, again thrown off the scent by the Austrian declaration of war, missed another chance to catch the Germans, who were delayed by the necessity for talking Enver Pasha into admitting the *Goeben* and her consort past the Dardanelles. Although, contrary to the intention of a treaty signed with Germany on August 2, 1914, Turkey had not dared to enter the war before making further preparations after the British participation on the side of her enemies had become apparent, on August 10 the Germans induced the desperate Enver to admit the *Goeben* past the freshly laid minefields now guarding the Straits. In fact, on August 3, Enver had been so beside himself with anxiety over his pressing need for naval protection against the Russian Black Sea Fleet that, momentarily, he had considered dropping his day-old agreement with Germany in favour of a new pact with Russia. It is probable that the *Goeben* had fled to Turkey precisely to thwart any such action.

On August 10 his German military advisers also persuaded Enver to agree to fire on the British battlecruisers, should they attempt to follow the *Goeben* up the Dardanelles.[14] For better or worse Turkey was now committed to the Central Powers, notwithstanding her belated stalling on a final entry into the war, an uneasy posture, anticipative of Winston Churchill's preferred Italian target in 1939–40. As Talleyrand had long ago observed, non-intervention is a metaphysical and political term meaning about the same as intervention.

For the overcautious British admirals in the Mediterranean, who were to face a court martial or retirement for what can hardly be considered their failure alone, there may have been some consolation that long before in these same waters Nelson and Collingwood had been similarly foxed by the enemy amidst a welter of confusing orders and false leads. Again in the Second World War, another half-hearted British admiral in the Mediterranean, cast as scapegoat for indecision or incompetence in the Cabinet or Admiralty, would receive a letter from Captain Lord Louis Mountbatten which read as follows: "I have heard of your fantastic treatment... I can well imagine what you are going through, knowing what my father [Prince Louis of Battenberg] felt from his enforced incapacity through no fault of his own in the First World War."[15] But in tense retirement an angry Kingfisher was already heard muttering about the need for shooting certain admirals *"pour encourager les autres"*.[16]

Within a month the British naval mission at Constantinople had to be withdrawn and, with a sense of misplaced chivalry comparable only to British policy in the Aegean during the Second World War, instead of Rear-Admiral Limpus being placed in charge of the British observation squadron off the Dardanelles in consideration of his unsurpassed knowledge of the defences of the Straits, Vice-Admiral S. H. Carden was called from command of the Malta dockyard to assume charge of the British ships in the Aegean.[17] In view of the time needed to reinforce the defences of the Suez Canal with Australian and New Zealand troops against a much overestimated threat of a Turkish attack, in mid-August Asquith rejected Churchill's "most bellicose" desire to send the British squadron up the Dardanelles to sink the *Goeben* regardless of the consequences to the shaky façade of Turkish neutrality.

Lord Kitchener, now Secretary of State for War, likewise resisted taking any initiative against the Turks, in part because of the tremendous Moslem population of the British Empire.[18] As with General Charles Gordon, whom he resembled in other ways, religion always played a role of unexpected importance in the mind of so pragmatic a realist as Kitchener. Moreover, it must be recalled that until June 1914 the protection of Egypt against her nominal Turkish suzerain had been Kitchener's direct responsibility. On the other hand, Kitchener did not accept a last-minute attempt by the Aga Khan to bring Turkey over to the Allied side, because of the dangerous probable consequences of such an action upon Russia's hopes of payment in Turkish territory as a compensation for upholding Entente grand strategy in Poland.[19]

If, notwithstanding the eager First Lord of the Admiralty, the Government had cause to delay action against the Turks, so also did the Turks against the British. Although the German Ambassador at the Porte, the formidable Baron Wangenheim, would boast happily on August 14: "We've got our foot on Russia's corn and we propose to keep it there," in requests, supported by Liman von Sanders, Enver Pasha was already begging Berlin for artillery, ammunition, rifles, mines, uniforms and even canned food. Several hundred German military personnel were also promptly sent, including a large naval group headed by Vice-Admiral Guido von Usedom, to help man the Bosphorus and Dardanelles forts with skilled technicians. Russian threats to Roumania would cut out this vital trickle of German aid to Turkey by early October, thus leaving the Turks very much on their own when they were finally induced to enter the war at the beginning of November 1914.[20]

Well before the Turkish entry, Winston Churchill had pressed for action in the Straits which went beyond that of merely sinking the *Goeben* and her consort. For that matter, while still a subaltern in India, in 1898, Churchill had written a novel whose *grande finale* consisted of "an ironclad fleet forcing a sort of Dardanelles to quell" a rebellious capital.[21] Asquith noted on August 21, on the eve of the battle of the Marne: "The real centre of interest [in the Cabinet], political, not military, at the moment is Turkey and the two darkest horses in the European stable, Italy and Roumania. The different points of view of different people are rather amusing—Winston violently anti-Turk; Kitchener strong that Roumania is the real pivot of the situation; Masterman eagerly pro-Bulgarian, but very much against any aggressive action *vis-à-vis* Turkey, which would excite our Mussulmans in India and Egypt; Lloyd George keen for Balkan confederation; Grey judicious and critical all around." With the other more Turkophobe members of the Cabinet, Churchill may have already reached the conclusion that a generous distribution of Turkish territory in a postwar settlement was a necessary catalyst to an effective Entente coalition conduct of the war.[22]

In this receptive atmosphere a Greek government offer to put all of her military resources at the disposal of the Entente, arriving almost simultaneously with the suggestion of Sir Louis Mallet, the British Ambassador to Turkey, that a combined operation could probably force and maintain control of the Straits, made the British Government seriously consider such an operation for the first time during the war. A momentary Russian acquiescence to the employment of Greek troops evoked discussions on August 31 and September 1 between Churchill, Kitchener and Lieutenant-General Sir Charles Douglas, Chief of the Imperial Staff, over the seizure of the Gallipoli Peninsula by a Greek expeditionary force to enable the British Fleet to pass through the Straits in the event of a Turkish declaration of war. On September 3 the Director of Military Operations, Major-General C. E. Callwell, reported for the General Staff that since the Staff appreciation of 1906 the Turkish position in the Straits had deteriorated to a point where a Greek force of 60,000 men with strong siege artillery might be able to seize the Peninsula from its Aegean side, although Callwell believed that any such assault was still "likely to prove an extremely difficult operation of war".[23]

On September 6, the pro-Entente Premier of Greece, Monsieur Venizelos, informed the British Government that, so long as Bulgaria remained neutral, the Greeks were sanguine concerning their proposed role in such an operation. Churchill thereupon asked Sir Edward Grey to put pressure on Russia to assist in an Anglo-Greek attack on Turkey by providing a corps from Archangel or the Far East for an amphibious assault on Gallipoli. Grey had to explain to the First Sea Lord that, fully engaged in Poland, Russia lacked troops for the sake of giving Constantinople to the Greeks and had no intention of allowing the Greeks "to drag" her into a war with Turkey in any event.[24] Presumably, like Churchill, Grey did not yet appreciate the logistic extravagance for Allied shipping of sustaining any troops in the Aegean, let alone those of the distant and soon vastly overburdened Tsar.

Sir Edward was already learning, however, as he subsequently put it, that "nothing so distorted perspective, disturbed impartial judgment, and impaired the sense of strategic values as the operations on Gallipoli". In his memoirs the sometimes overcautious Grey wrote that the Greek plan had ignored the probable resistance of the enemy, not to mention the eventually "disastrous" effect of any British obligation to Greece upon Great Britain's far more vital relations with the greedy and suspicious Russians. The First Lord and his still more outraged colleague, David Lloyd George, might never come to admit it,[25] but Russia had no intention of waiving her old dream of Tsargrad or Constantinople on behalf of the still older Greek chimera of reclaiming the former Byzantine seat on the Bosphorus as capital of a new Hellenistic Empire.

Still another small and disappointed aspirant for the source of Orthodox civilization and religion, Bulgaria, likewise had no intention of aiding either the Greeks or the Russians to occupy Constantinople. On September 8, 1914, Constantine, the cautious King of Greece, notified London that a Bulgarian promise of neutrality would no longer be enough to guarantee the security of the Greek Army during a Gallipoli campaign. The Bulgars now must actually join their recent enemy and aid Greece in a combined attack on Turkey to tie down more of the Turkish Army and, in all probability, to render more difficult abrupt changes of mind on the part of the Bulgarian Government regarding its always questionable relations with Greece. Since the Greek General Staff plan for operations against Turkey, submitted simultaneously with King Constantine's canny objections, now involved the indiscriminate employment of over 130,000 men in assaults ranging from Alexandretta and Smyrna through Gallipoli to that old point of Bulgarian General Staff interest in the First Balkan War, the lines of Bulair at the neck of the Gallipoli Peninsula,[26] King Constantine's anxieties would appear better justified than the more democratic aspirations of that resilient bearer of Greek gifts, Eleutherios Venizelos.

Indeed, so visionary does this notably elusive Greek war plan appear that its appeal to another great romantic in strategic matters, David Lloyd George, would seem to have been a forgone conclusion. Perhaps some variation of this particular *folie de grandeur* did lead the Hellenophile Welshman to disaster in Anatolia eight years later. For the moment, however, his erstwhile intimate at the Admiralty was compelled to remain, straining at the mouth of the Dardanelles with the warships, but no troops, for what all professional opinion still agreed would necessarily constitute a combined operation of great difficulty.

4

War by Sanhedrin

(August, 1914)

A nation that is liable to war requires men of war in its government, and, in the case of Great Britain, the place for them is in the Cabinet. The traditional practice of having a civilian minister inside the Cabinet with all the authority, and a soldier with all the knowledge outside the Cabinet, was devised for electioneering purposes, and not for war.[1]

SPENSER WILKINSON
DURING BLACK WEEK IN 1899

It is repugnant to me to have to reveal military secrets to twenty-three gentlemen [of the Cabinet] *with whom I am hardly acquainted.*[2]

LORD KITCHENER IN 1914

I quickly outgrew ideas. So I distrusted experts who were often intelligences confined within high walls, knowing indeed every paving-stone of their prison courts: while I might know from what quarry the stones were hewn and what wages the mason earned.[3]

T. E. LAWRENCE

He all their Ammunition
And feats of War defeats
With Plain Heroic magnitude of mind
And celestial vigour armed.[4]

MILTON

GIVEN the remarkably variegated and important military reforms undertaken in Edwardian Britain, by the standards of a later era it might be considered a matter for surprise that up to the outbreak of the First World War such inadequate methods had been devised for co-ordinating or reconciling opposing views on strategy. As Herbert Asquith asserted in a somewhat odd apology, the Cabinet rather than the Committee of Imperial Defence still remained the ultimate arbiter of such disputes, after, as well as before the commencement of hostilities. While this weakness of the C.I.D. as an institution was so zealously maintained following August 1914, the principal advantages of the Committee—its regular agenda, its carefully circulated minutes, its long-range strategic planning, and perhaps, above all, the equal and active participation of its military with its civilian members—were abruptly discarded at their moment of greatest need.[5] War might be too important to be left to the military, but it was now also far too complex to leave to what hereafter often amounted to an essentially civilian Council of War.

Three other basic deficiencies of the pre-war Committee of Imperial Defence, which similarly continued into the war with adverse consequences, had originated in a misconception common to all the belligerents of 1914, namely the inability to anticipate the prolonged and universal character of a general war in the twentieth century. These failures in the C.I.D. included a lack of planning for a serious expansion of either the armed forces or of the industrial bases for war, as well as a refusal to consider what organization would actually control the higher direction of war during hostilities. To be sure, the Esher Committee may have implied, and Hankey, the tireless Secretary of the C.I.D., unquestionably did appreciate, that the Committee of Imperial Defence alone could undertake this last function. But such a concept had remained in embryo, easily miscarried under the great shock of war, with consequences which would eventually result in David Lloyd George's overwhelming recognition that the war could not be won by a Sanhedrin.[6]

With customary indirection Hankey has cited Lord Curzon's celebrated description of the methods of Asquith's Coalition Cabinet of 1915–16 as applicable to the 1914–15 period. "There was," declared Curzon, "no agenda, there was no order of business . . . no record whatever was kept of our proceedings, except the private . . . letter written by the Prime Minister to the Sovereign. . . . The Cabinet often had the very haziest notion as to what its decisions were . . . cases frequently arose when the matter was left so much in doubt that a Minister went away and acted upon what he thought was a decision which subsequently turned out to be no decision at all, or was repudiated by his colleagues. . . . I do not think anyone will deny that the old Cabinet system had broken down, both as a war machine and as a peace machine."[7]

To accentuate the failure of the Cabinet, the General Staff of the Army, perhaps the most notable Edwardian military creation, was to be hopelessly submerged under the impact of war. Ignoring the still less desirable situation prevailing within his own rudimentary Admiralty War Staff, Winston Churchill has testified accurately of the Army in August 1914: "All the principal officers we were accustomed to work with went off to the war, and a new staff came in,"[8] sometimes consisting of what Churchill would shortly enjoy terming "dug-out trash" and "mediocrities who have led a sheltered life mouldering in military routine."[9]

A fortunate exception among such refurbished warriors, Major-General Charles Callwell, the new Director of Military Operations in August 1914, has testified that "the real reason why the General Staff ceased to exist was because it was not consulted."[10] And the first of the reasons for this lack of consultation may be found in the formidable character and reputation of Lord Kitchener.

Brought into the War Office as Secretary of State at the insistence of Lord Haldane to bolster the Liberal Cabinet with accretions on the Right to make up for its losses among the pacifists of its Left, Kitchener of Khartoum was more than a great recruiting poster. In a Cabinet of great men he was the greatest and the British public knew it. Northcliffe, the press magnate, might boast that he had made Kitchener; like two generations of detractors, Northcliffe would utterly fail to unmake him.[11]

Kitchener has been sharply delineated by Sir Osbert Sitwell, who, observing him in June 1914, wrote that he "plainly belonged to some different order of creation from those around him . . . he could claim kinship to the old race of gigantic German generals,

E

spawned by Wotan in the Prussian plains, and born with spiked helmets ready on their heads. As he sat there with the same suggestion of immense strength and even of latent fury . . . every trait of his appearance . . . proclaimed him to be English; not an English leader of the patrician type, such as Wellington, but one from that class that had, since the Reform Bill, monopolized power."[12]

A shy man and secretive, Kitchener was now thrust into a War Council of men belonging to a profession with which he had been struggling all his life, and for which, according to Lloyd George, "he had the usual mixture of military contempt and apprehension. His main idea at the Council table was to tell the politicians as little as possible of what was going on and get back to his desk at the War Office as quickly as he could decently escape."[13]

Asquith had embarked upon what he himself called the "hazardous experiment" of drafting the reluctant Kitchener as the first active professional soldier in a modern democratic Cabinet. From South African days, Kitchener was fully aware that no one man could cope with the burden of the War Office and had then written that he would sooner sweep a crossing than serve in it.[14] Incapable of easy teamwork with the silver-tongued civilians, in any event Kitchener preferred an independent command in a distant post of Empire where the romance of the exotic lent authority to his reputation. In his frantic efforts to escape from assisting the Edwardian reformers in cleansing the Augean military stables at home, he once told a member of the Cabinet: "I don't know Europe, I don't know England and I don't know the British Army."[15] However untrue, these words would be used against him.

In his close friend Ian Hamilton's phrase, this "Master of Expedients", who "hated" and "smashed organizations",[16] had recognized when he set up the General Staff and Staff College in India that "nothing is more essential . . . for successful operation in war than that an army should have a thoroughly trained and highly educated General Staff."[17] But Asquith himself admitted that Kitchener acted as his own chief of staff in 1914, a process enhanced by the War Office tendency to ignore the series of nonentities selected for this post prior to the appointment of Sir William Robertson. The conclusions of the Dardanelles Commissioners here are just. The Commissioners reported: "Lord Kitchener did not sufficiently avail himself of the services of his General Staff, with the result that more work was undertaken by him than was possible for one man to do, and confusion and want of efficiency resulted."[18] If, in truth, Kitchener was poorly suited for his new job, unlike most of his critics within the Cabinet he tended to be right in essentials.

The most important of these essentials involved the proper gauging of the course and duration of the war. One advantage of Kitchener's atypical but profound military mentality was that, distrusting, as he did, Henry Wilson and his continental school of strategic thought at Camberley almost as much as did his intimate, Ian Hamilton, Kitchener kept his distance from what Hamilton has called "a plague worse than those of a Pharaoh, a General Staff war". At the same time, much to the disappointment of his enemies in the Cabinet, Kitchener would get on with that eventual strong man of the General Staff, Sir William Robertson.[19] As usual, Lord Esher grasped the point about Kitchener, noting in August 1914: "There never was such a wild elephant. And yet! his instincts are true enough and he is far away from a pedant!"[20]

Well before Black Week in the South African War, Kitchener had warned his fellow officers that vast forces would be required to subdue the Boers in a long and laborious struggle. Now, taking his seat at the Prime Minister's right as his dominant adviser on grand strategy, in the beginning of August 1914, Kitchener proceeded to utter what Churchill himself has called "a series of inspiring and prophetic truths". Dissociating himself from the views of those about him, Kitchener declared that the war could be won only by great battles on the Continent. To such holocausts the British Empire must contribute its fair share in armies of millions of men, an unprecedented idea for a nation which so vastly preferred her traditional role as the principal seapower and paymaster of a coalition. Nevertheless, Kitchener said that armies of such size could be raised within the Empire, since the war might well last for several years. Last, but not least in the long run, Kitchener said that the war could not be limited in any way.[21]

The Cabinet took the shock rather well of discovering for the first time that they had just chosen to join the negative side of the twentieth century—no doubt, in part, because, like Sir Edward Grey, who did not wish to know about war, or like General Henry Wilson, who did not know about anything else, they did not yet really understand their new War Minister. They were still sleeping what George Orwell years later described as the deep, deep sleep of England, a sleep from which Orwell feared "we shall never wake till we are jerked out of it by the roar of bombs".[22] And when Kitchener told the Australians, several years before August 1914, that it would be "the last and not the first million England can put into the field that will give us the victory",[23] he was reflecting an outlook which transcended alike the stubborn insularity of the Admiralty, the continental parochialism of the General Staff, and the incorrigible innocence of the civilians. Here, if anywhere in Great Britain, the war had met its peer. Retrospective lamentation notwithstanding, no man would or could prove its master.

On August 5, 1914, the day following the British declaration of war, Prime Minister Asquith met with his War Council. Asquith opened what Henry Wilson once again called a "historic meeting of men, mostly entirely ignorant of their subject", by saying that he had convened this assemblage of seventeen statesmen, soldiers and sailors at the earliest possible moment.[24] Under the plausible assumption that British strategy should not be finally settled until her policy had been determined, Asquith's assertion might be considered true. Nevertheless, except in so far as delay on the formulation of her policy had affected the unfolding of her strategy, British strategy had been settled by Henry Wilson and the General Staff since 1911, if not earlier.

In short, the issue facing the War Council on August 5 was the issue already faced by all the other European belligerents in 1914: whether or not Great Britain's traditionally opportunist policy

52

could be related to an already thoroughly predetermined strategy. After the usual parallels to the similar agonies elsewhere in Europe, the War Council hurriedly thrust the horse of policy into its proper position ahead of the already rapidly accelerating cart of strategy. Not surprisingly, the horse was rather badly bruised in the process.

Significantly, however, at this stage in Britain the arguments over grand strategy were chiefly among the military. Unlike their continental counterparts, the British statesmen, still deluding themselves, in Esher's phrase, that they were flinging themselves into an absolute and general war "upon a plank of limited liability",[25] would require more time to appreciate the overwhelming repercussions of their seemingly most trivial actions on August 5, 1914. And, for that matter, so would the cocksure and conceited Major-General Henry Wilson, who was about to ridicule Kitchener for raising shadow armies for shadow campaigns at unknown dates at the expense of a supposedly rapid decision in France.

In the event, Kitchener proved right, and Wilson and his General Staff were in for the rude awakening sadly anticipated by Lord Esher, when he noted on August 27 that London society similarly tended to regard the war "as a sort of picnic, chequered by untoward incident", but there "will come a day when the flower of our manhood will have been gathered by the reaper, and when the casualty lists will contain none but plebeian names that convey nothing to anyone beyond the mourners in obscure homes."[26] Kitchener, for one, knew what he was doing on August 5 when he pushed through the decision to dispatch the bulk of Haldane's expeditionary force to the Continent at once.[27] With the naval situation unexpectedly favourable as a result of Battenberg's foresight and Churchill's courage, to Henry Wilson's rather pathetic gratitude, Churchill again "behaved like a hero" on August 5 in advocating the immediate dispatch of the entire expeditionary force to France.[28] As so often, hereafter, when action was concerned, Churchill's advocacy was more rapid and forceful than that of Kitchener.

Interestingly, the First Lord had not taken up what Henry Wilson naturally termed Sir John French's "ridiculous proposal" to send the British Expeditionary Force to Antwerp. Harking back to the prewar Admiralty position, Churchill had declared that the Navy could not guarantee the sea communications of so large a land force as the B.E.F. inside the North Sea. Moreover, the General Staff had worked out no alternative plans for a concentration on Antwerp, and even the original British proponent of Antwerp, Lieutenant-General Sir James Grierson, now spoke up in favour of decisive numbers at the decisive point, which with Kitchener, Douglas Haig, and Hamilton, he located on the French left flank in France.[29] Haig who, in any case, had a low opinion of the capacities of Sir John French, declared that he "trembled at the reckless way" in which Sir John had spoken about the "advantages" of the B.E.F. operating as a small detached force from Antwerp against the powerful and still intact German Army.[30] With good reason the pessimistic Haig, who with Kitchener anticipated a long war, feared a defeat "in detail", if the British were separated from the French Army.

Selected, to Kitchener's regret and his own gratified relief, rather than Hamilton or Haig as Commander of the British Expeditionary Force, Sir John French did not push his Antwerp suggestion after Sir Edward Grey explained that his hopes of Dutch aid were unlikely. In an attempted compromise, however, Sir John proposed sending the B.E.F. to France first, moving overland thereafter along the coast to Belgium. The tenor of Sir John French's more maritime than continental thought is already perfectly apparent from August 5, and it must not be forgotten that he was an intimate friend of Churchill, however divergent their strategies might momentarily appear on this day of dupes. As the commander of the B.E.F. himself very fairly recognized: "The vital element of the problem was speed in mobilization and concentration; change of plans meant inevitable and possibly fatal delay."[31]

With the generals at last in agreement on the necessity for going to France, on still another matter the self-proclaimed innocent on Europe and the British Army would manifest a remarkable foresight regarding the point on which the British Expeditionary Force should concentrate in France. Henry Wilson had long envisaged Maubeuge on the Belgian frontier as his *point d'appui*, but Great Britain had delayed in entering the war and, as Kitchener, if not Wilson, had anticipated, the Germans were coming through Belgium farther north, and thus much closer to Maubeuge than was desirable for the security of an assembly point. Therefore, on August 6, although not yet holding any official post, let alone the appropriate one of Chief of the Imperial General Staff, Kitchener persuaded Asquith to concentrate the B.E.F. upon Amiens, a town much farther from the frontier than Maubeuge. To Wilson's even sharper dismay, on August 6 Asquith also ruled that only four of the six infantry divisions of the B.E.F. should be sent into the maelstrom immediately. Kitchener had never liked to put all his eggs in one basket, and in certain respects had obtained a more realistic knowledge of the relative capacities of the French and German armies from first-hand observation of the Franco-Prussian War than Wilson had gleaned in his studies at Camberley or with that academic Bergsonian, General Ferdinand Foch.[32]

After a delay of another six days, on August 12, Wilson, Sir John French and the General Staff, all supported by the authority of General Joffre, confronted Kitchener on the issue of concentrating upon Maubeuge instead of Amiens. Following a three-hour wrangle, Kitchener gave in to the combined weight of the British and French experts. Confessing that the Anglo-French staffs had studied the problem for years, Kitchener reluctantly accepted Maubeuge as the British concentration point, subject only to the more or less automatic approval of a Prime Minister who did not believe in openly contradicting the experts. But, as Henry Wilson's first biographer has generously admitted, the direction of the German advance proved Kitchener right in favouring Amiens as the more secure point for the concentration of the B.E.F. Fortunately, the delay in movement and limitations upon the strength of the B.E.F. imposed by Kitchener's caution had discouraged Sir John French from sacrificing his small force with anything like the reckless audacity displayed by the far larger French armies in Lorraine. As a result, the British Expeditionary Force escaped from Mons to fight on another, more favourable, and far more decisive day during the battle of the Marne.[33]

Like Kitchener on the questions of the duration of the war, the need for great armies, and for caution in their employment, to some degree all men anticipate as probable or certain events, which, with that prior anticipation at heart, they then proceed to render so. Alignment as an integral part of the French left wing would henceforth make it impossible for the British Army to break loose from the Continent, except by inviting almost certain disaster for the Anglo-French armies. In the analysis of J. E. Tyler, an analysis representative of the disillusioned decades between the two World Wars, it was now definite that in the end Great Britain would be "obliged to raise the conscript army of Wilson's dreams. 'Amphibious strategy' gave way to a thoroughgoing land war in Europe with all the sacrifice entailed."[34]

Thus, as Kitchener perceived so clearly in 1914, bound irrevocably to France both from the desire for victory and from the need to stave off defeat, Great Britain was no longer granted much real choice on the degree of her participation in a general continental war. Only with the collapse of France in 1940 would Britain regain a measure of freedom of action in grand strategy and then only for three or four years.

5

Resurrected

(September—October, 1914)

We want a sea-going Army that we can launch forth anywhere AT AN HOUR'S NOTICE! Not six months![1]

ADMIRAL FISHER IN 1908

The second conclusion is that to make the navy an effective weapon we require a military instrument capable of being used in conjunction with it. . . . To this end a highly trained army for such over-sea work is essential.[2]

GENERAL SIR IAN HAMILTON IN 1911

It is Antwerp we shall seize, and not go fooling on the Vosages Frontier.[3]

ADMIRAL FISHER IN 1912

I feel I have it in me [to be a successful soldier]. I can visualize great movements and combinations.[4]

WINSTON CHURCHILL IN 1913

BEFORE the war shook down to a gruelling deadlock in that terrible main and decisive theatre in France, several efforts at an independent British maritime strategy were essayed. The first of these efforts—still extremely tentative in nature—appeared towards the end of August, when Fisher's man as the new Secretary of the Committee of Imperial Defence, Lieutenant-Colonel Hankey of the Royal Marines, proposed the employment of a brigade of Marines along the Belgian coast to distract the vastly overextended Germans inland with the possibility of a larger British follow-up. By September 18, following the German retreat from the Marne, General Joffre, the French Commander-

57

in-Chief, appealed for the further use of British Marines to cover the now threatened Channel ports of Calais and Dunkirk. Eager for some obvious and dramatic action by the Navy, Churchill soon had untrained Marine detachments ostentatiously parading London omnibuses through Northern France and Flanders, an operation which shortly became notorious within ministerial circles as the Dunkirk Circus.[5]

After the German retreat from the Marne, as the main forces of the belligerents began the race for the sea, with Kitchener's cordial approval Churchill opened discussions with Sir John French along the lines of the latter's proposal of August 5 for a sideslipping movement of the B.E.F. up the French coast towards the increasingly threatened Belgian citadel at Antwerp. On October 1 the Germans began to penetrate the outer forts of Antwerp, and Kitchener offered to relieve the beleaguered port with two newly formed but regular British divisions from the United Kingdom, if the French Army would offer a first-line division for so difficult and hazardous an operation.[6]

In the absence of the Prime Minister on the evening of October 2, Lord Kitchener and Sir Edward Grey decided to allow the more-than-eager First Lord of the Admiralty to go to Antwerp to dissuade the Belgians from surrendering their final stronghold. Churchill, who had been stressing the importance of Antwerp to the Cabinet for almost a month, brought across the North Sea in his wake, as a token of larger reinforcements in the offing, his own Marine brigade from Dunkirk. This Marine brigade would, in fact, be followed shortly by two other still more poorly trained Naval brigades extorted by Churchill from a Government as yet in no way organized for the fast moving circumstances of war.[7]

Once in Antwerp, as the still indulgent Asquith had anticipated, Churchill spurred the Belgians into a few more days' resistance, in a performance foreshadowing greater occasions to come. The Germans, thereby, may have been distracted from the vital Channel ports long enough for Sir John French to occupy these ports in strength, if not to relieve Antwerp itself. Unhappily, the intoxication of the event seems to have gone to the young First

Lord's head because, in Asquith's less amicable account a few days later, having "tasted blood", Churchill's mouth began to water at the thought of the glory and excitement of an independent Army command. To the astonishment and amusement of the Cabinet, instead of returning promptly from his Belgian adventure to his duties at the Admiralty, Churchill telegraphed London to suggest that he should resign the Admiralty and assume command of all the Entente forces in Antwerp. Although Kitchener, with whom Churchill was getting on splendidly in this period, was perfectly amenable to accepting such an unprecedented offer on the part of a member of the Cabinet, the more politically astute and rather disillusioned Asquith demanded the prompt return of his errant First Lord.[8]

Unfortunately for Churchill's reputation, not to mention that of Mr Asquith's Government, Henry Wilson's savage reaction proved representative of much Conservative and professional military opinion in Britain, when the loss of most of one of the brigades of the Royal Naval Division to internment in the Netherlands became apparent. "K. and Winston have so arranged their childish strategy," wrote Wilson, "that they have lost 2,000 Marines and some guns, and have not saved Antwerp."[9] Wilson's good friend and Churchill's inveterate enemy in the Conservative Opposition, Andrew Bonar Law, wrote of Antwerp that it seemed to him "an utterly stupid business", pushed through by a First Lord of "entirely unbalanced mind".[10] For a statesman whose deductions concerning continental strategy had already appeared "sound and straight" in Henry Wilson's view so early as 1912,[11] an Antwerp emphasis would obviously seem stupid, quite apart from Law's strong personal antipathy to Churchill.

More significantly, within the Royal Navy opinion was shifting against Churchill, if not often as violently as that of a particularly bitter naval collaborator of the First Lord in this period at the Admiralty, the Assistant Director of Operations, Captain Herbert Richmond. The erudite Richmond, who after the war would become the first Commandant of the Imperial Defence College, wrote of Antwerp that he did not mind Churchill's sending "his tuppenny untrained rabble" to Antwerp, but that he did object to their loss, since these few Marines constituted the Navy's "last reserve" for combined operations. Richmond declared that it was "a tragedy that the Navy should be in such lunatic hands at this time".[12] Leaving aside the friction of high-strung personalities at the Admiralty and the paucity of strictly naval means available to Churchill at the time, in principle it is difficult to imagine a more desirable combined operation than one which might save both the Channel ports and the Belgian Army; yet, as the disheartened[13] First Lord of the Admiralty was learning, defeat has few friends and men are judged by their achievements rather than by their principles.

Even before the seeming fiasco at Antwerp, a vainglorious speech by Churchill on September 21 concerning the need to dig the German "rats out of their holes" in the North Sea had been followed by apparent retribution in the form of the loss of three British cruisers in the North Sea to a single German submarine. Churchill's speech was reminiscent of Admiral Sir Arthur Wilson's old desire for a close blockade of German ports, a desire necessarily thwarted by the still unsolved problems of mines and U-boats, but which, to the great alarm of Captain Richmond, the First Lord had abandoned with notable reluctance.[14] Instead, in August, Richmond had called Churchill a "shouting amateur" for his proposal to seize a naval base in the neutral Netherlands. By the end of September the Assistant Director of Naval Operations had concluded more temperately: "There is no doubt that we are the most appalling amateurs who ever tried to conduct a war . . . we do not train our officers upon any principles of war, nor make them concentrate their minds on how war should be waged."[15]

The humiliating retirement of the Grand Fleet from its poorly protected main anchorage at Scapa Flow, and the augmented threat of the submarines to merchant shipping, provoked a serious warning from Churchill's warm admirer, Admiral Sir David Beatty. Beatty, who certainly could not be charged with lacking courage, wrote to the First Lord in a private communication: "The feeling is gradually possessing the Fleet that all is not right somewhere. The menace of mines and submarines is proving larger every day . . . and we are gradually being pushed out of the North Sea. . . . I think you know me well enough to know that I do not shout without cause . . . I would not write thus if I did not know that you with your quick grasp of detail and imagination would make something out of it."[16]

Two years later, when asked by Lord Riddell whether Beatty had taken the proper course of action at Jutland, Churchill would explain: "Yes, it was a brilliant affair—worthy of the best traditions of the Navy. The public do not understand naval warfare. They criticize naval losses more severely than military losses. The loss of a ship is regarded as a crime."[17] Throughout the First World War, as in the Second, Winston Churchill preferred to spend in warships in order to save the lives of soldiers, expendable though these may have appeared in comparison with *matériel* in 1914.

In 1916 Captain Richmond would conclude that, while Churchill had studied war, he did not understand sea war, and that Churchill's naval advisers were themselves "so ignorant that they could not keep him straight and make use of his really valuable qualities". At that time, Richmond reiterated that the "so-called" Admiralty War Staff set up by Churchill was so much "eyewash", constituting "a body which never was nor ever could be called a war staff, as it was deficient in all the characteristics that are needed for staff work".[18]

The lack of high officers trained in staff duties was unquestionably an important cause of the First Lord's difficulties at the start of the war and, as with Kitchener, this tended to push Churchill into attempting to exercise the functions of the First Sea Lord in controlling strategy and even tactics throughout his tenure of office at the Admiralty. In the words of another naval critic of this period, Churchill's "immense range of superficial knowledge beguiled him into believing that that knowledge was accurate and profound. In executive command in the field he would, in all probability, have earned undying fame, but, temperamentally, he was unsuited to fill the post of civilian head of a highly technical department in wartime."[19] And Churchill himself has made no bones regarding his conception of the role of the First Lord of the Admiralty. Replying to his critics even before the war he had declared: "The collective and corporate responsibility of the Board of Admiralty is a matter of high importance, but the swift and effective executive control of events is a matter of still higher importance."[20]

With a weak or acquiescent First Sea Lord, such an attitude might result only in friction within the Navy; with a strong First Sea Lord, such as Churchill now sought in Jacky Fisher to bolster his threatened political career, Churchill's assumption of the prerogatives of the obsolete office of Lord High Admiral could only lead to a public row and, in time of war, very possibly to naval disaster.[21]

Churchill was warned regarding the probability of such a clash, the King particularly opposing Battenberg's supersession by Fisher on the grounds that at seventy-four the latter was too old and had too many enemies within the Navy. The Prime Minister explained to his monarch, however, that in view of Battenberg's unpopular German background, the political advantages of the change, combined with Churchill's insistence that he could work only with Fisher, left him no choice in the matter. Fisher's comparative acceptability to the Conservatives, and Battenberg's lack of energy and capacity to stand up to Churchill, were also unspoken considerations in the mind of the Prime Minister.[22]

Churchill's own explanation to Lord Riddell two years later would concede that Fisher could not be trusted and that he could only work three or four hours a day, but even in 1916 Churchill would loyally proclaim the Kingfisher to be a man of genius whose three or four hours a day were worth more than the full time of any alternative First Sea Lord. Commodore Roger Keyes also subscribed to this view in spite of the jeopardy to his career afforded by Fisher's enmity, and Admiral Sir David Beatty wrote to his wife on November 2, 1914: "Prince Louis has gone. . . .

They have resurrected old Fisher. Well, I think he is the best they could have done, but I wish he was ten years younger. He still has fine zeal, energy, and determination, coupled with low cunning, which is eminently desirable just now. He also has courage and will take any responsibility. He will recognize that his position is absolutely secure and will ride the Admiralty and Winston with a heavy hand . . . and please God we shall change our present method for a strong offensive policy. . . ." In this connection Beatty blamed the incompetency of the Admiralty for the recent defeat of the Royal Navy at Coronel by the Germans. Beatty further complained that the Admiralty's current conception of strategy was infantile.[23]

In September Fisher had told Churchill that he was ready to do "any mortal thing, even to co-operating with Beresford! if [it would be] any good for the War." Shortly after his reappointment as First Sea Lord the old Admiral went to pray at Westminster Abbey and, upon leaving, was heard to mutter: "Resurrected! Resurrected! Resurrected! Again!"[24]

6

Special Fun

(October 30—December 28, 1914)

If there's a war, one man at the Admiralty will run the war! Don't make any mistake about that certain fact![1]

ADMIRAL FISHER IN 1912

What a good thing it is to have an optimist at the front!

WINSTON CHURCHILL

Excellent, provided you have also, as we have in K, a pessimist in the rear.[2]

HERBERT ASQUITH IN DECEMBER, 1914

What a hell of a time you must be having! It is a thousand pities that Winston should be so confident that his knowledge of the military art is profound when in fact he is so lacking in strategical judgment.[3]

FIELD-MARSHAL SIR JOHN DILL
TO THE C.I.G.S. IN 1944

I do wish Winston would give up strategy as his special fun, and interference in small military matters.[4]

MAJOR-GENERAL J. N. KENNEDY,
DIRECTOR OF MILITARY OPERATIONS IN 1944

FISHER returned to the Admiralty deeply grateful to his former pupil for his restoration as First Sea Lord and not inclined to make trouble regarding the faulty organization of the Admiralty, a faulty organization, indeed, for which he was largely responsible. Although, thanks to Haldane's and Battenberg's intervention in 1912, the Admiralty War Staff came under the authority of the First Sea Lord rather than the First Lord, contrary to Fisher's desire, both in 1912 and in 1914, the office of Chief of the War Staff remained separate from that of First Sea Lord. This separation of these necessarily interwoven offices by Winston Churchill in 1912 may have been an excuse for Sir Arthur Wilson's resignation as First Sea Lord: in any event, in 1914, notwithstanding Churchill's conciliatory gestures in replacing a Fisher enemy as Chief of the War Staff with a member of the so-called Fishpond, Rear-Admiral Henry Oliver, the friction inherent in unclear channels of authority was still there. Only after Churchill had left the Admiralty and Jellicoe became First Sea Lord could the two posts finally be combined.[5]

Something of Fisher's difficulties with his new civilian master, soon after resuming his old post at the Admiralty, are reflected in an unusually indiscreet letter he wrote to Admiral Jellicoe commanding the Grand Fleet, in December 1914.

My beloved Jellicoe . . . Winston has so monopolized all initiative in the Admiralty and fires off such a multitude of purely departmental memos (*his power of work is absolutely amazing!*) that my colleagues are no longer "*superintending Lords,*" but only "*the First Lord's Registry*"! I told Winston this yesterday and he did not like it at all, but *it is true!* and the consequence is that the Sea Lords are atrophied and their departments run really by the Private Office, and I find it a Herculean task to get back to the right procedure, and quite possibly I may have to clear out, and I've warned Winston of this. . . . The distribution of weak slow ships all over the world is disastrous. . . . It's too laughable! and yet Sturdee [former Chief of the Admiralty War Staff] [is] considered a great brain man! and he alone did it all! for Battenberg was a cypher and Winston's facile dupe![6]

Fisher had returned to the Admiralty only twenty-four hours ahead of the British defeat at Coronel. Even before hearing of the engagement, over the objection of Winston Churchill, Fisher's first action had been to order reinforcement of Rear-Admiral Sir Christopher Cradock's squadron. Upon receipt of the news of Coronel, Fisher promptly ordered two battlecruisers to be sent from Jellicoe's Grand Fleet without a moment's delay beyond the absolute minimum for preparation. Over the protests of the naval dockyards, and with workmen still aboard, the two battlecruisers sailed, arriving in the South Atlantic just in time to win the victory of the Falklands.

Well might Churchill write to the masterful old Admiral in heartfelt appreciation on December 10: "My Dear: This was your show and your luck. I should . . . have sent [fewer ships] . . . This would have done the trick. But it was a great *coup*. Your flair was quite true. Let us have some more victories together and confound all our foes abroad—and (don't forget) at home." Admiral Bacon, for one, has questioned whether Churchill's belief that fewer battlecruisers would have done the trick is justified. Bacon declares that, on the contrary, Fisher's two battlecruisers were essential as margin for error and that only Churchill's amateur grasp of tactics had kept him from understanding the real reason for Fisher's flair—not mere panache, but more than a half century of professional sea experience.[7]

The reason behind Fisher's ruthlesss dispatch in disposing of the German raiders in the outer oceans was to be found not only in the simple pleasure of vindicating his Navy, but still more in upholding (as he wrote Beatty on November 15) "the main object of all [British naval] strategy", the mustering of "overwhelming strength in the decisive area, and the decisive area is the North Sea".[8]

On the other hand, on October 20 the Cabinet had concluded that "we ought to take a vigorous offensive against Turkey and to make every effort to bring in Bulgaria, Greece and, above all, Roumania". Within three days British Indian troops were landed at the head of the Persian Gulf in order to protect the oil resources at Abadan; within a month these troops had inaugurated the first of several improvised campaigns against Turkey, in this instance the inglorious expedition against Mesopotamia.[9]

The German failure, increasingly apparent after the Marne, to destroy France in a quick campaign, induced the Reich, likewise, to reconsider the advantages of Turkish neutrality. Although their supply lines to Constantinople were about to be cut, the value of a

Turkish threat to distract the Russian armies from Germany's still weakly held Eastern Front was growing. Moreover, a Turkish entry into war would permanently interdict Entente trade with Russia through the Dardanelles, might provide a counterweight against the uneasy neutrality of Bulgaria, and, finally, could threaten British imperial communications at Suez with the appearance of an assault on the Canal.

Concerning this last possibility, in the words of the German Chief of Staff, General von Falkenhayn, so much like those of General Alfred Jodl in 1943, such a simulated Turkish threat to Suez would tend "to keep strong British forces away from the main theatre of war, whilst Germany's resources were not involved to any harmful extent by enterprises in Asia". If Falkenhayn had his way, Germany's resources would not be frittered away on so-called "Alexander the Great" campaigns in the Near East as long as romantics such as Field-Marshal von der Goltz, soon to be sent by Berlin to Constantinople, did not determine German strategy.[10]

If Mr Churchill had been active in promoting the parallel decision of the British Cabinet in favour of an offensive against the still nominally neutral Turkish state, Lord Kitchener was strongly opposed to adding another enemy to Britain's military commitments until additional troops from India had traversed the Suez Canal. The Director of Military Operations, Major-General Charles Callwell, also warned Churchill that the capture of the Dardanelles would be mainly an Army task, a conclusion similar to that of the Greek General Staff earlier in the autumn of 1914. Callwell added that in his opinion the operation would be extremely difficult in the face of Turkish entrenchments.[11]

Through chicanery, on October 30 the Germans induced the Turko-German Navy to shell Russian Black Sea ports, and Winston Churchill at last had an opponent in the Mediterranean. Alleging the need to test the ranges of the Turkish batteries at the entrance to the Dardanelles, and without apparent reference to the Cabinet, or even waiting for a formal British declaration of war, on November 1 Churchill ordered the British squadron covering the entrance to the Dardanelles to shell the outer forts. This action took place on November 3 for about ten minutes. Whether Fisher had concurred in this decision on the part of the Admiralty is unknown, but, in retrospect, British military opinion and the Dardanelles Commission alike have generally criticized this gratuitous warning to the Turks to mend their defences. Hankey, as usual, has blamed the incident upon the defective organization for the higher direction of war and, like others, has seen analogies with Churchill's provocative policies towards Norway[12] or Vichy France in the Second World War.

In fact, Turkey profited far more than the Royal Navy from this bombardment, because the Turks now heeded the suggestions of their professional German advisers to shift their main defensive strength from the vulnerable outer forts of the Dardanelles to a reliance upon a skilful combination of mine-fields within the Straits, supported by concealed and mobile artillery on the Gallipoli Peninsula. But not until February 1915 would the Turks reinforce their single division on the Peninsula with any of their numerous and nearby divisions in Thrace or Constantinople. Their ammunition was also in very short supply and their mines few in number.[13]

When Mr Asquith's War Council met on November 25 for a further discussion of a long-range strategy in the Mediterranean, to some extent its organization had been improved to fit the longer war which day by day was becoming more apparent, except to the professional optimists in France. Taking advantage of the tendency, manifest at Antwerp and before, for leading ministers to make rapid decisions without necessarily convening the whole Cabinet, the War Council of November 25 had only eight regular members, plus the ubiquitous Hankey as its secretary. Given Asquith's compromising nature, however, within four months it had again increased to thirteen.

Mr Asquith's insistence to the contrary notwithstanding, in other respects the official War Council established in November resembled the haphazard Cabinet committees of the first few months of the war rather than the well-organized machinery of the pre-war Committee of Imperial Defence. This was, in part, due to the Prime Minister's traditional Liberal fear of subordinating the Cabinet to a War Council, so that many vital decisions had to be referred back to the Cabinet for eventual approval, with inevitable and, as will be seen, on occasion disastrous delays. Moreover, in accord with the gentlemanly amateur traditions of nineteenth-century Cabinet procedure, and contrary to the practice of the C.I.D., neither an agenda nor arrangements for regular meetings were provided.

Most seriously, and again despite Mr Asquith's disclaimers, as the Dardanelles Commissioners would ultimately declare: "It was not the practice to ask the [professional military] experts attending the Council to express their opinions. The experts themselves did not consider it their duty either to express any opinions, unless they were asked to do so, or to intimate dissent, at the Council board, if they disagreed with the views set forth by the Ministers in charge of their respective Departments. [Thus] the Council was, in technical matters, guided wholly by the views laid before them by the Secretary of State for War and the First Lord of the Admiralty."[14] Finally, no machinery for joint staff planning was set up, with the result that each Department made its own plans without much reference to those of the other branches of the Government. War by and for gentlemen was breaking down as surely as had a Cabinet and Government derived from such principles, but Herbert Asquith lacked the temperament to make a rapid, let alone radical, break with the past here, as in so many other particulars.

Although without the benefit of an agenda, the still comparatively small War Council of November 25 met to discuss the problem of the defence of Egypt against the Turkish threat to the Suez Canal. In agreement with the Duke of Wellington's emphasis in 1839 upon the vulnerability of Turkish communications in Syria, and with the conclusion of Colonel Surtees, made during the C.I.D. study of the problem in 1906, that the defence of Egypt would be best realized by British amphibious attacks on such logistic bottlenecks as Haifa or Alexandretta, Kitchener had already opened discussions on this issue with his chosen instrument in Egypt, Lieutenant-General Sir John Maxwell. As former sirdar in Egypt, Kitchener had long been concerned with the possibilities of employing rebellious Arab irregulars against Turkish communications in the event of war and had contemplated the resulting possible dissolution of the Turkish Empire with considerable equanimity.[15] Indeed, earlier in November the British Government had announced the formal annexation of such former portions of the Ottoman Empire as Cyprus and Egypt; moreover, inaugurating the abandonment of the historic British position on the Straits, Sir Edward Grey had also given the Russians certain guarantees of compensation along the Bosphorus in return for their vital sacrifices on the Eastern Front.

After Kitchener had explained to the War Council that currently he lacked troops for any major operation in the Mediterranean (the Australian and New Zealand Army Corps—or ANZAC—was just arriving in Egypt and still lacked training and artillery) Churchill advocated a combined attack on the Dardanelles as the best method of protecting Egypt. That the First Lord's fancies had risen considerably beyond the simple defence of the Canal was made clear by his conclusion that the success of such a combined assault would "enable us to dictate terms at Constantinople".[16] Realistically, however, the First Lord had coupled this old dream of his hero Napoleon—to smash the Turks and "take Europe in the rear"—with the candid admission that such a combined operation by the British Army and Navy would be very difficult and would demand large forces. Churchill was never solely a demagogic Alcibiades to Kitchener's more prudent Niceas, although there are as many parallels between the Sicilian and Dardanelles campaigns as between the Peloponnesian and the two World Wars.[17]

An excess in candour has disadvantages, as the First Lord in time came to appreciate, and the War Council reflected small enthusiasm for so large and difficult an additional campaign in the Dardanelles at a moment when ammunition was already in desperately short supply on the Western Front. Churchill attempted to save something of his proposal by urging that shipping be collected in the Mediterranean against the contingency of future amphibious operations, but this stopgap was knocked out on the grounds that merchant shipping was also lacking. As a sop to the First Lord, in what Admiral Bacon has called a typical War Council decision, horse boats were to be sent to Egypt whenever opportunity offered.[18]

If Churchill found himself thwarted for the moment on his hopes for a combined assault against the Dardanelles, the return of Fisher to the Admiralty revived the possibilities of amphibious warfare within waters of far greater concern to the First Sea Lord: the North Sea. Although Captain Richmond had expressed the anxiety of the Admiralty War Staff in mid-November to the effect that Fisher might "dissipate our force" and depend upon only a slight margin of superiority in the North Sea, the latter was now in hearty support of a plan concocted by Churchill and Sir John French to recover Ostend and Zeebrugge by means of an amphibious operation along the Belgian coast, perhaps precisely for the sake of retaining his principal forces in his principal theatre.[19]

The lack of interest of Kitchener, who in any event wished to replace Sir John French with Sir Ian Hamilton, and a momentary hostility on the part of Joffre stalled this inclination towards a more maritime strategy. In December, despite his growing interest in the advantages of naval gunfire for combined operations, Churchill himself admitted to Fisher that he was "not quite happy" about the Zeebrugge operation on the Belgian coast. The First Lord added: "I am shy of landings under fire—unless there is no other way."[20]

Angry at Sir John French's efforts to procure more ammunition for his proposed coastal offensive, Kitchener now turned on Churchill and what he called the First Lord's "wild cat schemes" for amphibious operations. In a fury, too, over Churchill's irregular military formations, Kitchener submitted his resignation to the Prime Minister and suggested that Churchill take his post as Secretary of State for War and that Fisher become First Lord in Churchill's place. By December 22 Asquith had patched up relations between his two temperamental ministers,[21] and Churchill turned his attentions to trying to persuade Admiral Fisher to press more urgently the First Sea Lord's old scheme of seizing Borkum, one of the German Frisian Islands, as the first step in an amphibious invasion of the Baltic. But now neither the old Admiral nor his subordinates in the War Staff showed much zeal for such an impracticable plan, dependent as it was upon the prior annihilation of the German Navy.[22] Although not yet satisfied that the war would last beyond 1915, at least his consideration of Belgian and Baltic operations had induced Churchill to authorize Fisher's immense construction programme of light and landing craft; vessels which would be of the utmost value when at last the First Lord's restless search for amphibious action hit upon a target more or less acceptable to all.[23]

7

Ninepins

(December 28, 1914—January 13, 1915)

In war it is necessary not only to be active, but to seem active.[1]

BONAR LAW

L. G. wants a victory quickly, a victory while you wait. He does not care where. Somewhere where opinion will be impressed . . .[2]

SIR WILLIAM ROBERTSON IN 1916

This is a soft job—not like fighting the Germans. . . . What we want is a big show in the shop window. We should do this like the Germans did Norway. Remember how easy Madagascar proved to be?[3]

WINSTON CHURCHILL IN 1942

But the Eastern heresy has fast hold on the minds of men who have no faith in soldiers and no principles in war.[4]

LORD ESHER IN 1916

ON December 29, 1914, the Prime Minister noted that he had received "two very interesting memoranda", one from Churchill and the other from Hankey, regarding strategic alternatives to what the First Lord termed chewing barbed wire on the Western Front.[5] Kitchener had similarly been urged by that tireless exponent of a maritime strategy, Lord Esher, that "our greatest weakness is the want of co-ordination between the naval, military and political forces of the Empire. . . . The army of a maritime power loses half its effect when it is not employed in combination with its fleet and diplomatic service."[6] Two other

factors present at the end of 1914, which likewise favoured movement along the lines stressed by such influential advocates, included the release of several older capital ships for new tasks as a
consequence of the naval victory of the Falklands, as well as the
ever more desperate shortage of ammunition so essential to land
offensives in France.[7] On the other hand, the percentage of
the German Army on the Western Front, although declining,
still amounted to eighty per cent of the total strength of the
Reich.[8]

In essence, the Hankey memorandum of December 26–8 had
offered two methods of overcoming "the remarkable deadlock"
on the Western Front. The first involved a variety of new technical devices, such as those with which Churchill would come to
be associated; the second, which Hankey himself considered
more realistic, proposed following the traditional British policy of
conquering overseas possessions of the enemy to gain "assets to
barter against his successes on the Continent of Europe when
arrangements for peace came to be discussed". It is quite
explicitly implied here that the methods of traditional limited
warfare that Hankey favoured would lead to a mediated peace.
Such a peace, however, would remain unacceptable to either a
Cabinet or country only just surrendering the prospect of a quick
and inexpensive victory.

Doubting the possibilities of amphibious action against Germany in the North Sea so long opposed by the prewar General
Staff, Hankey had finally concluded that Germany could "perhaps be struck most effectively . . . through her allies, and particularly through Turkey." "Is it impossible," asked Hankey,
"now to weave a web round Turkey which shall end her career as
a European Power?" Assuming that the defeat of Germany was
hopeless, Great Britain might very well stand to gain a good many
bargaining assets amidst a disintegrating Turkish Empire in Asia
rather than in Europe, although the promise of Constantinople
might also win over Bulgaria, a pawn whose entry into the Entente camp Fisher had long considered the key to the problem of
seizing the Dardanelles. Hankey might be somewhat naïve in

diplomacy, for example in his hope that both the Greek and Bulgarian Armies could be induced to fight for an objective already practically promised to Russia, but, Constantinople aside, his conclusion that three British Army corps, in addition to the assistance of the Greek and Bulgarian armies, would be required for the operation[9] strikes a rare note of realism in this period of Oriental phantasmagoria.

Still adhering to his sentiments of September 1 that, so far as British troops were concerned, the Turks could be "better dealt with at the centre", i.e. that the West remained the decisive theatre, Churchill advocated Fisher's old plan to seize Borkum, close the Elbe, and ultimately invade the Jutland peninsula in order to open the Baltic. Even the Prime Minister grasped that this harebrained scheme would presumably involve the violation of Danish neutrality, although the hope of conjoining the real British superiority in warships with the visionary Russian superiority in effective manpower appealed greatly to Mr Asquith's pacific temperament.[10]

On the last day of 1914, lest the Prime Minister relapse into his customary practice of waiting upon events, Asquith received what the most prominent biographer of David Lloyd George has called an ultimatum from the Chancellor of the Exchequer. In effect, Lloyd George told Asquith that he had to do something and that the War Council should meet regularly and frequently and consider the Russian situation in particular. Two days later, on January 2, Lord Kitchener would receive an appeal from the Grand Duke Nicholas to arrange for some kind of demonstration against the Turks to divert the latter from the hard pressed Russian Caucasus.[11] Never had David Lloyd George's incomparable political antennae reacted more sensitively to the gentlest breeze of chance.

The Chancellor of the Exchequer followed up his veiled ultimatum of December 31 with a long memorandum on grand strategy on January 1, 1915. Since as late as 1938 this memorandum could evoke enthusiasm from Captain Liddell Hart and would, apparently, influence Winston Churchill's subsequently avowed principles of war,[12] a detailed examination of this new development in the strategic thought of the Chancellor of the Exchequer may seem in order.

Lloyd George opened his New Year memorandum with a sharp warning that the "superb" new armies which Kitchener was raising in Britain should not be "thrown away upon futile enterprises such as those we have witnessed during the past few weeks" or the "country will be uncontrollably indignant at the lack of prevision and intelligence shown in our plans". The Chancellor went on to affirm the need to gain "a definite victory somewhere", an argument which was valid in politics, if not in strategy. Otherwise, said Lloyd George, morale in France and Great Britain would suffer from the mounting casualty lists with few or no territorial gains to offset them.

Since there is no doubt that in the long run a war of attrition would prove desperately unpopular in the Western democracies, Lloyd George's conclusion that the solution to the Liberal Cabinet's political difficulties consisted of knocking out what he called the German "props" in Austria and Turkey is a perfectly valid theory in politics. But since, in military fact, Germany and the German Army were the sole props sustaining the Central Powers, clearly the Entente Powers were already attempting to knock out the essential enemy props.

The Chancellor was franker when he declared that two incidental advantages of his policy were that "something which could be called a victory would be thus within our reach, and the public would be satisfied to support with all their resources the conduct of the War for a much longer period without grumbling or stint". Italy and the potential Balkan Allies, so important in Lloyd George's concept of war, might also be won over by a formidable British "demonstration" or "dramatic victory" in the East. Against Turkey the Chancellor proposed the employment of 100,000 British troops in Syria, a plum unfortunately of equal interest to the French politicians. At least Lloyd George did wind up his memorandum with one orthodox military theorem when he wrote that "expeditions decided upon and organized with insufficient care and preparation generally end disastrously".[13]

One of the greatest ironies in a war of ironies coupled David Lloyd George as Prime Minister with Henry Wilson as Chief of the Imperial General Staff. But, of course, by 1918 the apostle of an exclusively political conception of war, like the high priest of an exclusively military conception, had learned a great deal, although neither the protagonist nor his biographers like to admit as much.

On January 2, the day on which he received the Russian appeal, Lord Kitchener, in the absence of the Prime Minister and after the usual hasty consultation with Churchill and Grey, informed the Russian Government that a demonstration would be made against the Turks but that it was very doubtful whether this could be counted on to relieve the Russian Army in the Caucasus.[14] On the same day Kitchener wrote to Churchill in a similar vein. "I do not see," he told the First Lord, "that we can do anything that will very seriously help the Russians in the Caucasus. . . . We have no troops to land anywhere. . . . The only place that a demonstration might have some effect in stopping [Turkish] reinforcements going East would be the Dardanelles. Particularly if, as the Grand Duke says, reports could be spread at the same time that Constantinople was threatened. We shall not be ready for anything big for some months."[15]

The busy Secretary of State for War managed to find time on this same January 2 to write to Sir John French to the effect that the feeling of the War Council was moving towards the employment in other theatres of all surplus British forces beyond what were required to hold the line in France. In this letter Kitchener expressed his conviction that the German lines in France could not be broken and that Italy and Roumania were the most likely providers of fresh troops with which the Allies might hope to break the Western deadlock by action elsewhere.

In reply Sir John maintained that, given enough artillery and ammunition, he could pierce the German lines. Moreover, in the event of a Russian collapse, he would need all the available new armies. Should the Government desire a strategic alternative, notwithstanding the difficulties of the appalling Balkan logistics, Sir John preferred an advance through Serbia from Salonika on the principles advocated by Lloyd George. As for Turkey, Sir John French felt that any British attack there would be "devoid of decisive result" because, at best, "it would only cause the relaxation of the [Turkish] pressure against Russia in the Caucasus, and enable her [Russia] to transfer two or three corps to the West—a result quite incommensurate with the [British] effort involved. To attack Turkey would be to play the German game, and to bring about the end which Germany had in mind when she induced Turkey to join in the war—namely, to draw off troops from the decisive spot, which is Germany herself." It goes without saying that Sir John was still eager to further his own long-contemplated version of a maritime strategy, a combined British Army and Navy operation against Zeebrugge on the Belgian coast.[16]

Sir John French was so suspicious of Kitchener's intentions that he sent a copy of this message to the Prime Minister. Asquith promptly circulated Sir John's message among all the members of a Cabinet which was already complaining of being kept in the dark by Kitchener. Kitchener then rebuked the Commander of the B.E.F. for by-passing him in official communications to the Cabinet and for his breach of security, and the always shaky relations of the two Field-Marshals worsened again. There is no doubt that Sir John feared with some reason that Kitchener would seize any alternative to immediate action and particularly an action as dangerous and difficult as that contemplated against Zeebrugge.[17]

Equally relieved to be let off the hook of an increasingly unpromising amphibious operation against the Germans at Borkum, Jacky Fisher, too, leapt at the possibility of a naval assault against the Turks, provided there were plenty of troops in the offing when matters became serious. In a formal letter to Churchill on January 3 Fisher wrote:

Dear Winston:

I've been informed by Hankey that the War Council assembles next Thursday, and I suppose it will be like a game of ninepins! Every one will have a plan and one ninepin in falling will knock over its neighbour! I CONSIDER THE ATTACK ON TURKEY HOLDS THE FIELD! But ONLY if it's IMMEDIATE! However it won't be! Our Aulic Council will adjourn till the following Thursday fortnight! . . . We shall decide on a futile bombardment of the Dardanelles. . . . What good resulted from the last bombardment? Did it move a single Turk from the Caucasus? . . . In the history of the world—a Junta has never won! You want ONE man!

In somewhat less frenetic language the First Sea Lord proposed that all the East Indians, as well as 75,000 seasoned British troops, be sent from France under the command of Lieutenant-General Sir William Robertson and landed on the Asian shore of the Dardanelles. Simultaneously there should be a Greek attack on the Gallipoli Peninsula and a Bulgarian assault towards Constantinople, as Hankey had suggested. Lastly, Fisher thought that Vice-Admiral Sir Doveton Sturdee should force the Dardanelles with the old battleships, at that time surplus.[18]

Churchill now saw Fisher taking the initiative in an amphibious attack, and the opportunity proved too much for him to resist. Discarding Fisher's essential corollary of a large body of seasoned troops, Churchill immediately cabled Vice-Admiral Carden in the Aegean to inquire whether he would consider as practicable the forcing of the Straits with old battleships and in the expectation of severe losses. Two of Mr Churchill's more vigorous critics have objected that such an action by the First Lord—who was overriding the normal conception of his functions here in any event—put undue influence upon Admiral Carden to bring in a favourable verdict to a plan which had never before been considered.[19]

That from the beginning Fisher only contemplated combined operations against the Dardanelles and never accepted, even momentarily, Churchill's idea of a purely naval assault may be seen in a confidential letter Fisher wrote to Lord Balfour, then a member of the War Council, on January 4. This letter opened with Fisher's now customary threats to resign because of what he described as the "junta" within the Admiralty, but the First Sea Lord soon made clear that his real purpose was to beg for Balfour's support for "Hankey's Turkey Plan". Fisher here urged that 100,000 trained British troops would be required as soon as possible, an increase of 25,000 over his estimate to Churchill the day before. The old Admiral concluded agreeably that none other than Balfour was his "ONE man to direct the war."[20] On this same day Fisher also told Churchill that Hankey's plan was "vital and imperative and very pressing".[21]

Admiral Carden's reply was received on January 5. It explained that, while the Dardanelles could not be rushed, "they might be forced by extended operations with large numbers of ships". After consultation with Admiral Oliver, the Chief of the Admiralty War Staff, and Admiral Sir Henry Jackson, who was already studying the problem, Churchill informed Carden on January 6, in a cable not shown to Fisher: "Your view is agreed with by high authorities here. Please telegraph in detail what you think could be done by extended operations, what force would be needed, and how you consider it should be used."

Thus, like Herbert Asquith a week later, Carden went ahead on his planning under the assumption that Churchill spoke for the Board of Admiralty as a whole. Moreover, Fisher's complaint that his role as First Lord was being supplanted by the redundant office of Chief of the Admiralty War Staff is amply justified on this occasion.[22]

It is still somewhat difficult to determine how much each of the authorities in the Admiralty, consulted at his own volition by Churchill, actually favoured the First Lord's conception of a naval assault alone, since after matters went sour what grudging approval Churchill had extracted diminished very rapidly indeed. But it is an overstatement on Churchill's part to say that Admiral Sir Henry Jackson favoured any such conception. On January 5, when asked by Churchill for his opinion, Jackson had just completed a fairly pessimistic memorandum (read by Churchill several days later) which emphasized the need for troops, if only

80

for the occupation of Constantinople, as well as the difficulties of a retreat by the Fleet back down the Dardanelles if the Turks did not cave in.

In retrospect, Jackson asserted that he had only wished to have the Navy test the outer forts and to await the Army before penetrating into the more difficult interior of the Straits. In a phrase that was frequently flung by the Tories at Churchill's head in the future, Admiral Jackson testified before the Dardanelles Commission that, in his opinion, to attack the strong inner Dardanelles forts with the Navy alone "would be a mad thing to do". Certainly both orthodox naval theory and repeated staff studies over the years—studies with which Fisher had agreed—were in complete agreement with Jackson's testimony on this issue in 1917. But, with whatever rationalizations in mind, by January 15, 1915, Admiral Jackson had generally concurred in Carden's plan for a naval assault alone.[23]

Admirals Oliver and Sir Arthur Wilson evidently were in essential agreement with Jackson in favouring no more than the testing of the outer forts while waiting for the Army to do the really dirty work, a not very proud position for any admiral to affirm under oath and, hence, a possible cause of their subsequent vagueness. Wilson testified only that he had "never recommended" the naval assault alone. In contrast, it is a relief to observe that the articulate Fisher would declare before the Dardanelles Commission in 1917 that he had been "dead against the naval operation alone because . . . it was doomed to failure". But, as the Dardanelles Commissioners have observed, in January 1915 Fisher made no such strong statements in opposition to the proposed operation.[24]

In fact, Fisher's opposition to a purely naval assault would take time to crystallize once he realized that he was being shunted aside by the First Lord on this issue. Meanwhile, concerning the next decisive week, Herbert Asquith could testify with apparent ingenuousness that the opinion of the naval experts, as presented to him, were "very favourable" to the plan of a naval assault alone. After all, declared Mr Asquith in 1917, "Mr Churchill told me so, and I thought they were".[25] While it is possible to believe a great deal regarding Asquith's incapacity for the conduct of war, he was a fine judge of men and he had known Winston Churchill for a long time.

If the concurrence of the Admiralty on the question of a naval assault alone was half-hearted or unreal, that of the Army General Staff was not invited at all, although the General Staff had considered the problem of the Dardanelles at length in 1906 and thereafter. For that matter, Churchill himself took a fortnight to switch over fully from his hopes for a combined operation against Zeebrugge to what he would eventually confess to have been a last resort, at best. In 1916 Churchill told Lord Riddell that his plan for a naval assault alone was due to Kitchener's "failure to move".[26]

In 1917 Churchill testified before the Dardanelles Commission that, had he known at the beginning of 1915 that a British Army of 80,000–100,000 men would be provided by May 1915, he would never have undertaken the naval assault alone. By the time he came to write his war memoirs, Churchill had further concluded that "nothing less than the ocular demonstration" of the naval attack on the Dardanelles "would have enabled Lord Kitchener to wrest an army from France and Flanders. In cold blood, it could never have been done."[27]

Ex post facto though it be, this pitilessly candid admission has the ring of truth; as Riddell had learned in 1916, Churchill's publicity for an enterprise which the Cabinet had declared could be abandoned in the event of difficulties would compel the Government to throw in unsupported troops where unsupported ships had already failed.[28] For Winston Churchill had proved to be Fisher's apt pupil on the techniques of calculated leaks and appeals to public opinion as a means of getting his way in naval matters. Unhappily the statesman's and sailor's achievements could no longer be measured out in votes and ship launchings as in Fisher's heyday before the war; by 1915 the results would be tallied up in a harder and less adulterable coin.

The reason that Lord Kitchener had said that he had no troops ready for operations, even within the Levantine reaches of his imperialist dreams, became more apparent at the meetings of the War Council on January 7-8, 1915. Here Kitchener explained that he was planning to send the well-trained Twenty-ninth British and the First Canadian divisions to France for the sake of Sir John French's proposed Zeebrugge offensive. The Secretary of State for War ruled out the Balkans as an arena for a British offensive in view of the neutrality of Italy or Greece, one of which was required as a secure base for such a difficult operation. At the time he lacked even the 30,000–50,000 troops needed for a small operation against the Turkish lines of supply in the Alexandretta region;[29] for a combined attack against the Dardanelles, which he favoured since the fleet could best help the Army there, Kitchener estimated that roughly 150,000 men would be demanded.

David Lloyd George expressed surprise at this conservative estimate of the manpower needed for the Dardanelles; from 1915 until 1918 Lloyd George would always feel that the surest way of halting offensives in France was to milk this principal theatre of its potential reserves of manpower in favour of practically any other region, including the United Kingdom. On the other hand, at this juncture Kitchener feared a new German attack in the West and did not yet dare strip Sir John French of an easily available reserve. It is hardly surprising that under these circumstances the War Council compromised by deciding against mounting the Zeebrugge offensive without at the same time sending any first-class divisions off to the Near East for a campaign in which, Mr Churchill was still assuring them, the divisions were not required.[30]

To Kitchener fell the painful duty of explaining the decision of the War Council to Sir John French on January 9. In a long message Kitchener wrote that the success of the Zeebrugge operation "would not be commensurate with the heavy losses involved, as well as the extension that would be thus caused to the lines of the Allies in Northern Flanders". The Secretary of State for War went on to point out that it was impossible to supply artillery ammunition on the scale necessary for the offensive and that under these circumstances the War Council had considered it "desirable to find some other theatre where . . . obstructions to advance would be less pronounced, and from where operations against the enemy might lead to more decisive results".[31]

On January 11 Vice-Admiral Carden submitted his plan to the Admiralty for a naval assault on the Dardanelles. Carden estimated that with a force of twelve battleships, three battle-cruisers and numerous smaller ships, he could sustain the losses involved in a gradual reduction of the forts over a period of about a month. While everyone would have preferred troops as well, within the Admiralty War Staff the consoling opinion prevailed that, in the event of failure, the naval attack could be treated as a mere demonstration and be broken off at any moment. A week later however, on January 19, the First Lord cabled the Grand Duke Nicholas of Russia to assure him that it was the British Government's intention to press the matter to a conclusion. Mr Churchill expressed the hope that the Russians would assist the operation with a subsequent combined assault of their own in the Black Sea against the Bosphorus.[32] In the history of war so many prevarications and delusions have seldom joined together to lead to failure.

On January 12 Admiral Fisher, evidently still under the impact of his original enthusiasm for Hankey's proposal for a combined operation against Turkey, approved a minute written by Churchill which granted Carden the fifteen capital ships which he had deemed essential for the systematic reduction of the Dardanelles forts; at Fisher's own suggestion one of these was the new *Queen Elizabeth*, the vastly exaggerated power of whose fifteen-inch guns would help to win over Kitchener, despite his occasional doubts regarding the effectiveness of naval guns against land forts.[33] Indeed, so determined a believer in combined operations as Captain Herbert Richmond wrote in mid-January: "With our modern long heavy guns we can outrange the Turkish forts, and a useful bombardment can be carried out. If we can force the passage, we have Constantinople open, and the result will, I hope, be a revolution in Turkey ".[34] When the professional pessimists of the Admiralty were indulging in such speculations, one cannot wonder that the amateur optimists carried the day.

Lord Kitchener had summoned Sir John French to the critical meeting of the War Council on January 13 in order to argue in person for his Zeebrugge offensive. Kitchener's ambivalence between the now squarely joined dispute of the Easterners and Westerners is unmistakable from this date, and his attitude reflects the fundamental position of the equally undecided War Council on this great debate. Although Sir John admitted to a good many reservations concerning his chances of obtaining a decision as opposed to an advance on the Western Front, Kitchener now proposed to provide four additional divisions for the Zeebrugge affair, including the soon-to-be-famous Twenty-ninth Division. Balfour and Lloyd George thereupon showed such strong opposition to this that, as usual, the final decision on Zeebrugge was postponed.

Sir Edward Grey next expatiated on the benefits of a strategy which would serve policy by keeping Bulgaria out of the war while bringing Italy into it on the Allied side. Since operations in the Balkans were impracticable without a base, the Foreign Secretary was inclined to see the virtues of an operation of some sort against the Dardanelles. With Kitchener, Grey would come to rationalize the conception of a purely naval attack on the then usual grounds that, should it encounter difficulties, it could be called off before any grave humiliation was sustained.[35]

At this favourable point of weary impasse, Churchill suddenly revealed Vice-Admiral Carden's plan for a naval attack on the Straits. In Hankey's words: "The idea caught on at once. The whole atmosphere changed. Fatigue was forgotten. The War Council turned eagerly from the dreary vista of a 'slogging match' on the Western Front to brighter prospects, as they seemed, in the Mediterranean. The Navy, in whom everyone had implicit confidence and whose opportunities had so far been few and far between, was to come into the front line. Even French with his tremendous preoccupations caught something of the general enthusiasm."[36]

Flanked by his silent septuagenarian seamen, Admirals Fisher and Sir Arthur Wilson, the First Lord declared to the War Council that his battleships and battlecruiser guns had longer range than those of the old Turkish forts which could fall, as those of Liège and Namur had fallen before the big German howitzers in August 1914. The not-so-fine distinction between the plunging fire of the Skoda howitzers and the comparatively flat trajectory of naval gunfire was not explained to the eager civilians by either Fisher or Wilson, and Mr Churchill went on to point out that the mobile field artillery—towards which the Turks were increasingly shifting their defence—would be "merely an inconvenience" to the Royal Navy.[37]

The Dardanelles Commissioners would eventually conclude that, by not dissenting at this stage, Lord Fisher may be held to have accepted the views of his civilian superiors and, in their words, "so far as we have been able to ascertain, he did not, before the meeting, express anything approaching strong disapproval save on the ground . . . that he feared the Dardanelles operations would interfere with the execution of other schemes which he favoured".[38] Rear-Admiral Rosslyn Wemyss—an eventual supporter of the Dardanelles campaign—would decide on a future day, too, that when Fisher acquiesced in an operation "in whose success he had no faith [this was] . . . a fact only to be accounted for by the ascendancy of political over naval and military influence, an instance of professional knowledge allowing itself to be overridden by political expediency".[39]

With characteristic facility the Prime Minister summarized the sense of the meeting of January 13 to the effect that all preparations should be made for a combined attack on Zeebrugge; that the Admiralty should consider actions in the Adriatic which might bring in Italy; that "the Admiralty should also prepare for a naval expedition in February to bombard and take the Gallipoli Peninsula, with Constantinople as its objective"; and that "if the position in the Western theatre . . . becomes, in the spring, one of stalemate, British troops should be dispatched to another theatre and objective, and . . . adequate investigation and preparation should be undertaken with that purpose. . . ."[40]

Hankey has explained the imprecise civilian language of this remarkable Cabinet consensus on strategy as follows: Asquith meant, by having a naval expedition "take" the Gallipoli Peninsula, that the successful passage of the fleet would presumably cut off and starve out the Turks on the Peninsula, while the Prime Minister's last point clearly implied the employment of troops in either the Dardanelles or at Salonika. But the conclusion of the Dardanelles Commissioners in 1917 is inescapable, namely, that if by the decision of January 13 "the War Council only pledged itself for the moment to naval action they were, in reality, committed to military action on a large scale in the event of the attempt to force the Dardanelles by the Fleet alone proving successful".[41] Or, as it would turn out, the same result would accrue should the Fleet prove unsuccessful.

So, within a fortnight of Cabinet ninepins, a brief and safe demonstration to aid the Russians had been transformed into a difficult and methodical naval assault, with the probability of troops following, for the sake of a variety of somewhat intangible interests in and about the Near East. The famous indictment of Churchill's role on this occasion by C. E. W. Bean, the official Australian military historian, should be paraphrased with the Cabinet as the protagonist-villain of the Gallipoli "tragedy" rather than the First Lord alone, although, as usual in those endeavours with which he has been associated, Winston Churchill had certainly played the catalyst.[42] And a catalyst, like any other force of nature, has no moral significance: it merely evokes great movements in one direction or another without caring at the time what their ultimate significance may be.[43] Only in retrospect did Churchill become an apologist for the Dardanelles, an apologist often more brilliantly effective than as a catalyst.

8

Fruits de Mer
(January 14—31, 1915)

The Duke of Newcastle was a man of a sanguine, eager nature, very prone to action. He had a good clear intellect . . . unwearied industry, and an astonishing facility of writing. In the assumption of responsibility he was generous and bold even to rashness. Indeed, he was so eager to have his views carried into effect, and so willing to take all risk upon his own head that there was danger of his withdrawing from other men their wholesome share of discretion.[1]

ALEXANDER KINGLAKE

When sailors get round a Council Board they are almost invariably mute. The Politicians who are round that Board are not mute; they would have never got there if they had been mute.[2]

ADMIRAL FISHER

No lesson seems to be so deeply inculcated by experience of life as that you should never trust experts. If you believe doctors, nothing is wholesome; if you believe theologians, nothing is innocent; if you believe soldiers, nothing is safe.[3]

LORD SALISBURY

It is true, I suppose, that the Americans consider we have led them up the garden path in the Mediterranean—but what a beautiful path it has proved to be. They have picked peaches here, nectarines there. How grateful they should be.[4]

ATTRIBUTED TO
WINSTON CHURCHILL IN 1943

I N France, the Russian appeal at the end of December 1914 had fallen upon unexpectedly receptive ground. To be sure, with the Germans fifty miles from Paris, Joffre could thwart any

88

serious theft of troops from his zealously guarded Western Front, but Poincaré, Briand, Viviani, and certain general officers as prominent as Galliéni, favoured an operation based upon Salonika to attack what Lloyd George termed the "ramshackle" Austro-Hungarian Empire. Like the British, the French readily agreed on the use of their navy at the Dardanelles instead of their army; the friendly neutrality of Italy had freed an adequate squadron of warships for what the French, too, enjoyed considering a naval assault which could be broken off in the event of any real embarrassment.[5] Once reassured regarding the Third Republic's political interests in Syria, the French Minister of Marine, who had "no great faith in the scheme", did not think it was his business to do anything to dissuade Mr Churchill from assaulting the Dardanelles, since the British were "taking almost all the risk".[6] Within two months the failure of this naval attack had so depressed the French, that London had to remind them that in war *"il ne faut rien prendre au tragique, et tout au sérieux"*.[7]

At the same time a Greek refusal to provide Salonika as a base because of the absence of two Entente Army Corps as a guarantee against Bulgaria put a damper upon Lloyd George's and Briand's desire for a large-scale land campaign towards the Danube. Nevertheless, although the flow of political events was moving strongly towards a naval assault on the Dardanelles, Admiral Fisher was now encountering the full force of the reaction within the Navy to the conclusions of the War Council on January 13. On January 14 Fisher had again concurred with a memorandum of the First Lord in which Churchill had written: "The attack on the Dardanelles will require practically our whole available [naval] margin."[8] On January 17 the Commander of the Grand Fleet, Admiral Sir John Jellicoe, wrote to Fisher: "It is astonishing how quickly our supposed superiority in Dreadnoughts and battle fleets vanishes. Today I have 19 battleships (Dreadnoughts), plus 7 'King Edwards' to meet 16 German Dreadnoughts and 8 'Deutschlands' plus twelve 4th and 5th Squadrons, which is what would come out if they meant business. . . . I am wiring to ask when I may expect another flotilla. . . . I WONDER I CAN

EVER SLEEP AT ALL. Thank goodness the Germans imagine we have proper defences. At least so I imagine—otherwise there would be no Grand Fleet left now."[9]

Inside the Admiralty, the Assistant Director of Naval Operations, Captain Richmond, was expressing the view of the Admiralty War Staff when he pointed out to his superiors: "Until the batteries covering the approaches where you want transports to go are destroyed, you have not got command of the sea. . . . Also, until you have made navigation safe as regards both mines and sandbanks, you cannot bring the transports in. You cannot remove the mines except by sweeping, and you cannot sweep until the batteries are destroyed." Richmond added that he thought the whole project was impracticable and ought not be attempted.[10] Richmond's career would soon suffer for such a plethora of unwanted advice.

Richmond's portrait of Fisher on the eve of his greatest trial is not without interest: he described the First Sea Lord on January 19 as "old and worn-out and nervous. It is ill to have the destinies of an empire in the hands of a failing old man, anxious for popularity [and] afraid of any local mishap which may be put down to his dispositions."[11]

Richmond's failing old man had written to Churchill on the day before this brutal characterization as follows: "I only repeat, when a good chance offers to attack, it should be made *instanter*! But I desire to emphasize the necessity of sticking to the enemy's vitals! I am not minimizing the coming Dardanelles operation, but I wish to aggrandize the big fact that 750,000 men landed in Holland, combined with intense activity of the British Fleet against, say, Cuxhaven, would finish the war by forcing out the German High Seas Fleet and getting in the rear of the German Armies." On the nineteenth Fisher replied to Jellicoe's *cri de cœur* of January 17 in a similar vein: "It is amusing how Winston makes out that in all types you are ever so much stronger than when you assumed command of the Fleet. . . . And now the Cabinet have decided on taking the Dardanelles solely with the Navy, using 15 battleships and 32 other vessels, and keeping out there three battlecruisers and a flotilla of destroyers—*all urgently required at the decisive theatre at home!* There is only one way out, and that is to resign! But you say '*no*' which simply means I am a consenting party to what I absolutely disapprove. *I don't agree with one single step taken*, so it is fearfully against the grain that I remain on in deference to your wishes. The way the War is conducted both ashore and afloat is chaotic! We have a new plan every week!"[12]

The Prime Minister promptly learned of Fisher's new worry through Hankey and, if he was inclined to consider Fisher as rather difficult, Asquith feared that there was some truth in the First Sea Lord's complaints regarding his being outargued by Churchill on naval problems of a purely technical nature. In no very good mood himself, Asquith observed in the privacy of his journal that there were "two fatal things in war. One is to push blindly against a stone wall; the other is to scatter and divide forces in a number of separate and disconnected operations. We are in great danger of committing both blunders. Happily K. has a good judgment in these matters—never impulsive, sometimes inclined to be over-cautious, but with a wide general outlook which is of the highest value".[13]

Churchill, who chose to believe that Fisher's growing dissatisfaction with the Dardanelles naval assault was based upon the First Sea Lord's current advocacy of a combined operation against Zeebrugge, refused to take the narrow margin of superiority of the Grand Fleet very seriously as an issue. To oppose what the Dardanelles Commissioners have considered Churchill's over-sanguine disposition, on January 25 Fisher submitted a long memorandum to Churchill, a memorandum which he had ordered prepared by the Admiralty War Staff as early as November 1914. The conclusion of this fundamental statement on British naval policy during the First World War read:

The pressure of sea power to-day is probably not less but greater and more rapid in action than in the past; but it is still a slow process and requires great patience. In time it will almost certainly compel the enemy to seek a decision at sea, particularly when he begins to realize that his offensive on land is broken. This is one reason for husbanding our resources. . . .

We play into Germany's hands if we risk fighting ships in any subsidiary operations such as coastal bombardments or the attack of fortified places without military co-operation, for we thereby increase the possibility that the Germans may be able to engage our fleet with some approach to equality of strength. The sole justification of coastal bombardments and attacks by the fleet on fortified places, such as the contemplated prolonged bombardment of the Dardanelles Forts by our fleet, is to force a decision at sea, and so far and no farther can they be justified.

So long as the German High Sea Fleet preserves its present great strength and splendid gunnery efficiency, so long is it imperative and indeed vital that no operation whatever should be undertaken by the British Fleet calculated to impair its present superiority. . . . Even the older ships should not be risked, for they cannot be lost without losing men and they form our only reserve behind the Grand Fleet.

Ours is the supreme necessity and difficulty of remaining passive except in so far as we can force the enemy to abandon his defensive and to expose his fleet to a general action.

. . . It has been said that the first function of the British Army is to assist the fleet in obtaining command of the sea. This might be accomplished by military co-operation with the Navy in such operations as the attack of Zeebrugge or the forcing of the Dardanelles, which might bring out the German and Turkish fleets respectively. Apparently, however, this is not to be. The English Army is apparently to continue to provide a small sector of the Allied front in France, where it no more helps the Navy than if it were at Timbuctoo.

Being already in possession of all that a powerful fleet can give a country we should continue quietly to enjoy the advantage without dissipating our strength in operations that cannot improve the position.[14]

Churchill has not minced matters regarding this memorandum. It was, he declared, "absolutely counter to all my convictions" since, in his subsequent opinion, it would have condemned the Navy to "complete inactivity". Churchill has further denounced this basic naval policy as leading directly to the submarine menace of 1917. In his immediate reply to Fisher, the First Lord offered continued hopes of the eventual seizure of Borkum. For the Dardanelles, Churchill said that "with care and skill" ship losses could be kept to a minimum, but that certain naval losses would be justifiable for the sake of sparing much greater casualties among the soldiers.[15] Much of this might be perfectly true; yet as an argument it was not particularly well designed to appeal to an Admiral passionately devoted to the so-called *matériel* school in the Navy and notorious among the soldiers for his belief that the Army existed to uphold and spare the Navy losses rather than vice versa.[16]

In a more conciliatory than accurate covering note to his reply to Fisher, Churchill said that there were "no differences in principle" between him and the First Sea Lord. Churchill then suggested that he send both Fisher's memorandum and his own reply to Asquith, instead of printing and circulating Fisher's memorandum to all members of the War Council as, it will be recalled, had happened to a recent protest on the part of Sir John French. Most unwisely Fisher consented to this suggestion and much of the War Council thus never became acquainted with the views of the First Sea Lord or of the Admiralty War Staff until it was too late.[17]

Fisher did, however, write to the Prime Minister on the morning of January 28 to explain his even more unfortunate resolve not to attend the meeting of the War Council that day. Although the Prime Minister insisted upon the First Sea Lord's attendance, he did agree to see Fisher with Churchill privately before the Council sat. Fisher's note to Asquith had read:

I am not in accord with the First Lord and do not think it seemly to say so before the Council. His reply to my memorandum does not meet my case. I say that the Zeebrugge and Dardanelles bombardments can only be justified on naval grounds by military co-operation, which would compensate for the loss in ships and irreplaceable officers and men. As purely naval operations they are unjustifiable, as they both drain our naval margin—not too large in view of collisions . . . mines and submarines . . . and fools as admirals. . . . We are at this moment vitally in want of destroyers, wrongly kept at the Dardanelles in opposition to my representations. We are sending our best submarine to the Dardanelles and our largest and most valuable battleship, the *Queen Elizabeth*, with the only 15-inch guns ready at present, besides sending other battle cruisers now there against my protest. . . . I am very reluctant to leave the First Lord. I have great personal affection and admiration for him, but I see no possibility of a union of ideas, and unity is essential in war, so I refrain from any desire of remaining as a stumbling block.

The British Empire ceases if our Grand Fleet ceases. No risks can be taken.[18]

So spoke the authentic voice of a Jellicoe, if not of a Beatty or Roger Keyes. Fisher was growing cautious in old age; still this letter was the truth as Fisher saw it, and it can be understood why he would write somewhat guardedly in his memoirs: "However, no politician regards truth from the same point of view as a gentleman. He puts on the spectacles of his Party. The 'suppressio veri' and the 'suggestio falsi' flourish in politics like the green baize tree.

'Sworn to no Party—of no Sect am I:
I can't be silent and I will not lie'."[19]

Although Fisher might not lie, unhappily he would be silent at the decisive moment in the War Council later this day. And it is evident that Asquith was no more innocent with respect to Fisher's charges than Churchill, whatever may be said for the other members of the War Council.

According to the Dardanelles Commissioners, in his private discussion with the Prime Minister and First Lord before the War Council meeting Fisher did "not criticize the [naval] attack on the Gallipoli Peninsula on its own merits. Neither did he mention to the Prime Minister that he had any thought of resigning if his opinions were overruled".[20] In Asquith's own account, however, the Prime Minister tried to reconcile the "mutual grievances" of Churchill and Fisher with one of his usual compromises, a compromise under which Churchill would give up for the present the bombardment of Zeebrugge, while Fisher should accept the operation against the Dardanelles. And in Asquith's account, far from being reasonably contented with this "compromise", as Churchill's story would have it, throughout the subsequent meeting of the War Council "old Jackie maintained an obstinate and ominous silence". Moreover, noted the Prime Minister on this same date, Fisher was "always threatening to resign and writes an almost daily letter to Winston expressing his desire to return to the cultivation of his roses at Richmond".[21] Of this meeting *à trois*, Fisher himself has said only—in his customary dispatch to Jellicoe the next day—that he had had "fierce rows with Winston and the Prime Minister" and that they had decided upon the Dardanelles naval attack in opposition to his opinion.[22]

The War Council meeting of January 28 was opened with a statement by Mr Churchill explaining that both the Grand Duke Nicholas and the French Ministry of Marine had approved of his proposed naval attack on the Dardanelles and that the French Navy had promised to assist in the operation. Needless to say, Churchill did not add that the Russian Foreign Ministry had been forced against its will by the desperate Russian military headquarters to accept the British plan or that, at Sir Edward Grey's suggestion, this reluctant Russian consent may have then been used by Churchill as a lever to obtain the agreement of Victor Augagneur, the French Minister of Marine. Apart from the no longer acute problem of the Turkish threat to the Caucasus, the Russian Foreign Minister and soldiers both regarded a naval seizure of the Straits in any event "as difficult, almost impossible to achieve" and consequently could safely welcome the British diversion without seriously having to fear the loss of Constantinople to their ally in the process.[23]

Building upon this rather questionable Entente approval, in the War Council meetings of January 28 the First Lord went on to cite Vice-Admiral Carden's estimate of the time required for a methodical approach and added that the Admiralty had already put ships under way for the Mediterranean. Mr Churchill thereupon inquired whether the Council attached importance to the operation "which undoubtedly involved some risks".

At this point Admiral Fisher declared that he had understood that the question of a decision would not be raised on this occasion. The Prime Minister replied that, in view of the steps which had already been taken, the question could no longer be left in abeyance. According to the subsequent recollection of Admiral Sir Arthur Wilson, who was also present, Churchill told the War Council that the Navy could carry through the operation by itself and that he only wanted the Army to come in later as an occupation force to "reap the fruits" of naval endeavour.

Under these circumstances Lord Kitchener declared that the naval attack was "vitally important", since its success would be equivalent to a victorious campaign by his New Armies. Kitchener was obviously delighted at the prospect of having to expend neither his still poorly trained new armies nor his grievously short supply of ammunition. More cautiously, Kitchener added that a particular merit of the naval plan was that, failing satisfactory progress, the naval assault could easily be called off. Although uncomfortable, on principle, about both subsidiary operations and his role as the sole member of the Conservative Opposition in the War Council, Lord Balfour was even more enthusiastic. He pointed out that success in the assault would cut the Turkish Army in two, give Constantinople to the Entente, and open the Straits to the Russian trade and to the Danube. In summary, Balfour found it "difficult to imagine a more helpful operation".

The Foreign Secretary, Sir Edward Grey, felt that the plan would finally determine the attitude of Bulgaria and, with that pivotal country, the whole of the Balkans. Grey had decided that diplomacy was futile without a military success and that victory in the Dardanelles would win over most of the Balkans to partake in a slice of the Turkish Empire.[24] There is no doubt that, if it ever came to the carving up of Turkey, there would be as much eagerness among the Balkan gluttons as in those of the War Council, although why Grey should look forward to such a nightmare of diplomatic adjudication is more difficult to surmise. Meanwhile, as Mr Churchill said in reply to a question on the part of Lord Haldane, the real difficulties in the operation would appear only when the inner forts of the Narrows were encountered. Some losses "must be expected" from mines.[25] It is a pity that there were not more Haldanes on the War Council and more enthusiasts at the Straits.

The generally favourable response of the War Council to Churchill's argument may well have intimidated Fisher. Instead of protesting against the operation, a protest which Sir Arthur Wilson might then have supported, Fisher abruptly rose from the table and started for the door, intending to write his resignation on the spot outside. With remarkable agility, Kitchener intercepted the old Admiral and drew him aside to a window where he urged Fisher not to resign. Kitchener told the First Sea Lord that he was the sole dissenter and appealed to his sense of duty. After some further discussion of the overwhelming political reasons for making the attempt on the Straits, in his own words Fisher "reluctantly gave in to Lord Kitchener and went back to the Council table". Most significantly, neither the Prime Minister nor any other member of the Council asked for either Fisher's or Wilson's opinions or objections.[26]

The Dardanelles Commissioners have vigorously condemned what they called "a mistaken sense of duty" on the part of Fisher and Wilson in not volunteering their objections, whether asked for or not. Of course, as Field-Marshal Sir William Robertson later remarked, when he took the opposite course from that of Fisher with the Government in 1918 he was sacked for his temerity.

Fisher's own explanation for his conduct—which the Dardanelles Commissioners, so courageous for others, refused to print in their two reports—is based upon the perfectly valid tenet that the chief technical advisers of a Government can hardly be expected to resign on every occasion on which they disagree with the Government, "unless they are of the opinion that the operation proposed must lead to disastrous results". As yet, neither Fisher nor any other naval officer had reached such a positive conclusion regarding the naval assault alone, and, in addition, Fisher understandably hoped, by staying on at the Admiralty, to protect his North Sea and Baltic projects against mounting criticism.[27]

The Dardanelles Commissioners went further: they criticized Mr Churchill for not having insisted upon Fisher and Wilson expressing their views freely before the Council and concluded that the First Lord had been "carried away by his sanguine temperament and his firm belief in the success of the operation which he advocated". Yet, as we have seen in Churchill's admission to Lord Riddell in 1916, the First Lord had advocated the naval assault only as a last resort in view of Kitchener's steadfast refusal at this stage to provide troops for a combined operation.

The Dardanelles Commissioners, likewise, criticized the Prime Minister, and to a lesser degree the other members of the Council, for not having insisted upon the experts present contributing their opinions, particularly as it was "common knowledge that naval opinion generally condemned the attack on forts by ships unaided by any military force".[28] Like Mr Churchill, Mr Asquith remained unrepentant, saying in Parliament in 1917 that the "whole naval expert opinion" available at the end of January 1915 had considered the naval attack alone as a practical operation.[29] Before such misconceptions so representative of political life, little need be said, except that at least Herbert Asquith did not attempt to construct a philosophy of war based upon the denial of elementary logic and of professional military advice. But then he would only have another two years in office and, unlike the Heavenly Twins, his heart was never really in the row with the military.

During the afternoon of January 28 two important events took place which enabled the War Council to reach agreement that evening. Mr Churchill had a long, private conversation with Fisher, during which the First Lord has frankly conceded that he put "great and continuous pressure" upon the old Admiral, a pressure which had already been increased by Kitchener's entreaty, the collective influence of the War Council and the obvious decision of the Prime Minister himself. In the end Fisher gave up resistance and, in his characteristically exaggerated phrase, went into the Dardanelles operation up to the moment of his resignation, "whole hog, *totus porcus*."[30]

During the same afternoon, under the chairmanship of Lord Kitchener, a sub-committee of what was termed for the occasion the Committee of Imperial Defence, met to consider a General Staff memorandum on the employment of British troops in the Balkans for the sake of aiding Serbia. Since the Zeebrugge operation had now lapsed as part of the Prime Minister's price for conciliating Fisher, in theory several divisions might thereby become available for this pet project of Lloyd George. At the evening session of the War Council on January 28 the objections of the French Government to any such simple strategic solution were brought up and Kitchener got his way again on the retention of most of the divisions in question within the United Kingdom, while the Council waited on events.[31]

Here the Secretary of State for War has often been criticized for apparent indecision, for what was, in fact, a deliberate and consistent policy on his part. Kitchener always preferred to retain as large a reserve as possible in his own hands. At home the training of the new armies could proceed apace, ammunition would be saved, and the invariable tendency of active theatres to expand operations be most effectively checked. Long observation of statesmen had taught Kitchener that soon enough there would be plenty of claims upon his precious military hoard. And, as an immensely experienced soldier, he had come more and more to be impressed by the advantages which Germany derived from her central position.[32] Unlike the unco-ordinated or too fully committed reserves of the Entente, at almost any time the Germans could concentrate overwhelming strength at what might for the moment be the decisive point. Alone among the Great Powers of the Entente, Britain might hope to preserve this same inestimable advantage in war and in diplomacy.

In effect, if only tacitly, the War Council had now decided to make an unsupported naval assault on the Dardanelles; if necessary and possible, troops contemplated for Salonika could be employed along and beyond the Straits when occasion demanded. As for Fisher, unnerved by the blunt exposure of his total isolation within the War Council, the First Sea Lord secretly sent a copy of his memorandum of January 25 along to Bonar Law, leader of the Conservative Opposition and Churchill's inveterate personal enemy. Fisher justified this action on the grounds that the Prime Minister had not circulated his memorandum among the War Council (as he had done with Sir John French's protest against Kitchener's policy).[33] The First Sea Lord doubtless felt the need for a new anchor to starboard, considering his current circumstances among the Liberals, but it would seem that low cunning was not entirely confined to the ungentlemanly politicians. In the desperate struggle shaping up along Whitehall, Fisher was laying the foundation for his ultimate demonstration that he alone was tough enough to meet Winston Churchill on equal terms.

9

Miasma-ed

(February 1—March 10, 1915)

Put all the elements of a problem before a civilian of first-rate ability and enough imagination, and he would reach the right solution, and any soldier could afterwards put this solution into military terms.[1]

WINSTON CHURCHILL IN 1899

I am grieved beyond measure at the unpatriotic conduct of The Times *in . . . proclaiming to the Emperor [Nicholas] the attack on the Crimea.*[2]

THE DUKE OF NEWCASTLE
TO LORD RAGLAN

Winston was all to start out at once without thinking much of the consequences. He does not think that Germany will react strongly. We, the Chiefs of Staff, thought she would. Lord knows what the consequences may be and we are not ready in the Army for any hurried action. We have warned the Cabinet against this halfcock scheme in Scandinavia. . . . It is the Dardanelles over again.[3]

SIR EDMUND IRONSIDE, JANUARY 2, 1940

Winston was always in a hurry. He didn't like to wait for the pot to boil, you know.[4]

CLEMENT ATTLEE

BY the beginning of February 1915 what Major-General Call-well, the Director of Military Operations, would describe as drifting into a big military attack on the Dardanelles was under way. The Dogger Bank naval action in late January had relieved British opinion of some of its anxieties concerning invasion across the North Sea, thus releasing more troops from the United Kingdom, while the serious Turkish defeats by the Russians in the

Caucasus offered hopes that Turkey might prove equally weak at her heart. On January 29–30 Churchill had endeavoured to talk his friend, Sir John French, out of some of his prospective reinforcements from the United Kingdom for the Balkans. Sir John was warned to prepare to face the loss of two of these new divisions toward the end of March, if the possibilities of a British force in the Balkans seemed likely to trigger a larger movement towards the Allies within that enigmatic peninsula.

Regarding such seductive possibilities, French himself told the War Council on February 9 that "speaking as a strategist, I thought if such a result was made sure by landing arrangements, such a detachment would be justified . . . but if all this was not *absolutely certain* to result it would be a great strategic error".[5] Like most commanders, Sir John would demand certitudes for operations in all theatres but his own. However, Mr Asquith, too, unexpectedly noted that "from a purely strategic point of view it is a pity to divide your forces instead of concentrating them". Then, as if shocked by his utterance of such unpolitical sentiments, the Prime Minister hastened to add that, of course, the current instance was "one of the cases where policy overrides mere strategy", since the entry of Greece and Roumania on the Entente side would mean "an addition of perhaps 800,000 men to the Allies". Mr Asquith also noted that "Winston is for the moment as keen as mustard about his Dardanelles adventure".[6] The old Liberal dream of a Balkan catalyst was thus reborn separately from that of the Dardanelles naval operation, as it would die separately; however, only during their brief mating did either concept stand much chance of achieving effective results.

On February 6 that embodiment of policy-at-all-costs, David Lloyd George, returned from Paris with a most sympathetic colleague in tow, Théophile Delcassé, architect of the Entente Cordiale and Foreign Minister of France. As Foreign Ministers so generally do, Delcassé thought that France could contribute a division to the Balkans imbroglio, assuming that Great Britain did likewise. On the same day two battalions of Marines sailed from the United Kingdom for a destination which soon turned out to be Lemnos, a Greek island just off the mouth of the Dardanelles, ceded for the occasion by Premier Venizelos of Greece. To the great disgust of Captain Richmond, at this point, Churchill, possibly remembering Antwerp, had refused to send the whole Royal Naval Division to Lemnos, still believing, according to Richmond, that he could capture the Dardanelles without troops. Although Richmond considered the Naval Division to be "pretty rotten", none the less it is worth noting that he felt that the division "ought to be good enough for the inferior Turkish troops now in the Gallipoli Peninsula".[7]

When the War Council next assembled on February 9, the first news it received from Sir Edward Grey was that the likelihood of Bulgaria joining the Central Powers appeared almost imminent. The Turks were consequently moving forces from the Bulgarian frontier to the Gallipoli Peninsula, and the Greeks were cooling so rapidly regarding the unpleasant possibilities of a war with both Turkey and Bulgaria, that Entente hopes of using the Greek army for any purpose, as usual, were being undermined.

Given these circumstances Lord Kitchener abandoned his opposition, expressed as late as January 28, to the employment of British troops in the Aegean, and now agreed to match the proposed French division for Salonika with his best division on hand, the Twenty-ninth. Kitchener declared that it would be "very useful" for the Fleet at the Dardanelles to have some "good troops" in the vicinity[8] and went on to say that, should the Navy require the assistance of land forces at a later stage in the naval assault on the Straits, "that assistance would be forthcoming". With Sir Edward Grey, Kitchener drafted a telegram to Athens, offering the Greeks two Anglo-French divisions immediately and asking, in return, for their military intervention to aid Serbia.[9]

Striking while the iron was hot, Colonel Hankey had already circulated the account of the naval historian, Julian Corbett, relating the passage and ignominious re-passage of the Dardanelles by Admiral Duckworth in 1807. Corbett alluded to the conclusion current at that time that with a sufficiency of troops Duckworth might have achieved success. Instead, according to Corbett, Duckworth's failure to intimidate the Turks resulted in "a severe blow to our prestige in the Near East, and, what was worse, our relations with Russia were poisoned. So far from the operation strengthening the alliance, as was intended, the Tsar began to give us up in despair, and a few months later signed the peace of Tilsit with Napoleon."[10] As a Marine in the C.I.D., Hankey had had long experience in explaining military fundamentals in language calculated to appeal to the statesmen. At the same time, Fisher, too, was bombarding Lloyd George with memoranda to the effect that operations at the Straits would be both futile and deplorable without soldiers to exploit them.[11]

Although, like Kitchener, the Prime Minister was reluctantly coming to recognize the need for British troops at the Dardanelles, on February 13 he could not forbear a complaint that "if only these heartbreaking Balkan states could be brought into action, the trick [at the Dardanelles] would be done with the greatest of ease. It is of much importance that in the course of the next month we should carry through a decisive operation somewhere, and this one would do admirably for the purpose."[12] No better summary of Asquith's conception of the conduct of war can be found. In his refusal or inability to distinguish between a purportedly "decisive" operation and a true decision, between ephemeral diplomatic victories and a fundamental military victory, the Prime Minister foreshadowed the outlook of all of his successors in both the First and Second World Wars.

At the same time, in collaboration with Corbett and Hankey, on February 14 Captain Richmond submitted a paper to Fisher which, after a lengthy attack on the continental strategy of the Army, asserted that "the bombardment of the Dardanelles, even if all the forts are destroyed, can be nothing but a local success, which without an army to carry it on can have no further effect". Richmond recommended that an adequate land force be prepared at once or otherwise the Turks might soon discover "the real limitations of sea power divorced from military power". Fisher's approval of so nautical a statement was a foregone conclusion, but

Richmond's paper seems, in part, to have been based upon information just received at the Admiralty from Russian sources to the effect that both the Turkish Army and its German advisers were pessimistic about the defences of the Straits and the morale of the Turkish soldiers.[13]

The revolt among the second echelon of naval experts against the proposed naval assault on the Dardanelles culminated in an Admiralty War Staff memorandum on February 15 issued under the name of Admiral Sir Henry Jackson and sent to Admiral Carden. In strict accord with orthodox naval opinion it was affirmed in this memorandum that "the pressure of a strong field army of the enemy on the [Gallipoli] Peninsula would not only greatly harass the [British naval] operations, but would render the passage of the Straits impracticable by any but powerfully armed vessels, even though all the permanent defences had been silenced. The naval bombardment is not recommended as a sound military operation, unless a strong military force is ready to assist in the operation, or at least to follow it up immediately the forts are silenced."[14]

Jackson's memorandum, along with the C.I.D. and General Staff conclusion of 1906–7 that even a combined operation against the Gallipoli Peninsula involved "great risk", was presented to an informal meeting of most of the War Council on February 16.[15] Under the obvious impact of such professional studies, as well as an outright Greek refusal on the same day to provide troops to assist Serbia, the Council took what Hankey testified was "the all-important decision" to send the Twenty-ninth Division to Lemnos with accompanying horse boats and lighters. Arrangements were also made for reinforcements from Egypt in case they were needed, and shipping was to be assembled for the conveyance of a force of no less than 50,000 men. But, notwithstanding the presence of the C.I.G.S. at this meeting, the General Staff was not notified until March 11 of these supposed decisions of the War Council.[16] As it turned out, this was hardly an accidental omission on the part of Lord Kitchener.

Still more remarkable, at least in retrospect, although the

overture of the naval assault on the Straits had been held up for more than a week through accident and bad weather, nobody suggested delaying this assault until the Army could be ready. Either the Navy was more optimistic than the memoranda of the Admiralty would seem to imply, or else, in spite of such strong support, Fisher was not yet digging in his heels against the naval attack; later on, in his own plaintive euphemism, the First Sea Lord explained that he was still "miasma-ed" by that "subtle dialectician" who could "talk a bird out of a tree".[17] So long as Fisher was committed *totus porcus* to Winston Churchill, Admiralty studies could be overridden with not much more than guilty gestures in their direction.

To be sure, on the evening of February 16 Fisher had written Churchill to plead: "I hope you were successful with Kitchener in getting divisions sent to Lemnos *tomorrow*! Not a grain of wheat will come from the Black Sea unless there is a military occupation of the Dardanelles, and it will be the wonder of the ages that no troops were sent to co-operate with the Fleet with half a million soldiers in England. The war of lost opportunities! Why did Antwerp fall?" Despite the unerring aim of Fisher's last query, Churchill refused to be budged. According to his memoirs, he still anticipated that a naval passage of the Straits would be followed by a Bulgarian entry into the war and a flight or surrender of the Turkish government.[18] In reality, it seems probable that Churchill had already surmised that without a public naval commitment Kitchener would still be able to wriggle out of what remained for him a most unwanted military enterprise.

If Fisher was eager to drag Kitchener's only trained reserve into the Dardanelles, his attitude was naturally very different so far as his own reserves for the principal theatre were concerned. On February 18 he complained that the naval assault on the Straits was holding down four capital ships and a destroyer flotilla, all urgently requested by Admiral Jellicoe for the North Sea. Similarly, Kitchener was subject to great pressure from Sir John French not to divert the Twenty-ninth Division from its originally scheduled berth in France. As an American officer has observed, from its inception until its denouement, for the British soldier and sailor alike, the Dardanelles expedition was "an illegitimate child, importunate in its demands and annoying by the very fact of its existence".[19]

On February 19—ominously enough, the anniversary of Admiral Duckworth's ill-fated passage in 1807—the first and inconclusive naval bombardment of the outer forts of the Dardanelles had commenced. At a full meeting of the War Council, ostensibly because of the threat to France resulting from new Russian reverses, Lord Kitchener refused for the moment to release the Twenty-ninth Division for the Dardanelles. Instead he offered the still under-equipped Australian and New Zealand Corps in Egypt, claiming that since this Corps was nearer the Straits it could be employed there earlier. The usual War Council wrangle followed regarding whether the German reserves, freed by their latest victory over the Tsar, would be sent to mount new offensives against France or Serbia. Now for the first time Churchill insisted upon the necessity for British troops, and troops of the quality of the Twenty-ninth Division, ostensibly only to help the fleet keep the Straits open to merchant ships in the event of a naval breakthrough.[20] What the Admiralty War Staff could not achieve by memoranda, Kitchener's first attempt to cut bait in the Dardanelles evoked rapidly enough from the First Lord. And what the landing ship tank would mean to Mr Churchill's far-flung amphibious projects during the Second World War, the Twenty-ninth Division would constitute in the more modest and penurious reckonings of the Dardanelles.

Although on February 20 Kitchener notified General Maxwell in Egypt to instruct the 30,000 Australians and New Zealanders under the command of Lieutenant-General Sir William Bird-wood to prepare for service in the Dardanelles in March, the type of service the War Minister had in mind may be seen from his message of February 24 to Maxwell saying that: "The operation is to be effected mainly by naval means, and when successful will doubtless cause the retirement of the Gallipoli garrison. According

to our information it would not be a sound military undertaking to attempt a landing in force on the Gallipoli Peninsula,
whose garrison is reported to be 40,000 strong, until naval operations for the reduction of the forts have been successful and the
passage has been forced."[21] In short, in the Kitchener conception the under-equipped and under-trained Anzacs would be
adequate as garrison troops following an essentially uncontested
landing. And for this reason combat loading of amphibious
lighters would not be required; the Navy would have won the
battle long before such a tedious process could be completed.

On the other hand, Churchill, who since Antwerp had learned
to value high quality troops for amphibious operations of a desperate nature, was furious at learning that, unknown to him,
Kitchener had cancelled the transport for the Twenty-ninth
Division in a private arrangement with Fisher and the Admiralty
War Staff. Throughout the Second World War Mr Churchill
was exceedingly suspicious of what he termed a military "frame-
up" arising behind his back.[22] The type of operation growing up
in the First Lord's mind, so he informed Kitchener on February
20, would demand at least 50,000 men in the Aegean "either to
seize the Gallipoli Peninsula after it had been evacuated or to
occupy Constantinople if a revolution takes place".[23] Kitchener
almost certainly suspected that, once on hand at the Straits, so
formidable a body as 50,000 men, especially if it included the
Twenty-ninth Division, would be used for rather more than
occupation.

Renewed bad weather off the Straits delayed Admiral Carden's
next naval bombardment until February 25 and rendered the
Admiral more interested in General Maxwell's offers of troops.
Carden's optimistic belief that a mere 10,000 men would be
sufficient for an occupation force puzzled Kitchener in view of
the 40,000 Turks reported to be on the Gallipoli Peninsula, and
so on February 23 he ordered his old friend General Birdwood to
go from Egypt to consult with Carden at the Straits regarding
what land force was actually required and how it should be employed.[24] Within three days, General Maxwell telegraphed

Kitchener to say that the former French military attaché in Constantinople had described a landing on Gallipoli as "extremely hazardous" and the Peninsula as "very strongly organized for defence". Messages of such import, furthermore, must have accentuated Churchill's eagerness for, and Kitchener's reluctance to provide, high quality troops for the operation.[25]

The meeting of the War Council on February 24 opened very much aware of the fanfare with which the naval attack on the Straits had been launched on February 19. What some critics have considered an inspired leader in *The Times* called for "that touch of imagination which has been conspicuously lacking in the war" and made clear that "the one thing that the Allies dare not risk in a persistent attack on the Dardanelles is failure. If the Peninsula of Gallipoli could be seized and safely held, the worst stage would be over." The one thing which Kitchener had most feared and fought about to suck him into the Dardanelles miasma. Through the political devices of publicity and the consequent commitment of national prestige, Kitchener was to be drawn, unready and against his better judgment, into a new, unnecessary, ever-expanding and exceedingly difficult theatre of operations.[26] In 1942 an American War Minister and his Chief of Staff again would learn the hard way of the impact of publicity and national prestige upon their careful, long-range and rational plans for war.[27] And at the end they would be called stupid and stubborn, if not (as Kitchener was) vacillating, for their pains.

With characteristic clarity Colonel Hankey has summed up the impact of these influences upon the War Council by February 24. Churchill declared that Britain was "absolutely committed" to the naval attack; Grey believed that "failure would be morally equivalent to a great defeat on land"; most conclusively, Kitchener himself said that if the Fleet could "not get through the Straits unaided, the Army ought to see the business through. The effect of a defeat in the Orient would be very serious. There could be no going back. The publicity of the announcement had committed us."[28]

Lloyd George disagreed, holding that the British commitment

only extended to some operation in the Near East, an operation which could include his preferred Salonika project just as well as that in the Dardanelles. In his dissent, however, Lloyd George bared the painful truth that gradually the operation was turning into one in which the Army was being used "to pull the Navy's chestnuts out of the fire" rather than merely assisting in an essentially naval operation.[29] Winston Churchill's deliberately improvident naval assault was paying off.

Perhaps it was for this reason that two days later at another meeting of the War Council, according to his own account if not that of Mr Churchill, the Prime Minister supported Kitchener on keeping the Twenty-ninth Division at home until it became more apparent over the course of the next week or two how matters were developing both on the Eastern Front and in the Dardanelles. Churchill now again informed the War Council that the Navy could no longer guarantee success and that the most difficult part of the naval attack was still ahead. He asserted that with the Twenty-ninth Division "we can make certain of taking Constantinople by the end of March", and capture or destroy most of the Turkish Army in Europe before the Germans had conquered Serbia. His plea rejected, the First Lord entered into the records a formal disclaimer of any responsibility if a disaster occurred in the Dardanelles because of the insufficiency of troops.[30]

Meanwhile in Egypt General Maxwell, a purposeful pessimist, had not been idle. On the same day as the War Council meeting which had witnessed Churchill's disclaimer of responsibility, Maxwell had telegraphed Lord Kitchener an appreciation by a French Colonel who had been military attaché for five years in Constantinople. In accord with the subsequent French military line, this experienced officer had advocated landing the Allied expeditionary force on the Asian side of the Straits, since the Gallipoli Peninsula was too heavily fortified, and included in his estimate some 30,000 Turkish troops.

Replying on the evening of February 26, Kitchener reiterated to Maxwell that "the forcing of the Dardanelles is being undertaken by the navy, and as far as can be foreseen at present the task of your troops, until the passage has been actually secured, will be limited to minor operations". Kitchener's minor follow-up operations, however, were already allowing for a minimum of 64,000 troops, including the French, the Anzacs, and most of the Royal Naval Division. Finally, on February 28, the doleful Maxwell wrote to Kitchener to complain of the silence and optimism of the Navy at the Straits in the face of seven lines of mines and any number of howitzers, apart from the guns of the forts.[31] With such agents in the Near East, Kitchener had little enough cause for cheer, even before he received the reports of his trusted intimate, General Birdwood, direct from the scene of action.

Up until the beginning of March the Silent Service had, indeed, been optimistic. By March 2 naval bombardment had effectively silenced the outer forts of the Straits or approximately twenty per cent of the whole. In response to inquiry from Churchill, Admiral Carden estimated that only another fortnight would be required to take care of the more difficult inner forts. But two days later, on March 4, demolition parties, landing at the forts from the British warships and supported by Marines, were driven off by superior Turkish formations, covered by mobile field artillery.

During the next two weeks repeated efforts by unprotected fishing trawlers against a stiff current to sweep the minefields in the Straits while under shellfire resulted in the demoralization of their largely civilian crews. At the same time the weather remained atrocious, the Allied warships could not locate the concealed Turkish field artillery and their ammunition expenditure was restricted in any event. Although Fisher, who had long distrusted the capabilities of Admiral Carden, gallantly offered to take command in the Straits, the Dardanelles were proving a naval trap. As Fisher wrote to Jellicoe despairingly on March 15, "Things are going badly at the Dardanelles! We want military co-operation, as pointed out by me in January last, but it was ignored by everyone. Now we are held up for want of soldiers."[32]

The Army observer at the Straits, General Birdwood, less inhibited by an enthusiastic superior in London, had reached conclusions similar to Fisher somewhat earlier. On March 4, 5 and 6,

Birdwood telegraphed Lord Kitchener that Admiral Carden, who in his opinion was "very second-rate", lacked initiative and was "too sanguine" in his forecasts. Moreover, Birdwood found it "very doubtful" whether the Navy could force the passage without assistance.[33] As for the Army, Birdwood was careful to assure his master that he had "no intention of rushing blindly into the Gallipoli Peninsula" and he stressed that before any troops could be landed it was "absolutely necessary to have settled weather" in view of the "indifferent" nature of the landing sites.[34]

Now that at last one of his own trusted subordinates on the spot had, in effect, called for a large-scale Army campaign of a systematic kind against the Dardanelles, Kitchener finally took the plunge. On March 10, the first day of the battle of Neuve Chapelle in France, Kitchener released the Twenty-ninth Division for embarkation on or following March 15, enough time to see how Neuve Chapelle shaped up. On March 13 he would write Churchill that "no operations on a large scale should be attempted until the Twenty-ninth Division has arrived or is ready to take part in what is likely to prove a difficult undertaking, in which severe fighting must be anticipated". Even if this much-sought division had left three weeks earlier, it still could not have been employed any earlier at the Straits, as Churchill has claimed, both because of the persistently bad weather until late April and because, like all of the other units already *en route* to the Aegean, it was not combat-loaded by the Navy, and hence could not have been employed in a contested landing immediately upon arrival.[35]

In short, whatever might be asserted to the contrary later by Mr Churchill's more innocent admirers, no effective combined operation could have been mounted before late April, long after the Turks had been amply alerted by the purely naval assault. Yet without the ever-growing likelihood of a naval failure staring Kitchener in the face, by his own admission Churchill could never have extorted the troops necessary for a successful combined operation. In other words, no matter how the Dardanelles-

Gallipoli campaign is considered, it was not likely to have succeeded given any of the conditions actually available.

There was good reason for Winston Churchill to write in 1949, in his often-misunderstood last word on this great campaign: "It is always a misfortune when number two or three has to initiate a dominant plan or policy. He has to consider not only the merits of the policy, but the mind of his chief, not only what to advise, but what is proper for him in his status to advise; not only what to do, but how to get it agreed, and how to get it done. . . . I was ruined for the time being in 1915 over the Dardanelles, and a supreme enterprise was cast away, through my trying to carry out a major and combined operation of war from a subordinate position. Men are ill-advised to try such ventures."[36]

10

Moment of Truth
(March 3—27, 1915)

Operations once decided on in principle must lie in the hands of the commanders chosen, who have to back them with their reputations and lives.[1]

CHURCHILL TO KEYES
SEPTEMBER 30, 1941

Why could I not find someone of his mould? I would have made of him our Nelson, and things would have taken a different turn. . . . There is the naval profession a specialized, technical mentality which blocked all my plans.[2]

NAPOLEON

To get anything done in any highly articulated organization, you have got to carry people at all sorts of levels. It is their decisions, their acquiescence or enthusiasm (above all, the absence of their passive resistance) which are going to decide whether a strategy goes through in time.[3]

C. P. SNOW

On the actual day of battle naked truths may be picked up for the asking; by the following morning they have already begun to get into their uniforms.[4]

GENERAL SIR IAN HAMILTON IN 1907

THE auspicious naval operations in the Straits up to the beginning of March 1915, had produced the expected diplomatic repercussions. Yet, when they came to a head, these diverse diplomatic developments would, like the military operations, be incompatible with each other and, thus, prove equally nugatory. On February 28, Russian Army Headquarters had overcome its reluctance to undertake operations in the Black Sea to the extent that it agreed to provide a corps of troops for the occupation of Constantinople when the allied navies had broken through the Straits. Equally alert to dividing the remains of the presumably expiring Turkish Empire, on March 1 Premier Venizelos of Greece again offered a Greek corps with which to occupy the Gallipoli Peninsula.

Meeting in a mood of high anticipation on March 3, the War Council also looked forward to an immediate Bulgarian action against Adrianople, and within a few days the Italian Government, beside itself with anxiety lest it enter the war too late, made definite overtures to the Allies concerning the compensations for her participation. Certainly the First Lord of the Admiralty was ready to take advantage of these diplomatic trends as eagerly as he had exploited domestic circumstances on behalf of his campaign. On March 5 he wrote to Sir Edward Grey: "The attitude of Italy is remarkable. If she can be induced to join with us, the Austrian Fleet would be powerless and the Mediterranean as safe as an English lake. Surely some effort should be made to encourage Italy to come forward." The Foreign Secretary replied that he would neglect no opportunity, happily unaware of a still more urgent letter drafted by Mr Churchill on March 6 but never sent because of the fall of the Venizelos Government that same day.

Churchill's draft must be quoted in full for, like so much of his undelivered correspondence, it reveals his true motives in war far better than does the official record. Wrote the already desperate First Lord to Grey:

> I beseech you at this crisis not to make a mistake in falling below the level of events. Half-hearted measures will ruin all, and a million men will die through the prolongation of the war. You must be bold and violent. You have a right to be. Our fleet is forcing the Dardanelles. No armies can reach Constantinople but those which we invite, yet we seek nothing here but the victory of the common cause.
>
> Tell the Russians we will meet them in a generous and sympathetic spirit about Constantinople. But no impediment must be placed in the way of Greek co-operation. We must have Greece and Bulgaria, if they

will come. I am so afraid of your losing Greece, and yet paying all the future into the Russian hands. If Russia prevents Greece helping, I will do my utmost to oppose her having Constantinople. She is a broken power, but for our aid, and has no resource open but to turn traitor—and this she cannot do.

If you don't back up *this* Greece—the Greece of Venizelos—you will have another which will cleave to Germany.[5]

As so often in future decades, Churchill was manifesting diplomatic insights of a very high order indeed. His naval assault might no longer be going well, but in a crisis there is no doubt that Sir Edward Grey could benefit from a certain back-straightening from home; like the soldier, the diplomat who offends nobody rarely wins wars. Infinitely more important than the First Lord's attempt to make Grey favour a small and still neutral Greece over a large and belligerent Russia is the revelation that Churchill's motive in bringing aid to the Tsar was to save lives and particularly British lives.

As in the Second World War, in Lloyd George's phrase of December 1914, Winston Churchill was already looking for something which could pass as a victory without at the same time paying a price for this achievement which would effectively negate its benefits. Perhaps alone with David Lloyd George in the Cabinet, in effect, Churchill may have been seeking a compromise peace in policy by means of a strategy of limited war; the bulk of the Cabinet, dedicated with various degrees of enthusiasm to an absolute victory, did not yet recognize that, against an enemy coalition of roughly equal strength, such a victory could be realized only by an absolute strategic means, that is by a blood bath on the Western Front.

At this juncture, Arthur Balfour, too, was complaining about Russian hostility to the acquisition of new Balkan allies, and with customary subtlety suggested diverting the Greeks into Smyrna, both to reassure the Tsar and to provoke a more rapid entry into the war by the jealous Italians. Balfour believed what he called the Admiralty plan for fighting up the Gallipoli Peninsula "inch by inch" to be "altogether absurd".[6]

In the event, the Russian Government proved too weak to make the territorial concessions in Turkey necessary to bring the Greeks or the Bulgars into the war on its side. To the great disgust of such an advocate of limited war as Hankey (as subsequently to Captain Liddell Hart), the Tsarist Government preferred suicide to giving up what the French Ambassador to Russia caustically termed the "Byzantine mirage".[7] Since Nicholas II could not in any circumstances consent to Greek co-operation in the Dardanelles with the prospect of Greek rewards ensuing, on March 6 the Venizelos Government in Athens was dismissed to be replaced by a covertly pro-German Ministry. In fact, the Russians would even complain about the undesirability of Italy joining the Entente. Well might Hankey write: "*Quem deus vult perdere prius dementat.*"[8]

To avoid further antagonizing the Russians, once the will-o'-the-wisp of Greek aid had again receded, on March 10, in agreement with leaders of the Conservative Opposition, the British Cabinet decided to promise Constantinople to Russia in the postwar settlement. The French were eventually induced to accept this reversal of a historic British policy, notwithstanding their greater interests at the Golden Horn. Suspecting a political trap, Bonar Law refused to accept Churchill's proposal for the organization of a Coalition Government at this time, and the Prime Minister was equally unforthcoming concerning the need for such a drastic political change.[9] It is easy to gain the impression that the First Lord was as isolated within the Cabinet on his forebodings of stormy weather ahead as Fisher had been a month earlier.

At any rate Churchill was now up against it: his untenable promises regarding the naval assault were coming home to roost, and his hopes for a combined operation as a solution to his difficulties, in practice, were dependent upon either a clear-cut naval victory in order to win back the potential Balkan freebooters or upon an obvious naval defeat, which would induce Kitchener to commit his gradually assembling forces in the Aegean.

Although the Prime Minister noted the next day that he thought Admiral Carden was quite right in proceeding cautiously up the Straits, on March 11, and again on March 15, Churchill persuaded the Admiralty War Staff to notify Carden that he must now push ahead hard without regard for his losses. Carden got the point, and promised to do so at the first favourable break in the weather. Something of his real attitude showed, however, in his request on March 13 for more troops for large-scale land operations after he had penetrated the Straits. Before he had to go through with the attack, however, Carden collapsed from anxiety, leaving the task to his second-in-command, Rear-Admiral John de Robeck.[10]

As early as March 4, the first day when matters really began to go wrong for the naval assault, Churchill had mentioned the name of General Sir Ian Hamilton to Lord Kitchener as an excellent commander for the troops in the Aegean. On or before March 10 Kitchener had decided to supersede Lieutenant General Birdwood, his initial choice for the operation, in view of the likelihood of other Allied forces entering the ever more probable land campaign and the consequent need for a general officer of greater seniority and renown. An old friend and admirer of Kitchener from South Africa, Ian Hamilton had written to Kitchener regarding the lessons of the Russo-Japanese war, and more recently had served in close, if somewhat uneasy, collaboration with Kitchener in nearby Egypt, when Hamilton was the General Officer Commanding at Malta in the Mediterranean.[11]

On the morning of March 12, without warning Kitchener called Hamilton to his office and gave him command of what at Hamilton's insistence was called the Mediterranean rather than Constantinople Expeditionary Force. Informing Hamilton of the intensity of the opposition at Sir John French's and Joffre's headquarters to what these powerful organizations considered the theft or waste of the Twenty-ninth Division, Kitchener told Hamilton to treat this élite unit only as a temporary loan, repayable to the Western Front as soon as its services could be spared in the East.

The Director of Military Operations, Major-General Callwell, then explained what he believed to be the Greek plan for operations on Gallipoli, although Callwell had not actually been able to obtain the plan. Hamilton was to have 80,000 men with which to seize the Gallipoli Peninsula from an estimated 40,000 Turks. Half such a force, Kitchener said, would do Hamilton "handsomely", since the Turks were "busy elsewhere". At the same time the Secretary for War added "I hope you will not have to land at all; if you *do* have to land, why then the powerful Fleet at your back will be the prime factor in your choice of time and place. . . . We soldiers are to understand we are string number two. The sailors are sure they can force the Dardanelles on their own and the whole enterprise has been framed on that basis; we are to lie low and to bear in mind the Cabinet does not want to hear anything of the Army till it sails through the Straits. But if the Admiral fails, then we will have to go in."[12] Kitchener was obviously hanging on to his original conception of the Army aiding the Fleet to break through the Straits, however irresistibly the operation was being inverted to one of the Fleet aiding the Army.

Three small incidents in Kitchener's office that morning further indicated the questionable status of Hamilton's hastily assembled command. First, Hamilton's desire for the services of Major-General F. G. Ellison as his Chief of Staff was refused; secondly, the disconcerted C.I.G.S., Lieutenant-General Sir John Wolfe Murray, was informed, apparently for the first time, of the whole operation; and finally, Hamilton's assigned Chief of Staff, Major-General W. P. Braithwaite, was furiously turned down by Kitchener on a perfectly reasonable request for some modern planes so essential for reconnaissance over Gallipoli. The distraught War Minister only offered Hamilton the consolation that Turkish morale was low and that the Turks could never endure a Fleet bombardment of their capital.

Churchill evidently got in touch with Hamilton on the afternoon of March 12 to urge him, contrary to Kitchener's intention, to try to rush the Straits by a *coup de main* with the 40,000 lower grade troops already assembled in the Aegean. Lest there be any misunderstanding on this point, Kitchener informed Churchill the next day that, unless the Turks on the Gallipoli Peninsula were weaker than he anticipated, "no operations on a large scale should be attempted until the Twenty-ninth Division has arrived and is ready to take part in what is likely to prove a difficult undertaking, in which severe fighting must be anticipated."[13]

Hamilton's formal instructions from Kitchener on March 13 reiterated the latter's, rather than Mr Churchill's, idea of whether, when, and how a combined operation at the Dardanelles should be conducted. Hamilton's instructions opened:

(1) The Fleet has undertaken to force the passage of the Dardanelles. The employment of military forces on any large scale for land operations at this juncture is only contemplated in the event of the Fleet failing to get through after every effort has been exhausted.

(2) Before any serious undertaking is carried out in the Gallipoli Peninsula, all the British military forces detailed for the expedition should be assembled so that their full weight can be thrown in.

(3) Having entered on the project of forcing the Straits, there can be no idea of abandoning the scheme. It will require time, patience and methodical plans of co-operation between the naval and military commanders. The essential point is to avoid a check which will jeopardize our chances of strategical and political success.

Kitchener also "strongly deprecated" the occupation of the Asian shore of the Straits, which his French Corps commander, Lieutenant-General D. D'Amade, would shortly advocate to Hamilton. Although operations on the Anatolian mainland would have offered ample room for manœuvre and not simply compelled repeated assaults upon entrenched positions within the narrow limits of the Gallipoli Peninsula, Kitchener had spelled out to Hamilton, the day before, his fears of the implications of a campaign on the Asian side of the Straits. Such a campaign would cease to be one of "limited liability", and, said Kitchener, "once we began to march about Asia Minor the liability would become unlimited, and I would very likely have to make demands on him for reinforcements of all descriptions, which in the present state of affairs would be very difficult to give."[14] Unfortunately, as so often in future campaigns sponsored by Winston Churchill within the confines of narrow and rugged peninsulas, the resources demanded for advances under such difficult conditions would prove almost unlimited, although the results open to such campaigns would remain very restricted indeed.

Kitchener terminated his cautious instructions with an injunction which the over-chivalrous Hamilton would take too literally, namely, to address all his communications hereafter to the Secretary of State for War. Kitchener neither liked the Cabinet nor trusted much the activities of his ubiquitous colleague and rival in charge of the Admiralty, who he well knew was also an old friend of Hamilton from South Africa and India. At their parting, Kitchener relented somewhat, telling Hamilton as he left the War Office for the Dardanelles on March 13: "If the Fleet gets through, Constantinople will fall of itself and you will have won, not a battle, but the war."[15] One can see why, among all the terrified newcomers at the War Office, Kitchener could still hold the affection and loyalty of his subordinates from an earlier and happier day.

At Churchill's insistence Hamilton was hurried off to witness the great naval attack on the Straits with no time for the proper and complete assembly of his staff or even, for that matter, for an opportunity to read the General Staff Memorandum of 1906 on the problem of a combined operation against the Gallipoli Peninsula. As the official historian has concluded, the dispersion of Hamilton's staff resulting from this haste was a misfortune from which the expedition never quite recovered. Churchill did come to the railway station to see Hamilton off on Friday, March 13: this was his last chance for any direct contact with the Army Commander.[16]

Hamilton arrived in the Aegean on March 17 in time for a conference with the new commander of the naval attack scheduled for the next day, Rear-Admiral John de Robeck. Promoted Vice-Admiral for this mission, de Robeck had just assured the First Lord that he personally approved of his predecessor's plans for the naval assault. The new naval commander had stressed to Mr Churchill that everything depended upon silencing the Turkish forts long enough to allow the clearing of the minefields by the unprotected mine-sweepers.

Two years later, however, de Robeck would tell the Dardanelles Commissoners that "everyone thought it was better to have a combined operation, but one was not consulted [on this possibility] . . . we were told to bombard the forts, so we did it". The Admiral estimated that if he broke through to the Sea of Marmara without the aid of troops, his ships could hold out there for two or three weeks before being forced to return down the Straits in the event that no revolution occurred in Constantinople.[17] De Robeck's testimony has been supported by Admiral Limpus, who, having helped to plan the Turkish defences of the Straits, opposed the March 18 attack because the forts were too strong and a naval failure would simply alert the enemy.[18]

At their first conference on March 17, de Robeck informed Hamilton that the Gallipoli Peninsula was being rapidly fortified by thousands of Turks who worked at night "like beavers". All landing beaches were protected with trenches skilfully sited by German experts and covered by a constantly increasing number of concealed pieces of artillery and searchlights of the latest model. The relatively flat trajectory of naval artillery had little effect on these emplacements.

In a private letter to Lord Kitchener the next day Hamilton wrote: "Here, at present, Gallipoli looks like a much tougher nut to crack than it did over the map in your office. . . . My present impression is that, if it eventually becomes necessary to take the Gallipoli Peninsula by a military force, we shall have to proceed bit by bit." Hamilton also recommended that Alexandria would make a much more effective staging base from which to mount a large-scale operation against a hostile shore. The improvised facilities of Mudros on the island of Lemnos were utterly inadequate, apart from the constant disruption caused by bad weather, while none of the ships of the Royal Naval Division already there were combat-loaded for a contested landing.[19]

As Hamilton returned on the afternoon of March 18 from a reconnaissance of the uninviting Gallipoli coastline, he observed the later stages of Admiral de Robeck's great naval attack. When this day was done, three Allied capital ships had been sunk, three more badly disabled, while the civilian crews of the vital mine-sweepers had become completely demoralized from shell fire. De Robeck had lost one-third of his major ships from an unlocated minefield and, talking in terms of disaster, expected to be super-seded the next morning.

Little did he gauge the temper of his civilian, if not nautical, superiors at the Admiralty. At a sombre meeting of the War Council on March 19, Admiral Fisher declared that it was im-possible to "explain away" such losses, that he had always anti-cipated the loss of twelve battleships in an effort to force the Straits, and that, in any event, he would prefer to lose battleships elsewhere. Nevertheless, with the concurrence of Fisher and Admiral Wilson, Churchill had already set about replacing de Robeck's losses.[20]

Opinion differs regarding the impact of the Allied bombard-ment upon the inner Turkish forts. The proponents of the cam-paign affirmed that the damage to key forts was serious, the Turks were running low in several important categories of ammunition and their government was about to flee Constantinople. Con-versely, the opponents of the whole operation have emphasized the Allied shortage of naval ammunition, the still somewhat unknown and unlocatable menace of fixed and drifting mines, as well as the continued inaccessibility of the Turkish field guns to naval artillery.[21] Since the naval assault was not to be seriously renewed, no judgment on the issue can ever be final, particularly in matters so fickle and intangible as those of civilian morale. But the opinion of the German Commander, General Liman von Sanders, that, even with a naval success, the benefits for the British would have been largely illusionary unless they had staged a simultaneous army landing on Gallipoli, cannot be easily gainsaid.

On March 19 Hamilton informed Lord Kitchener concerning

his close reconnaissance of the Gallipoli Peninsula and on his impressions of the naval action of the previous day. Hamilton terminated his telegram to Kitchener: "I am being most reluctantly driven towards the conclusion that the Dardanelles are less likely to be forced by battleships than at one time seemed probable and that, if the Army is to participate, its operations will not assume the subsidiary form anticipated. The Army's share will not be a case of landing parties for the destruction of forts, etc., but rather a . . . deliberate and progressive military operation, carried out in order to make good the passage of the Navy."

Kitchener replied immediately: "You know my view that the passage of the Dardanelles must be forced, and that if large military operations on the Gallipoli Peninsula by the Army are necessary to clear the way [for the Navy], they must be undertaken, after careful consideration of local defences, and must be carried through."[22] The Secretary of State for War's continued emphasis upon helping the Navy would inhibit Hamilton's choice of landing beaches almost as much as his original instructions from Kitchener forbidding large operations on the Asian shore or landing in detachments.

At the same time in London on March 20 Colonel Hankey sent the Prime Minister a memorandum urging adequate staff preparation "so as to avoid repetition of [the] naval fiasco". Hankey made clear that the opportunity for a swift and casual Army *coup de main* on Gallipoli had already passed and that a serious siege operation of a combined nature would require more time for study and preparation by a joint army-navy staff in the United Kingdom.[23] Hankey's rather revolutionary suggestion for the parochial Services of that period got absolutely nowhere, however essential it would seem today for success in the simplest of amphibious operations. At the Admiralty Hankey also found both Fisher and Admiral Sir Henry Jackson angry at Churchill for having pushed through the naval attack without the aid of troops.

On March 22, in Hamilton's account at least, Admiral de Robeck asked for the assistance of all of Hamilton's troops. Since piecemeal landings were forbidden by Kitchener's instructions, without difficulty de Robeck agreed with Hamilton that the earliest date a combined assault could be mounted would be mid-April. By this date the haphazard expedition assembling at Lemnos could be reloaded for combat in Egypt, and reasonably good weather might be expected during the landings.[24] Repressing alike Commodore Keyes' passionate desire for a prompt resumption of the naval assault and General Birdwood's inclination for a rapid *coup de main* with what military forces were available, in effect, Hamilton upheld Admiral de Robeck's telegram of March 23 to the Admiralty. In this bombshell to Winston Churchill, de Robeck explained that the solution to the unexpected menace of mines would take time to achieve, but that, rather than risk "half measures", it would be better to make adequate preparations, while waiting for the Army to get ready.[25]

Churchill immediately convened a meeting of the Admiralty War Group and advocated sending orders to de Robeck to resume the naval attack as soon as possible on the grounds that the Turks were low on ammunition and that the old British battleships involved would soon be scrapped anyway. Although Churchill was supported by Admiral Oliver, backed by Sir Arthur Wilson and Sir Henry Jackson, Fisher now refused point-blank to concur in the resumption of the naval assault. High words were exchanged and the First Lord had to appeal to the sympathetic Prime Minister.

While Balfour and Kitchener, too, would have preferred another naval effort, none of these leading members of the War Council were willing to overrule both the admirals in London and the admiral on the spot on what appeared to them to be a question of professional naval judgment. For that matter, Asquith himself was becoming rather worn out by what he believed to be Churchill's political intrigues with the Conservative opposition, and in this connection would observe on March 25: "It is a pity that Winston has not a better sense of proportion. I am really fond of him, but I regard his future with many misgivings. I do not think he will ever get to the top in English politics with all his wonderful gifts."[26] It may also be seen why the Prime Minister did not choose to call together another session of his squabbling War Council until his growing anxieties regarding Winston Churchill came to a head some two months later.

By March 27 the grief-stricken First Lord had surrendered to the revolt of the Admiralty and the passivity of the Government. His telegram to de Robeck, saying that he "clearly" understood the necessity for a combined operation, was in reply to a long explanation from the Admiral on the same day which had pointed out that the assumption on which the naval assault had been based, namely that forts could be destroyed by naval gunfire alone, had now been "conclusively disproved".[27] Pressing his advantage, de Robeck declared that "the assistance of all naval forces available will, in my judgment, be needed to land the Army of the size contemplated, in the teeth of strenuous opposition". If Kitchener did not yet admit it, Fisher's and de Robeck's Navy was already engaged in assisting the Army in what had at last become an essentially military campaign.

The Cruellest Month

(March 29—April 25, 1915)

The advantage of time and place in all martial actions is half a victory;
which being lost is irrecoverable.[1]

SIR FRANCIS DRAKE

When it was decided to intervene in Greece [General Sir Archibald]
Wavell did not raise his voice against such an action. Being the good soldier
he was, he must have known it would not succeed. He did not say so. Indeed,
he gave the impression that he reckoned there were reasonable prospects of
success.[2]

FIELD-MARSHAL MONTGOMERY

This is going to be worse than Gallipoli.

LIEUTENANT-GENERAL JOHN LUCAS
BEFORE ANZIO

If that's how you feel you had better resign.[3]

ADMIRAL SIR JOHN CUNNINGHAM

If I had asked for a three-division lift, I should not have got anything.
How often in life must one be content with what one can get. Still, it would
be better to do it right.[4]

WINSTON CHURCHILL
ON THE ANZIO OPERATION, IN 1944

ALTHOUGH the sailors had finally succeeded in handing over
their unwanted Dardanelles baby to a gallant but still somewhat bemused soldier, the atmosphere within the Admiralty did
not noticeably improve—moments of truth may be salutary, but
they are rarely appreciated very much at the time. In this

atmosphere of nautical recrimination, Captain Richmond wrote that Churchill's "personal vanity occupies so large a place in the arrangements that the operation is either a fiasco or is most wasteful in lives or *matériel*—or both". Hankey talked Admiral Fisher out of one of his frequent threats of resignation, on this occasion because Churchill kept sending telegrams to various naval authorities marked as private, when according to Fisher they really dealt with public matters under the exclusive authority of the Board of Admiralty. (The Prime Minister eventually halted this practice on the part of the First Lord.)[5] And so normally serene an officer as Admiral Wemyss, after watching a week-long gale knock about his wretchedly impromptu facilities on Lemnos, complained that "amateur strategists and amateur warriors is what we are suffering from".[6]

To do the Admiralty justice, the cold aftermath of March 18 was now evoking second thoughts regarding a Dardanelles campaign under any guise, notwithstanding its somewhat belated assumption of respectability as a combined operation. What a subsequent critic would call vicious, absurd, and utterly irrational,[7] namely, launching an army attack after the naval failure had alarmed the Turks, had already occurred to Fisher in two letters which he submitted to Winston Churchill on March 31.

The first of these letters terminated with a request for a reconsideration of all the Dardanelles plans "before the final plunge is made"; the second, less reflective of Hankey-panky, reiterated "that we have now descended to the bare minimum of superiority in Home Waters, and . . . to dispatch any more fighting ships of any kind to the Dardanelles operations would be to court serious losses at home. . . . Consequently, I desire now to state my definite opinion that we must stand or fall by the ships now out in the Mediterranean or on their way there. . . . We can recover from an indecisive or even unsuccessful result of these operations in the Dardanelles; we can recover from an abandonment of the operations if this should be necessary; but we could never recover from a reverse to our main Fleets in the decisive theatre at home. *It would be ruin.* . . . I therefore beg you to forward my previous memorandum . . . and this communication also, to the War Council, in order that immediate deliberation may take place."[8] Thanks to the decision of the Prime Minister, no meeting of the War Council could consider the Admiralty's internal struggle until May 14—three weeks after the Army had landed on Gallipoli. If Herbert Asquith would not take positive steps to make the campaign in the Aegean effective, he would certainly take negative steps to render it possible.

Fisher's efforts to break away from his commitment to Churchill to back the Dardanelles led him into inconsistencies regarding the operation seemingly as ambivalent as those of Kitchener. Nevertheless, like those of Kitchener, Fisher's inconsistencies are perfectly intelligible once his position is properly understood. For example, in a letter to Churchill on April 5, playing up a supposed German threat to the Netherlands in the vain hope of distracting the First Lord's attention from the Aegean, Fisher broke out: "You are just simply eaten up with the Dardanelles and cannot think of anything else! Damn the Dardanelles! They will be our grave!" The day before, Fisher had written Jellicoe in a similar fashion: "I have time for little else now but increasing anxiety over the Dardanelles situation. I know so very little of de Robeck and Ian Hamilton that I am not able to rely on their judgment and Keyes is very shallow. . . . No good purpose would be served by my resigning. My opinions are known. But the politicians took the bit between their teeth and decided it was a Cabinet and not an 'expert' question, and Kitchener unwittingly led on by thinking it was going to be a purely naval operation, which Carden undoubtedly said but I never agreed to, and so here we are!"[9]

On the other hand, on April 7, the Second, Third, and Fourth Sea Lords requested a formal minute from Fisher reassuring them on the adequacy of the strength of the Grand Fleet as a consequence of the Dardanelles effort. Fisher answered his fellow Sea Lords that he had consented to the Dardanelles operation "with hesitation" in view of the shortage of ships and naval ammunition and the general incertitude concerning the project, but that "subject to the strict limitations of the naval forces to be employed" in the operation, British naval supremacy in the North Sea was not yet jeopardized.[10] In other words, subject to a swift and decisive victory by the Army, Churchill and his Dardanelles enterprise were still safe from Fisher.

His apparent effort, through Fisher, to forestall the Army attack having failed, on April 7 Colonel Hankey approached the Prime Minister directly. Hankey suggested that since Italy was about to join the Allies, while the success of the Gallipoli operation was very doubtful, it would be wise to postpone the attack. In a remarkable reversal of his "Boxing Day Memorandum" of the previous December, Hankey now inferred that a delay in the proposed combined operation might bring in not merely Italy, but also Greece and Bulgaria, thus altogether "obviating the hazardous attack on the Dardanelles".

Not surprisingly, Mr Asquith did not respond too well to such a display of flexible reasoning and objected that, after all the publicity, the attack must go through. In no way daunted, Hankey rejoined that "on military grounds" this was the best possible reason for dropping the assault altogether and attacking elsewhere, such as at Haifa, against the overextended Turkish lines of communication.[11] Unfortunately, by themselves, military grounds were rarely persuasive enough to win over statesmen, even those as relatively sympathetic as Asquith, when the political grounds were patently unfavourable. After all, as Bonar Law wrote to General Henry Wilson two days later with grim Presbyterian satisfaction, he was now certain that "the Government had jumped into all this without at all counting the cost".[12]

Henry Wilson had already spelled out something of the potential cost of the Dardanelles when in mid-March he had sent word to Law from France that "the way to end this war is to kill Germans and not Turks. The place where we can kill most Germans is here, and therefore every man and every round of ammunition we have got in the world ought to come here. All history shows that operations in a secondary and ineffectual theatre have no bearing on major operations—except to weaken the force there engaged. History, no doubt, will repeat her lesson once more for our benefit."[13]

On April 8 Hankey broached his Haifa idea to Captain Richmond at the Admiralty and arranged for the trusting Richmond to forward the suggestion to Admiral Fisher. Fisher promptly relayed to Churchill what then appeared to be Richmond's suggestion for treating all the Dardanelles preparations "as a gigantic feint", covering a real attack on Haifa. The outraged First Lord thereupon blamed his *bête noire*, Richmond, for by all odds the cleverest ploy ever bandied about the Pandora's Box of the Dardanelles. The indefatigable Hankey next put pressure on Churchill through Kitchener, Balfour, and Esher.[14]

Hankey's little-known struggle for a fundamental reconsideration of the campaign was, of course, much assisted by the usual pressure from the generals in France. Sir John French, who had just received a letter from Hamilton recounting his difficulties, described the proposed operation against Gallipoli as madness; General Sir William Robertson considered it the most difficult enterprise in the world; and Henry Wilson thought that Churchill should be sacked for still insisting upon it.

Hamilton himself was upset over his shortage of ammunition, his lack of authority over his main base in Egypt and the uncontrolled publicity in the Egyptian press regarding the destination of the expedition. Indeed, among his gloomy subordinates, the Commander of Hamilton's vital Twenty-ninth British Division, Major General A. G. Hunter-Weston, had concluded that there was not "in present circumstances a reasonable chance of success" at Gallipoli and had recommended delaying the expedition for more adequate preparation and more favourable circumstances elsewhere. Apart from the Haifa concept, at this juncture the British Army may have considered a landing on the then friendly seacoast of Bulgarian Thrace as an alternative to the increasingly unappetizing assault on the Gallipoli Peninsula.[15]

According to Hankey, on April 9, apparently with Churchill's consent, the Prime Minister decided to postpone the combined attack on the Dardanelles until Italy had clarified her intentions.

After consultation with the Army and Navy Staffs on the twelfth Hankey presented Mr Asquith with an appreciation in which he reached a masterly straddle: "If the Turkish troops are prepared to fight and if they are well supplied with ammunition and supplies of all kinds, success must be considered extremely doubtful. Fortunately, however, it is supposed that the Turks are short of ammunition and that they did not fight very well in the recent Balkan wars. . . . The military operation appears, therefore, to be to a certain extent a gamble upon the supposed shortage of supplies and inferior fighting qualities of the Turkish armies."[16] Of course, Mr Asquith was neither the first head of government nor the last to find that the final decision on a matter which no amateur could possibly judge had, nevertheless, been passed up to his desk by his cautious professional advisers.

In practice, Hankey's desperate intervention in London does not seem to have delayed the expedition any longer than the weather and the necessity for reloading would have demanded in any event. But, on the Turkish side, as so often in war, energetic last-minute efforts by the new German commander on the Gallipoli Peninsula, General Liman von Sanders, were about to weight the terms of Hankey's gamble decisively against Ian Hamilton.

Firmly anticipating the forthcoming British landing, on March 25–6 Enver had appointed von Sanders to command the Fifth Turkish Army along the Straits. He was given 84,000 men in some six and one-third divisions, most of which he placed at each end of the Gallipoli Peninsula poised for rapid movement in any direction. The German commander was particularly concerned with protecting his communications bottleneck at Bulair at the head of the Peninsula where the Turks had recently halted the Bulgars in the old British fortifications which still survived from the Crimean War. If the Bulgarians proved friendly to Turkey, von Sanders could count upon another twelve or fourteen divisions, taken from nearby Turkish Thrace, as reinforcements against any assault aimed through the Dardanelles at the centre of Turkish military power and security.[17] Thus, while in the upshot the four weeks granted von Sanders enabled him to accentuate the improvement of the tactical defences of the Straits, there was always a much larger untapped source of Turkish strength in reserve, should the British threat ever promise to bring about serious results.

If, on the eve of the landings, Hankey found Churchill officially optimistic regarding the prospects, by the third week in April Hankey and Kitchener had become more anxious than ever concerning what Fisher, too, now described as a "huge gamble" into which Churchill had "shoved" them all. On April 19, Kitchener had telegraphed Hamilton an account of tough Turkish resistance against the British in Mesopotamia, the implications of which for Hamilton's marginal operation on the Gallipoli Peninsula were at any rate plain to the professional soldier.

Taking as few chances as possible, in his plan of operations Hamilton had settled for landings on and near the tip of the Peninsula in the hope of simply getting ashore at all.[18] In theory, landings in such locations could be rationalized as helping the Navy break through the Straits as enjoined by Kitchener's instructions; in practice, Hamilton may have really given up the game before he started since, while an attack up a long and mountainous peninsula from its foot might achieve a tactical surprise because the enemy would expect nothing so futile, in the long run strategic surprise would, thereby, be lost and the enemy would simply reinforce his units entrenched in the rugged terrain. The analogy with the Italian campaign of the Second World War is striking, although the latter would also always reflect the potential of the somewhat more rational example of the Korean War in view of the far greater size of these two peninsulas. In short, in peninsular warfare, small peninsulas constitute the least promising arenas for offensive operations, as even the medium-sized Crimea has demonstrated on several occasions.

On April 23 and 24, at about the earliest date permitted by the weather, Ian Hamilton's expedition finally sailed for Gallipoli. The Germans simultaneously inaugurated a more Eastern emphasis to their grand strategy with a crushing blow against the Russians at Gorlice in Poland. As an inauspicious omen for a campaign commanded by a general whom Kitchener had once affectionately termed a "bloody poet",[11] Rupert Brooke had died of an infection on the afternoon of April 23. He was buried by his grieving companions of the Royal Naval Division on the Aegean island of Skyros, where traditionally the subtle Ulysses had discovered Achilles, disguised as a girl against the trials of war. Mr Churchill sent an eloquent tribute to Brooke to *The Times*. One of Brooke's comrades recalled that the burial of the poet was like witnessing the origin of some classic myth, as, indeed, it would prove to be. Shortly before his death Brooke had written an epitaph perhaps as sweet and fitting for his entire generation as for his comrades:

> I would have thought of them—
> Heedless, within a week of battle—in pity,
> Pride in their strength and in the weight and firmness
> And link'd beauty of bodies, and pity that
> This gay machine of splendour'ld soon be broken,
> Thought little of, pash'd, scatter'd. . . .[20]

12

The Fall of Icarus
(April 25—May 25, 1915)

But when the sun came up again to light the dawn, we saw the Aegean Sea blossoming with dead men. The men of Achaea, and the wreckage of their ships.[1]

ÆSCHYLUS

In a country like ours, governed by discussion, a great man is never hanged. He hangs himself. Therefore, pray be Machiavellian, and play upon the delicate instrument of public opinion with your fingers and not with your feet —however tempting the latter may be.[2]

LORD ESHER
TO FISHER IN 1906

The Prime Minister perceived at once that something much more important than the life of Gordon or the safety of Khartoum was now imperilled. The existence of the Government was at stake. And for the first time in the long chapter of procrastinations he acted swiftly.[3]

LORD ELTON

The first essential for a Prime Minister is to be a good butcher and there are several who must be poleaxed now.[4]

HERBERT ASQUITH
TO WINSTON CHURCHILL IN 1908

B Y sacrificing most of his hope for future advance Sir Ian Hamilton pulled off the difficult feat of landing on the Gallipoli Peninsula on beaches where he was not particularly expected. Despite the relative effectiveness of his feints, giving him a temporary superiority in strength at the moment of landing, rudimentary amphibious techniques and poorly trained troops and commanders lost Hamilton much of the advantage of surprise in the decisive first hours of the operation. As the Russians had complained at Plevna in 1877, the Turks fought a lot better than their enemies had been led to believe, and in Mustafa Kemal the Turkish Army had discovered a commander of great tactical presence. But, in the last analysis, as Field Marshal Kesselring would remark of a future amphibious project of Winston Churchill—that at Anzio in 1944—the British landing forces were too weak: "it was a half-way measure as an offensive that was your basic error".[5]

At the end of April Churchill was ready enough to concede to Hankey that great risks had been taken in the landings and, on the frantic Aegean base of Mudros, Admiral Wemyss recorded: "Never has a big campaign been so hastily organized and got together and never has such an undertaking had so little consideration given it from home. . . . I now realize that I never really believed that we should succeed. . . . the apparently impossible has been accomplished."[6] Already running short of ammunition, Hamilton noted in his diary: "Officialdom at the Admiralty is none too keen on our show. If we can get at Winston himself then we can rely on his kicking red tape into the waste paper basket; otherwise we won't be met half way. As for me, I am helpless. I cannot write to Winston—not on military business; least of all on Naval business. . . . The worst loss is that of Winston's ear; high principles won't obtain high explosives."[7]

Following repeated unavailing attacks against the rapidly hardening Turkish positions, on May 9 Hamilton was forced to inform Kitchener: "I might represent the battle as a victory, but actually the result has been failure, as the main object remains unachieved. Our troops have done all that flesh and blood can do against semi-permanent works, and they are not able to carry them. More and more munitions will be needed to do it. I fear this is a very unpalatable conclusion, but I can see no way out of it."[8] Kitchener's reply alluded to the shortage of merchant shipping and requested Hamilton's views regarding future operations. On May 10 Hamilton wrote Kitchener that Admiral de Robeck was in agreement with him that "the only sound procedure is to hammer away until the enemy gets demoralized". For this cheerless proposal, so reminiscent of the Western Front, Hamilton asked for two more divisions.[9]

On May 11 Kitchener telegraphed Hamilton that he was sending out one division with some additional artillery and ammunition. To obtain this ammunition Kitchener ordered Sir John French to send 25,000 rounds to the Dardanelles at once, or about one quarter of what Sir John had just expended in his unsuccessful offensive at Festubert. Beside himself with rage at this demand in view of his scanty remaining ammunition stocks, and angry in any event with the Prime Minister for having publicly denied the existence of any shortage of ammunition, Sir John French, through intermediaries, informed the leaders of the Conservative Opposition, Arthur Balfour and Bonar Law, and Kitchener's bitter enemy on the new Shell Committee, David Lloyd George, of the situation. Little wonder that when Northcliffe's press broke this news on May 14, Lord Kitchener confessed in a mood of heartfelt revulsion, shared by Hankey because of the parallel situation within the Admiralty: "I am deadly sick of this system of intrigue, [but] I am out to fight the Germans, and not to fight Sir John French."[10]

To the official historian of Gallipoli, however, goes the last word on this desperate internecine struggle now precipitated by Mr Churchill's campaign in the Aegean. Wrote General Aspinall-Oglander, who had actually participated in the planning for Gallipoli: "This was the acid test. There could be only one decisive theatre. Either it lay in the Dardanelles, in which case, owing to the limited means available, the strategical defensive should have been temporarily imposed upon the Army in France; or, if a spring offensive on the Western Front, as urged by the French High Command, was held to be of greater importance, or, if the obligations to the French were considered paramount, every available man and gun should have been concentrated in France, and the landing in Gallipoli should not have been undertaken.

"But neither of these courses had been adopted. For lack of a careful Staff study beforehand, Sir Ian Hamilton was ordered to enter upon a new campaign without a sufficient reserve. Sir John French, with a strength even less adequate for his task, was permitted to persevere with his plans for a spring offensive in France. With barely enough ammunition for one theatre, an offensive campaign was sanctioned in two, and both ended in failure."[11]

The Army failure gave Roger Keyes another chance to advocate a renewal of the original plan for a naval attack. Long identifying with Winston Churchill under their common lucky star, Orion the Hunter, on May 9 Keyes talked de Robeck and his subordinates into making a half-hearted suggestion to the Admiralty for a resumption of the naval assault on the Straits. In a long memorandum to Churchill on May 11, Admiral Fisher again rejected the whole concept of a naval attack, stressing the narrow British naval margin in the North Sea and his disbelief that the Fleet could force the Narrows before the Army had occupied the heights on each side of the Straits. Churchill replied immediately, informing Fisher that both Great Britain and Fisher personally were "absolutely committed" to success in this enterprise. On May 12 Fisher repudiated any commitment to what he termed a "repetition of March 18" until the Army had seized the Narrows. At the same time, Fisher sent the Prime Minister a copy of his memorandum of protest with a request that it be circulated to the still dormant War Council.[12]

Through Hankey's good offices, on May 11 the Prime Minister had already promised the First Sea Lord that no naval attack would be permitted without Fisher's concurrence, and, over Kitchener's violent protests, on May 12 Fisher even managed to procure the withdrawal of the new Dreadnought, *Queen Elizabeth*, from the Aegean for the North Sea. Fisher's soon justified fear of the long anticipated arrival of German submarines in the Mediterranean had made him particularly adamant on this point, while the French Ministry of Marine supported Fisher in opposing a resumption of the naval attack. The need for detaching several more capital ships and cruisers from de Robeck's squadron for the sake of guaranteeing Italy naval supremacy in the Adriatic at the moment of her expected entry into the war afforded the *coup de grâce* to Keyes' hopes for a resumption of the naval attack.[13]

As a consequence of Fisher's success in withdrawing the *Queen Elizabeth* from the Dardanelles, Lord Kitchener directed an indignant letter at the Prime Minister on May 13. The gist of the Secretary of State for War's ominous epistle read: "Lord Fisher said he would leave the Admiralty if the *Queen Elizabeth* was not at once withdrawn, as he could not stand the fear of losing the ship. I may say that I have had to face the loss of some 15,000 men in this operation to help the Navy. . . . This desertion of the Army after coming to the assistance of the Navy when they failed to force the passage of the Dardanelles, will undoubtedly have a very unpleasant effect on the confidence that ought to exist between the Services. . . . We may have to consider under these circumstances whether the [Gallipoli] troops [had] better not be taken back to Alexandria, as there may be a Moslem uprising in Egypt. . . ."[14]

While Kitchener's reference to the possibility of a revolt in Egypt was a patent fraud, the implications of his threat to abandon the whole Gallipoli operation rather than continue it solely as an Army show could hardly have been lost upon the much harassed Mr Asquith. In a minute for the files, however, Kitchener explicitly stated that although he would have liked to give up the operation, he realized that this was impossible. Kitchener was too much of an Orientalist to make clear-cut decisions against campaigns in the East, and besides, whatever may be said regarding Fisher, Kitchener and his Army's prestige were now irrevocably committed to a few thousand yards of bloodstained beachhead on Gallipoli.

On the same day on which he faced Kitchener's threat, the Prime Minister was once again the target of a similar communication from Fisher. In this eruption the First Sea Lord stated that he distrusted Churchill's willingness to abide by Asquith's veto of a renewed naval assault on the Straits, and that, instead of allowing the Admiralty to concentrate on the submarine menace, the First Lord was distracting everyone with his "ceaseless *prodding* . . . in every department afloat and ashore" in the interest of the Dardanelles. Fisher concluded his letter on his usual note of an impending resignation.

A pleasing interview with Herbert Asquith promptly ensued, which, preceded by a waltz with the Prime Minister's wife, Margot, put the old Admiral into a fine enough fettle to carry him through another twenty-four hours with Winston Churchill. Almost as alarmed as the First Sea Lord, the other Sea Lords now agreed with Fisher on the undesirability of forcing the Straits and requested that they be kept up-to-date on the Dardanelles decisions at all times.[15]

Appreciating at last that his suspicious and angry gods of war and of the sea might well destroy the Government, if not the Turks, Mr Asquith ordered the War Council to assemble on May 14 for the first time since late March. In preparation for this meeting Kitchener engaged in another old Army game when he wrote a memorandum for the War Council which laid stress upon the increased danger of a German invasion of England as a result of the recent Russian reverses in Galicia. Here, Kitchener was merely observing his customary practice when in doubt, namely keep as many of his reserves as possible on hand, uncommitted to any course of action.[16]

In the words of Winston Churchill, the atmosphere of the resurrected War Council meeting of May 14 was sulphurous. The Army had been stopped with heavy casualties both in France and at Gallipoli, the Navy would not go ahead in the Straits, and the shell scandal was breaking in the Press that very morning. To top matters, the great passenger liner, the *Lusitania*, had just been sunk by a German submarine in the Atlantic. A British battleship had met the same fate at the hands of a Turkish torpedo boat in the Aegean and a Russian collapse in Poland appeared ever more imminent.

Lord Kitchener opened his remarks with the complaint that he had been let down by the Navy and referred again to the departure of the *Queen Elizabeth*. Fisher interrupted to comment that he had been against the Dardanelles operation from the beginning, as the Prime Minister and Secretary of State for War well knew. As no one contradicted this statement, Kitchener resumed his jeremiad with a description of the appalling rate of shell expenditure and what he called the increasing German threat to France and the United Kingdom. Uncertain about the future, he opposed sending more troops out of the United Kingdom to any active theatre of war.

Faced by a hostile audience Churchill then advocated halting the unrewarding British offensive in France in favour of the concentration of all available reinforcements and ammunition on Gallipoli. Although his arguments may now have become tenable, as in 1944–5 with the Americans, Churchill had discredited himself too much with his earlier, more specious, pleading to be accepted when logical necessity—let alone the course of future events—may well have been on his side. Nevertheless, the War Council lacked the courage either to reinforce Hamilton as Churchill desired, or to cut bait and abandon the Dardanelles, as Kitchener and Fisher favoured, if only by implication. In an effort to conceal the usual compromise, perhaps even from themselves, the War Council eventually authorized Kitchener to ask Hamilton what forces he required, upon the highly improbable supposition that such resources would then be placed at his disposal.[17]

A letter sent by Churchill to the Prime Minister following the meeting of the War Council, if somewhat *de haut en bas* in tone, defines the play of personalities against events at this stage very well. Justifying Fisher's suspicions that he would never abide by the Prime Minister's veto of a renewed naval attack, Churchill wrote to Asquith on May 14:

> I am attached to the old boy [Fisher] and it is a great pleasure to me to work with him. I think he reciprocates these feelings. My point is that a moment will probably arise in these operations when the Admiral and General on the spot will wish and require to run a risk with the Fleet for a great and decisive effort. If I agree with them, I shall sanction it, and I cannot undertake to be paralysed by the veto of a friend who, whatever the result, will certainly say, "I was always against the Dardanelles."

You will see that in a matter of this kind *someone* has to take the responsibility. I will do so—provided that my decision is the one that rules —and not otherwise.

It is also uncomfortable not to know what Kitchener will or won't do in the matter of reinforcements. We are absolutely in his hands, and I never saw him in a queerer mood—or more unreasonable. K. will punish the Admiralty by docking Hamilton of his divisions because we have withdrawn the *Queen Elizabeth*; and Fisher will have the *Queen Elizabeth* home if he is to stay.[18]

That evening of May 14 Mr Churchill had a relatively friendly conversation with Fisher concerning fresh naval forces for the Dardanelles in lieu of those so recently removed. At the end of the conversation the departing First Lord said to the old Admiral: "We have settled everything, and you must go home and have a good night's rest. Things will look brighter in the morning, and we'll pull the thing [i.e. the Dardanelles] through together." Fisher thereupon informed his naval assistant not to pack up his effects "just yet", although he added that, notwithstanding his momentary agreement with Churchill on the question of replacements for the Dardanelles, he supposed that the latter would soon be at him again.[19]

Fisher did not have long to wait, for later that evening Churchill added two submarines as well as other naval *matériel* to the forces agreed upon in the early evening with the First Sea Lord. According to Fisher's biographer at least, Churchill capped this injury with the insult of a gratuitous covering note on a telegram regarding the movement of additional British naval units to Italy, a covering note which read that the First Sea Lord should see it only after it had been sent out. Whether so or not, Churchill would seem to have had a pretty good suspicion that he might be provoking Fisher into resignation because, disregarding the warning of Fisher's naval assistant, Captain T. E. Crease, that this would be the automatic consequence, Churchill still went ahead with the order for the inclusion of the new naval *matériel* for the Dardanelles, not yet discussed with Fisher.

The next morning, that of May 15, when Fisher, who often

arose almost as Churchill retired to bed, read of the First Lord's unilateral action with respect to the new naval additions for the Dardanelles, he instantly wrote a letter of resignation to the Prime Minister. A very similar note which Fisher sent to Churchill at the same time went as follows:

First Lord,
  After further anxious reflections, I have come to the regretted conclusion I am unable to remain any longer as your colleague. It is undesirable, in the public interests, to go into details—Jowett said "never explain"— but I find it increasingly difficult to adjust myself to the increasing daily requirements of the Dardanelles to meet your views. As you truly said yesterday, I am in the position of continually vetoing your proposals.
  This is not fair to you, besides being extremely distasteful to me.
  I am off to Scotland at once, so as to avoid all questionings.[20]

Yours truly,
FISHER

Like Rudolf Hess, Jacky Fisher would find it harder to reach the Duke of Hamilton's estate in Scotland than he had anticipated and, like Hess, he would soon be called insane, if not worse, for his effort.

Shortly discovered in the questionable sanctuary of the Charing Cross Hotel, Fisher immediately received an order from the Prime Minister to return to his post in the King's name: the German High Seas Fleet was believed to be at large. To be sure, at first Mr Asquith did not take Fisher's resignation very seriously, any more than Churchill did, because of the too frequent previous threats of such action on the part of the temperamental First Sea Lord. When another personal discussion with Fisher proved fruitless, in order to avoid adding a further political complication to the augmenting shell crisis, Asquith asked Churchill to urge Fisher in writing to return to the Admiralty.

Churchill's appeal to Fisher was eloquent. Unhappily, it was also not entirely honest, although Fisher might forbear from saying as much to his superior. Churchill wrote:

In order to bring you back to the Admiralty [in 1914] I took my political life in my hands with the King and the Prime Minister, as you

143

know well. You then promised to stand by me and see me through. If you go now at this bad moment and thereby let loose on me the spite and malice of those who are your enemies even more than they are mine, it will be a melancholy ending to our six months of successful war and administration. The discussions which will arise will strike a cruel blow at the fortunes of the Army now struggling on the Gallipoli Peninsula, and cannot fail to invest with an air of disaster a mighty enterprise, which, with patience, can and will certainly be carried to success.[21]

While it is perfectly true that the King and Mr Asquith had been dubious concerning Fisher's return to the Admiralty in 1914, Churchill's motive in insisting upon this action had been to improve his own weakening position in the public gaze with the aura of Fisher's prestige—not vice versa. Furthermore, it was exceedingly doubtful whether Fisher's enemies among the Tories were anything like as numerous as those of the First Lord. Finally, an appeal for yet more patience for the sake of carrying the Dardanelles operation to success, when the whole point was that Fisher had long considered the operation an ever-growing threat to the supremacy of the Grand Fleet, can hardly have been an argument of a very convincing nature to the old Admiral. In short, Churchill's appeal smacks more of an epitaph to a definitely played-out relationship than of a sincere call for a renewal of what, at best, had been a difficult and demanding collaboration.

Fisher replied to Churchill in kind, that is in the manner of an unforgiving spouse who knows that she had been rejected. He wrote on May 16:

You are bent on forcing the Dardanelles and nothing will turn you from it— NOTHING. I know you so well! I could give no better proof of my desire to stand by you than my having remained by you in this Dardanelles business up to this last moment against the strongest conviction of my life, as stated in the Dardanelles Defence Committee Memorandum [of 1907].

You will remain. I SHALL GO. It is better so. Your splendid stand on my behalf with the King and the Prime Minister I can NEVER forget, when you took your political life in your hands and I really have worked very hard for you in return—*my utmost*—but here is a question beyond all personal obligations.[22]

The old Sea Lord was still grateful, he was reasonably polite, and he was absolutely determined not to accept another paper treaty, shielding the next inevitable attempted evasion by Churchill and resultant humiliation on his part.

On this same day the three junior Sea Lords submitted a minute to Churchill and Fisher in which they said that Fisher's resignation appeared to be a result of his disagreement with the First Lord on the conduct of the Dardanelles operation and of his dissatisfaction with Churchill regarding the procedure employed for the executive control of the movements of the Fleet. On the Dardanelles issue the junior Sea Lords acknowledged that their imperfect acquaintance with the political considerations at stake prevented them from judging the rightness of the policy of the Government. So far as the question of the disposition of the Navy was concerned, the junior Sea Lords declared that operations in the Dardanelles "most certainly jeopardize the crushing superiority of the Grand Fleet which is essential to the successful prosecution of the War".

On Fisher's second point the junior Sea Lords also agreed with the First Sea Lord and wrote that the present method of allowing the control of the movement of the Fleet and its supplies to remain largely under the aegis of the First Lord was "open to very grave objection". Nevertheless, despite their disapproval of Mr Churchill's activities both in strategic theory and in actual operations, the junior Sea Lords did agree to continue as a Board under Churchill's leadership. And to Churchill's acknowledged surprise, not to mention Fisher's intense chagrin, Sir Arthur Wilson accepted the post of First Sea Lord under Churchill, replacing Fisher.[23]

Perhaps it was this last mortification which precipitated Fisher's next action, because he now sent the Conservative leader, Bonar Law, a not very anonymous note implying his resignation. Law promptly called on David Lloyd George, who confirmed the former's surmise regarding Fisher's intent. Law then informed the Chancellor of the Exchequer that the Conservative Party would revolt if faced with Churchill's effective rule over a tame

L

Board of Admiralty. Acting on Lloyd George's brandy more like a spark than the water of Mr Harold Macmillan's well-known metaphor, Law's warning evoked an instant trip on the part of the Chancellor next door to the Prime Minister's residence at 10 Downing Street. Mr Asquith, too, at once realized the necessity for a Coalition Government in order to avoid a damaging Parliamentary debate at a moment of extreme vulnerability for the Liberals. And, of course, Churchill's surrender of the Admiralty was the first price demanded by his old enemy, Andrew Bonar Law, for Tory participation in the Government.

At the Prime Minister's request, Law wrote him a letter in which the Conservative leader said that, since the imminence of an Italian entry into the war made it undesirable to have a public debate on Fisher's resignation, the Conservatives would maintain silence so long as Fisher's resignation was postponed. To guard against any weakening by Bonar Law with respect to Churchill's elimination from the Admiralty, the terms of Fisher's continuance as First Sea Lord were spelled out in a signed but secret letter which Fisher sent Law later on May 17, Fisher wrote:

My *definite decision* is that I am absolutely unable to remain with W.C. (HE'S A REAL DANGER!) *But he is going to be kept* (so I go! at once, TODAY), only they are "forking" me till Parliament rises for 3 weeks or more. I regret to say that your A. J. B[alfour] has been backing W.C. ALL THROUGH and I have refused to have anything to do with him (A.J.B.) in consequence! *Keep this private.* I must not see you, BUT PARLIAMENT SHOULD NOT RISE TILL THE FACT OF MY GOING IS EXTRACTED.

Don't be cajoled *privately* by the P.M. to keep silence . . . I don't want to stay, but W.C. MUST go at all costs! AT ONCE . . .

Be prepared for the *suppressio veri* and *suggestio falsi.* . . . *W.C. is leading them all straight to ruin . . . a very great national disaster is very near us in the Dardanelles!* against which I have vainly protested and did resign long ago, but Kitchener persuaded me to stop. *I was a damned fool to do so* (HE ought to have resigned also). . . . Yesterday a member of the Cabinet told me that the present Government is on the verge of being smashed by my going! I DOUBT IT, BUT I WILL GO?

Please burn and don't mention. . . . This evening Winston sent Lambert, the Civil Lord of the Admiralty, to offer me a seat in the Cabinet if I

would return as First Sea Lord with him (Winston) as First Lord! I
rejected the 30 pieces of silver to betray my country.

The furious old Admiral had also told Sir Edward Grey that he
would serve under McKenna or Grey, but not with Balfour or
Churchill.[24]

Fisher's style might be eccentric and his practice on this, as on
a good many earlier occasions in his career, one of low cunning,
but he was not mad nor had he undergone a nervous breakdown,
as Churchill and Asquith have suggested in explanation of his
behaviour over the next few days.[25] When Prime Minister in
the next war, Mr Churchill's strenuous and demanding personality would again repeatedly infuriate and exhaust his subordinates,
and even political colleagues, to the point of tears or of collapse,
if no longer to an effective revenge. As Fisher complained to
Hankey in language almost identical with that of Sir John
Dill or of Sir Alan Brooke in the future, managing Churchill
took most of the energy he wished to devote to fighting the
Germans.[26]

On the afternoon of May 17 the still unsuspecting Churchill
arrived at the House of Commons, prepared to defend his new
Board of Admiralty against all Tory challengers. There the Prime
Minister gave him the news that he would no longer be in charge
of the Admiralty in the forthcoming Coalition Government. His
opinion being requested on the question of his successor, Churchill
recommended Arthur Balfour, who was in thorough agreement
with him on the need for a campaign in the Dardanelles. Stunned
by the abruptness of his fall, Churchill has written that the Prime
Minister instead should have accepted a debate over the conduct
of the war in a secret session of the House of Commons, much as
Churchill himself would in the very different circumstances of
July 1942. But in 1915, and for long thereafter, Winston Churchill
evidently did not appreciate the extent to which he had been discredited in the eyes of Mr Asquith and of his associates
in the Liberal Party during the period of his tenure at the
Admiralty.[27]

The dismissal of Churchill galvanized Fisher into frantic intrigues to regain the position with the Tories which he had just thrown away with the Liberals. When on May 19 Sir Arthur Wilson refused to accept the post of First Sea Lord except under Churchill, in truth Fisher did stand a chance of returning to the Admiralty. After all, as a consequence of an outburst of public opinion during this political crisis, Kitchener, who had also been menaced with the loss of his Cabinet post, found himself suddenly spared and, in fact, signally honoured by his old friend, the King. Nevertheless, even the idolized Secretary of State for War was soon to be stripped of his control over munitions, a control which was transferred to a new Ministry set up under his bitter enemy, David Lloyd George.[28]

The prospect of Arthur Balfour replacing Churchill may have thrown Fisher's judgment off balance, for the letter which he sent the Prime Minister on May 18 utterly destroyed any chance he stood of a triumphant vindication at the expense of Winston Churchill. In terms intolerable to the weakest of Prime Ministers and, indeed, to any democratic government, Fisher promised Mr Asquith a successful termination of the war only on the basis of his obtaining sole and absolute authority in the Admiralty, with the powers of the civilian First Lord reduced to those of an undersecretary. Moreover, Churchill, Balfour and Sir Arthur Wilson were to be excluded from the Admiralty in any capacity whatever. Faced with this ultimatum, the Prime Minister had no choice but, finally, to accept Fisher's resignation on May 22.[29]

Fisher's fatal overbidding of his hand with the Prime Minister on May 18 gave his rival another lease on nautical life. Swallowing his pride, Churchill appealed on May 20 and 21 to various Tory leaders, including his old opponent Bonar Law. From before the war Churchill had maintained a point of social intercourse with Law and several prominent Conservatives in the so-called Other Club which he had founded with his friend F. E. Smith. And in 1911, in 1912, and with the outbreak of war in 1914, Churchill had advocated a Coalition Ministry as a method of strengthening his position with the still scornful Tories.

THE FALL OF ICARUS

All of these efforts had been unavailing in the past and un-availing they remained. Notwithstanding so unpolitical a state-ment in his plea to Law as "we are coming together not to work on public opinion but to wage war, and by waging successful war we shall dominate public opinion", the cautious, self-abnegating, and pragmatic Presbyterianism in Law distrusted the glittering rhetoric of his great Liberal enemy as part and parcel of a roman-tic, but not always very real, sense of *noblesse oblige*. Austen Chamberlain likewise turned Churchill down.[30]

On May 22, with the aid of Fisher's old friend Reginald McKenna, Colonel Hankey finally managed to bundle the reluc-tant Fisher off to an already undesired exile in Scotland. There Hankey, if not McKenna, hoped that the old Admiral would gradually accept the collapse of his illusions and, in any event, have fewer opportunities for further indiscretions. With some annoyance the Prime Minister accepted this solution, thus leaving the Admiralty with neither a civil nor a naval chief.

The next day, May 23, the Prime Minister and Mr Churchill doubtless consoled themselves for the embarrassments of their Dardanelles venture with the entry of Italy into the war. On May 24, and again on May 25, Admiral Fisher, in his turn, found justi-fication when the German submarines which he had so long pre-dicted were about to enter the Mediterranean, sank two more of Winston Churchill's expendable old battleships at the mouth of the Dardanelles with unhappy results for naval assistance to the Army. Fortunately, in the betwixt-and-between dimension of strategy, the battleship *Queen Elizabeth* was safely on her way north to join Jellicoe, a year in advance of that infinitely more important encounter off Jutland so long awaited by Churchill's erstwhile naval friend and associate.[31]

Both Lord Hankey and Arthur Marder have summed up the collaboration of Churchill and Fisher as a failure of two men too much alike in temperament: in imagination, in drive, and in occasional lapses of judgment. Indeed, each would continue to appreciate the other on a personal level; in 1915 Churchill said that he did not bear Fisher any grudge, and in 1916 Fisher asserted that he would back up Churchill again to the point of resignation because, in Fisher's unstinting appraisal, his former First Lord was "a War Man!"[32]

With respect to their common superior, a despairing Churchill had cried out to Lord Riddell on May 20 that Herbert Asquith had been "terribly weak—supinely weak. His weakness will be the death of him." For himself Churchill said that he was the victim of a political intrigue and he was finished for all he cared for: the waging of war and the defeat of the Germans.[33]

Two days later that wise old member of the Genro, Lord Esher, had a long talk with Sir John French. Politicians, Esher pointed out to the embarrassed soldier, were "utterly untrustworthy" in their support of any man, since they existed only by popular favour "to which, from the nature of their being, they are primarily obliged to look". Instead of statesmen, Esher recommended that Sir John rely upon Lord Kitchener and General Joffre.[34] Churchill has noted that at the moment of his abandonment Kitchener was almost alone in calling on him with sympathy. The Field-Marshal had then said to his frequent trial and tribulation: "Well, there is one thing at any rate they cannot take from you. The Fleet was ready."[35]

It was David Lloyd George, however, who, in agreement with Esher on the lack of true friendship at the top of political life, had properly gauged the significance of Churchill's fall for the future, when he told Riddell on May 23 that the blow would really be the making of the First Lord. As the politically prescient Welshman wrote in his memoirs so late as 1933–4, Churchill's subsequent career "will depend on whether he can establish a reputation for prudence without losing audacity".[36] Even then the question would remain open for another decade.

13

Failure in Command

(May 19—August 15, 1915)

Alas! I struggle from Pride. Yes! It is Pride that now prompts me, not ambition. They shall not say that I have failed.[1]

DISRAELI

Really, when I reflect upon the character and attainments of some of the General officers of this army, and consider that these are the persons on whom I am to rely . . . I tremble; and, as Lord Chesterfield said of the Generals of his day, "I only hope that when the enemy reads the list of names he trembles as I do."[2]

THE DUKE OF WELLINGTON

They [the Dutch] were seeking the impossible; they wanted a general who would be strong against the enemy, but weak and submissive towards themselves.[3]

WINSTON CHURCHILL

There is nothing so restful as taking orders from fools.[4]

T. E. LAWRENCE

ON May 19 Ian Hamilton noted in his diary that he had received "a queer cable" to his request to Kitchener for four more divisions; in fact, to the overly sensitive Hamilton, Kitchener's message sounded "uncommonly like a cry for help" against the politicians, "ever . . . a British Commander's bane". Kitchener had expressed his serious disappointment at discovering that his "preconceived views as to the conquest of positions necessary to dominate the forts on the Straits . . . with the active help of naval bombardment were miscalculated". Kitchener

151

added: "The question whether we can long support two fields of operation draining on our resources requires grave consideration. I know I can rely upon you to do your utmost to bring the present unfortunate state of affairs in the Dardanelles to as early a con-conclusion as possible, so that any consideration of a withdrawal, with all its dangers in the East, may be prevented from entering the field of possible solutions."

Still more ominous from Hamilton's point of view were the rumours that Churchill was leaving the Admiralty. Hamilton wrote: "This would be an awful blow to us out here . . . alas, how grievous is the set-back to one who has it in him to revive the part of Pitt, had he but Pitt's place. Haldane, too! Are the benefits of his organization of our army to be discounted because they had a German origin?"[5] The poet in Hamilton may have sensed, as impassioned civilians do not, that, in André Malraux's phrase, the hot embrace of war is no more than a negative approach to so fascinating an object as an enemy.

In fact, Churchill was fortunate to have retained his seat in the Cabinet at all, albeit in the sinecure of the Duchy of Lancaster, carefully removed from any control over naval operations. His fall was further broken by the appointment of his recommendation and sympathizer, Arthur Balfour, as First Lord of the Admiralty, and Admiral Sir Henry Jackson as First Sea Lord. Presumably, to guard still further against any tendency on the part of the articulate and knowing Mr Churchill to go into opposition, the artful Prime Minister had allowed him to retain a position on the new Dardanelles Committee, shortly to be set up as the lineal heir of the War Council.

In the Dardanelles Committee Churchill similarly faced another restraint upon his powers of persuasion in the persons of its new Conservative members, particularly Bonar Law, and, with his subsequent entry, Sir Edward Carson. But notwithstanding the accession of fresh blood, the Dardanelles Committee retained the major defects of the old War Council, namely the lack of an agenda and the power to make decisions binding upon the rest of the Cabinet.

Like its predecessor, the Dardanelles Committee was also in-augurated with too many members, and under the lax and com-promising rein of Herbert Asquith inevitably grew still larger. At first, however, no regular seats were found for the Service mem-bers, although under Hankey's spur they were increasingly per-mitted to attend to provide information on particular issues. At least the new Committee met more regularly (its Tory com-ponents saw to that) and from sheer necessity dealt more and more with the daily running of the war as a whole rather than its titular subject matter of the Dardanelles.[6]

It is indicative, however, of the continuing influence of Winston Churchill upon grand strategy that the organization for the higher direction of the war would flaunt no more than the name of his swiftly growing Dardanelles offspring. In one sense, of course, such a parochial title was just, since the Dardanelles would de-mand most of the time and care of the Dardanelles Committee, amidst all the customary turmoil and vexation attendant upon the fostering of this natural child of the necessarily somewhat prom-iscuous process of strategic natural selection.

In a memorandum largely prepared by Hankey, the reluctant Kitchener was now called upon to propose a new course of action *vis-à-vis* what he already considered the Dardanelles millstone across his shoulders. On May 28 Kitchener suggested three courses of action to the Cabinet: to withdraw, to seek a decision, or to accept the present stalemate. Since withdrawal would un-questionably involve a great loss of life, this course was not recommended. On the other hand, neither the trained troops nor, which was even more important, the necessary ammunition, could be spared from France for an all-out offensive against the Turks on Gallipoli. Hence, it followed, to Kitchener at any rate, that the prolongation of the current impasse was the only solution open, particularly because, with the aid of certain reinforcements, such a course might serve equally well to encourage the Balkans and discourage the Turks from operations elsewhere.[7]

On June 2 Hamilton tightened the east-west vice in which Kitchener was gripped by cabling that as a result of the Russian reverses and Bulgaria's increased coolness, he anticipated that vast reinforcements would soon reach the Turks on Gallipoli. Hamilton asked for either Greek assistance or for the full four divisions which he had already requested.

Working in collaboration, if presumably not in communication, with Hamilton, in a public speech at Dundee on June 5 Churchill called for a victory "such as this war has not yet seen", the seizure of Constantinople. Declared the bloodied but yet unbowed Minister: "There was never a great subsidiary operation of war in which a more complete harmony of strategic, political and economic advantages has combined, or which stood in truer relation to the main decision, which is the central theatre. Through the Narrows of the Dardanelles and across the ridges of the Gallipoli Peninsula lie some of the shortest paths to a triumphant peace."[8] The German Commander at the Straits, General Liman von Sanders, has expressed his appreciation for the warning granted him by this speech. What Kitchener said concerning Mr Churchill's view of the felicitous relations prevailing between the main and subsidiary theatres of war, unfortunately, has not been recorded.

To the great distress of the anxious Hamilton, the necessity for educating certain of the new Conservative members of the Government on the desirability of providing reinforcements for the Dardanelles delayed the first meeting of the Dardanelles Committee until June 7. Here, in spite of Kitchener's half-heartedness, unexpectedly aided by a new Tory colleague, Lord Selborne, Churchill pushed through the acceptance of Hamilton's request for four additional divisions (one had already been dispatched). In a paper dated June 1, Churchill had argued that there was little chance of either side breaking the stalemate in France, while a small part of the high explosive expended in France could achieve a victory against the Turks. With still stronger logic Churchill warned against the disadvantages of piecemeal reinforcements which would always enable the Turks to match the British build-up.

To be sure, the battle won in the Dardanelles Committee

against the opposition of Bonar Law on the seventh had to be refought again on June 9 in the whole Cabinet, but on this occasion the opposition of Sir Edward Carson and others was likewise overcome and Hamilton gained his reinforcements. Three days later, however, Law charged that Hamilton himself lacked confidence in his projected landings at Suvla Bay.[9]

Reactions to this remarkable recrudescence of Churchill's strategy varied: Ian Hamilton expressed gratified relief, his fears regarding Kitchener's apparent indecision on the operation momentarily allayed. Hamilton did note, though, that two new Turkish divisions had already arrived on Gallipoli. In France, Henry Wilson, who had spent the recent political crisis at his old tricks of intriguing with the Conservatives against Asquith, raged: "It is simply incredible. This makes, I think 9 [divisions] there [at the Dardanelles] and 22 here, and not a single Boche facing the 9. How they will laugh in Berlin."[10] Kitchener's own attitude is, perhaps, best defined by his statement to Riddell later in the month that he would not let the Navy, which had started the campaign in the Dardanelles, evade "their share of the blame and trouble".[11]

Writhe as he might, Kitchener could no longer escape from the implacable dilemma of the Dardanelles. Emboldened by his success of June 7–9, Churchill now assailed both the Dardanelles Committee and the Secretary of State for War with demands for still further reinforcements for Hamilton. As with the Americans in the Second World War, having committed the prestige of his country and his colleagues to an ever-expanding campaign in the Mediterranean, Churchill could effectively proceed to extort more troops and still more from what would soon enough cease to be the main, let alone decisive, theatre in France. In the short run, Churchill's strategy of reinforcing Hamilton made good sense, but in the long run, as Henry Wilson's fury proclaimed, the divisions sent East, if victorious, in all probability would never return West for the sake of achieving a military decision in France.

In a memorandum in mid-June, strikingly evocative of his calculated appeals to President Franklin Roosevelt's political need for immediate action in 1942, Churchill wrote: "Here [Constantinople] is the prize, and the only prize which lies within reach this year. It can certainly be won without unreasonable expense, and within a comparatively short time. But we must act now, and on a scale which makes speedy success certain."[12] Whether an effort on a scale necessary to render success certain in the Straits could be defined as an unreasonable expense or not depended of course upon the observer's over-all conception of the war; in any event, success on Gallipoli probably could never have been realized without a prolonged halt to most British operations in France, and this Kitchener was unable to face. Since, as Prime Minister from 1917–18, David Lloyd George would prove equally incapable of preventing such offensives in the West, the limitations upon Kitchener's power rather than simply the vacillations of old age may be inferred as the primary explanation for his conduct.

Following a meeting of the Dardanelles Committee on June 25, Kitchener resolved to curtail the supply of ammunition for Sir John French in order to swell the amount available for Hamilton's next attack on Gallipoli. He also offered Hamilton another division and informed the Government that Hamilton might call upon further reinforcements from the Egyptian garrison should this prove necessary.[13]

As a consequence, the limited extent of Kitchener's authority soon became apparent. Although on June 30 he repeatedly promised the doubtful Henry Wilson that all the current reinforcements for the Dardanelles would eventually be returned to the West, two days later Wilson repaid the Government for his new knighthood by persuading three new Conservative members of the Cabinet, Bonar Law, Walter Long and Sir Edward Carson, to oppose sending any more troops to Gallipoli. Sir Henry had concluded smugly that both Kitchener and the Government were frightened and no longer knew what to do.[14] Like that worsted advocate of a nautical concentration in the West, Jacky Fisher, Wilson always knew where to turn when threatened unduly by the Dardanelles. Unhappily for Winston Churchill's great project, Sir Ian Hamilton would not stoop to similar means of attaining his ends.

On July 6 at a conference between the British and French Governments at Calais, Kitchener was reduced privately to cajoling Joffre into an ostensible postponement of his proposed offensive in Champagne until 1916. In reality, Joffre appears only to have agreed with Kitchener to delay his offensive long enough for the results of Hamilton's next attack on the Peninsula to become obvious. But, as Hamilton would note in mid-July, stopping all operations in France was "the very kernel of the question" of success in his theatre.[15] And like Fisher before him, the weary Titan at the War Office was recognizing ever more sadly that the interests of the Eastern and Western theatres, far from being complementary, were fundamentally irreconcilable.

In mid-July, also, the united Austro-German drive against Russia was launched. This pushed the British Government into sustaining a constantly expanding effort at the Dardanelles and the French Government into backing Joffre's proposed August offensive in Champagne. If the strategies of the Western Entente Powers remained unrelated, well-justified pessimism reigned behind their lines regarding the chances of success of either of the two offensive actions ostensibly designed to bring aid to the Tsar. Both Herbert Asquith and Bonar Law, although antagonistic in temperament—the former an optimist and the latter a pessimist— were in agreement that this was the last chance for the Dardanelles. Should Hamilton fail this time, he would not be reinforced again, the Prime Minister assured Sir Henry Wilson at the end of July.[16]

In July Churchill proposed going on a tour of inspection of the Dardanelles, but a suspicious Kitchener had insisted that Colonel Hankey accompany him. To take no chances with the former First Lord, Kitchener informed Hamilton that Churchill should "in no way interfere with military operations". Churchill refused to depart under these unflattering conditions and so Hankey went off by himself as an agent of the Prime Minister.[17]

In his first report from the Gallipoli Peninsula at the end of

July, Hankey dwelt on the difficulties of the exhausted and under-manned units about to resume the assault. Weak from diseases of the East and under constant enemy daytime observation and shellfire, the increasingly demoralized divisions already at Galli-poli had run out of most of their never ample cadres of competent regimental officers. For the reinforcements this situation was not much better. The green and hastily raised territorial or new army divisions were led by old, inexperienced or lethargic commanders, commanders who for the most part had been imposed upon Hamilton by Kitchener against the always mild protests of Sir Ian.

This difficulty was compounded by Hamilton's natural but excessive desire for secrecy, which would leave too few officers on the spot with an adequate knowledge of what to do. Yet in current British military doctrine the officers on the spot were entirely responsible for achieving results; moreover, during the actual landings Sir Ian was to defer too long to the ill-advised judgment of some of his subordinates out of unnecessary con-sideration for their feelings. At least the lighters or landing craft so carefully constructed by Admiral Fisher for his proposed amphibious operations in the North and Baltic Seas would make possible a British amphibious assault on a scale, and with a theoretical impact, which alone could offer some promise of achieving decisive results.[18]

To oppose Hamilton's twelve scratch divisions, Liman von Sanders had some fifteen somewhat smaller Turkish divisions, many veterans of several years of combat. Like the British, his troops were short of ammunition; indeed, while it is questionable whether a more adequate supply of ammunition would have given victory to the British, it is almost certain that an adequate amount of Turkish ammunition would have forced an almost immediate British evacuation. Only wretched logistics and the narrowness of the peninsula prevented Sanders from reinforcing his fifteen divisions with the bulk of the Turkish army, which was always stationed in nearby Thrace as a precaution against the Russians or Bulgars. Nevertheless, it was for this fundamental reason, and not only because of delays caused by the Cabinet's or Kitchener's indecision, that the British could never best the Turks in their reinforcement of the Peninsula: the Turks were defending their heart with the best and largest portion of their army against what, so long as the Western Front existed, would necessarily remain a subsidiary operation for the British.[19]

Accounts of the Suvla Bay landing and the other offensive operations launched by Hamilton on August 6, of course, vary greatly so far as their ultimate implications are concerned. One British correspondent—already something of a gadfly to Hamilton with his own concepts of strategy—in an undercover letter to the Prime Minister portrayed a disorganized and soon thirsty mob landing at Suvla, simply waiting without effective leaders or orders for something to do.[20] On the Turkish side, however, Sanders and Mustafa Kemal acted with characteristic promptitude to halt the British flanking attempt, Sanders stressing to his own credit the narrow margin by which he succeeded.

Possibly, had Hamilton possessed the essential brutality of character of his opponents, he might have successfully exploited his advantage in surprise and seized the Narrows before the Turks could stop him. Yet, apart from the many remediable deficiencies in the British landings, the question arises whether, without the developed amphibious and support techniques of a later era, any such primitive operations could have moved so very much faster than the enemy. In any event, as Compton Mackenzie remarked on the evening of August 6, Great Britain had lost her "amateur status" in the conduct of war that night.[11] Such might well be termed the *leitmotif* for the whole Dardanelles campaign.

14

War as We Must

(August 16—October 31, 1915)

We seem to be falling into all the errors of the last war by starting subsidiary theatres and frittering away our strength. However, there is still hope that those we propose to help will elect to be left alone and may well decline our assistance.[1]

SIR ALAN BROOKE, FEBRUARY 8, 1940

I expect ministerial ingratitude will be displayed, as in all countries and all times has been usual, to remove the blame from the order to its execution.[2]

GENERAL JOHN BURGOYNE

Power, power? You may think you are going to get it, but you never do.[3]

HERBERT ASQUITH

The great defect in the management of the war, however, has, in my opinion, been the want of a determinate object for which you have been contending.[4]

CHARLES JAMES FOX

B Y August 17 the optimistic Hamilton had brought himself to admit in a cable to Kitchener that his "coup had so far failed". He now wanted a total of 95,000 new men in replacements and reinforcements to continue offensive operations against a Turkish force of an estimated 110,000, a force which had not merely obtained a moral ascendancy over some of the British units, but was also being continually strengthened with fresh drafts of men. Hamilton concluded: "I have thought it best to lay the truth fully before you. . . . We are up against the Turkish Army, which is well commanded and fighting bravely."[5]

The Prime Minister was exasperated, deeming the failure at Suvla Bay his worst disappointment since the beginning of the war. He wrote Kitchener on August 20 to say in a most untypical fashion: "I have read enough to satisfy me that the generals and staff engaged in the Suvla part of the business ought to be court martialled and dismissed from the Army." Asquith was particularly annoyed at Kitchener's selection of Hamilton's inferior commanders because he had consented to the recent heavy reinforcements for Gallipoli upon the representation that success was all but certain, and now he was back again facing the old struggle between Eastern and Western theatres of war.[6]

The Army's failure was the eager Commodore Keyes' opportunity. On August 20 Keyes had it out again with Admiral de Robeck, trying to shame him into a resumption of the naval attack. Although backed by a recent convert to such action, Rear Admiral Wemyss, as well as by a more favourable spirit within the Admiralty, Keyes failed to talk de Robeck into changing his mind. The too tactful Sir Ian Hamilton had not rendered Keyes' gallant effort any easier with his refusal to demand aid directly of the reluctant Admiral. Almost everyone who dealt with Hamilton personally liked him, but not enough found it necessary to defer to his silent entreaties. Under the circumstances, it is hardly surprising that Hankey had written the Prime Minister saying that Hamilton was dominated by his Chief of Staff, General Braithwaite.[7]

Two general officers somewhat less insistent upon agreeable relations with others, Joffre and Douglas Haig, had meanwhile informed Kitchener that for the sake of French political morale and in order to bring immediate aid of an effective nature to the rapidly retreating Russians, an autumn offensive on the Western Front was imperative. Sir Edward Grey had likewise reached the conclusion that Russia would feel deserted by her Allies unless some such action was taken, the Dardanelles alternative having failed. Bad weather in the Aegean after September 15 would also

M

inhibit the normal supplying of Gallipoli, let alone the mounting of a new amphibious offensive. Consequently Kitchener's decision in the Dardanelles Committee on August 21 in favour of the offensive in France is not surprising, however disappointing it was to Winston Churchill. Although in no sense hopeful for a decisive victory in the West, in a classic summing up of their differing philosophies, Kitchener said to Churchill, "unfortunately we have to make war as we must and not as we should like to".[8]

No sooner had the decision been reached to support the French offensive than the British Government was again reduced to its customary state of indecision by a most unexpected French offer, made on September 1, of four divisions for the Dardanelles. It shortly turned out, in Joffre's bitter description, that this offer was no more than an expensive method of removing that "factitious" Dreyfusard, General Maurice Sarrail, from a politically dangerous retirement in France. To play safe, in happy collusion Kitchener and Joffre agreed on September 11 that in any case Sarrail's intention of landing on the Asian shore of the Dardanelles should be thwarted, lest it lead to further calls for British and French divisions from the West. At the same time Kitchener turned down Churchill's plea for the command of an Army corps in the Dardanelles.[9] Kitchener no more trusted Churchill as Hamilton's subordinate than as his superior.

Perhaps resentful of such necessary decisions on the part of their still rather sovereign War Minister, in Kitchener's absence on September 22 the Cabinet decided to surround him with a strengthened General Staff, a Staff which would draw up a weekly military appreciation for the benefit of the Government. Nevertheless, statesmen otherwise so little in harmony as Bonar Law, Curzon, and Lloyd George were united upon desiring Kitchener's removal. Perhaps suspecting that the departure of his politically popular War Minister might soon be followed by his own, the Prime Minister resisted these pressures, and with Kitchener's support for several reasons successfully postponed the ever more pressing issue of conscription and thus a more vigorous conduct of the war.[10]

Unhappily for General Sarrail's ambitious plans, as a result of the British failure at Suvla Bay, on September 6 Bulgaria signed the Treaty of Maritza with the Turks, a treaty in which Turkey undertook to make certain territorial concessions to the Bulgars. The next day Enver told United States Ambassador Morgenthau that the deal would release 200,000 Turkish soldiers for service at the Straits, and that renewed supplies of German ammunition would stop any attempt by the allies to resume their assaults up the Gallipoli Peninsula. The *deus ex machina* of this arrangement, the German Chief of Staff, General von Falkenhayn, had made clear to his more reluctant Austrian Ally that "the Dardanelles should be secured", while the Bulgarian iron was still hot.[11]

The imminent threat of being overrun by the Central Powers evoked a frantic appeal for aid from the Serb and Greek Governments to London and Paris. In view of the great Allied offensive then under way in France, the principal source from which Entente troops might be dispatched to assist the Balkan states lay in Ian Hamilton's embattled footholds on Gallipoli. The enemies of Kitchener, Churchill, and, ultimately, Asquith in the Cabinet, namely Bonar Law, Lloyd George, Carson, and Austen Chamberlain, now all came out in favour of a partial evacuation of Gallipoli to provide troops for a Balkan expedition based upon Salonika. On September 25 the blow fell upon Hamilton: Kitchener told him to prepare to send two or three divisions from his sickly and depleted forces to Salonika.[12]

To confound the issue still further, as the first Allied troops from Gallipoli were landing at Salonika, on October 5 the pro-Allied government of Premier Venizelos was dismissed by King Constantine. To the extreme chagrin of Sir Edward Grey, the Allies thus appeared in the role of the invaders rather than saviours of the Balkans. In no way deterred by the Allied action, nine days later Bulgaria attacked Serbia which, also assaulted by a dozen German and Austrian divisions sent against her by Falkenhayn, would be conquered by the Central Powers in short order. Nevertheless, although that brutal realist, Georges Clemenceau, had warned General Sarrail that he was "being drawn into a trap. . . . We haven't enough troops in France. The Germans are at Noyon, and England will never follow us into such a harebrained scheme," on October 7 Sarrail eagerly sailed for Salonika, far from Paris and farther from Joffre.[13]

So confused had the Cabinet become that on October 6, for the first time in 1915, it called for the joint opinion of the Army General Staff and the Admiralty War Staff regarding its course of action. The combined Staffs replied on October 9 deprecating the dispatch of more troops to Salonika, since it was probably too late to save Serbia. Instead they recommended a new emphasis upon the offensive in France. Failing this, the combined Staffs urged a renewal of the attack on Gallipoli with eight more British divisions from France under a new commander. As an appendix to this memorandum, Admiral Sir Henry Jackson proposed what amounted to a combined assault by both services upon the Straits as soon as possible and regardless of losses to the Navy.[14]

The combined Staffs apparently did not mention another defect of the Salonika plan, namely that, as Falkenhayn was well aware, the terrain of the Balkans was extraordinarily favourable to a defensive action by the Central Powers and not to an offensive action on the part of the Western Allies. In any case the Dardanelles Committee would not accept conclusions even so hedged as those of the combined Staffs. On October 11 the Committee decided to send most of the eight British divisions recommended by the Staffs as reinforcements for Gallipoli from France to Egypt, there to wait upon events. Characteristically, as during the Second World War in the Middle East, Winston Churchill's exuberant solution to the dilemma of inadequate resources for one campaign was to advocate the support of all three, that in France on a reduced basis, with expansion for those in Salonika and at Gallipoli.[15]

Similarly racked by indecision, the French Government half-heartedly condoned the Salonika operation, to some extent because of its enthusiasm for getting General Sarrail out of France. Through his close connections with Briand and the other French Easterners, and with strong support from Bonar Law and Carson,

Lloyd George would use this desire of the French to put forth his case again for a campaign in the Balkans. Unable to bring itself to facing the abandonment of the Straits, on October 11 the Dardanelles Committee compromised. Kitchener was ordered to send eight divisions from France to Egypt to be employed at Gallipoli or Salonika as circumstances might dictate. Yet, indicating which way the wind was blowing, Kitchener asked Hamilton to estimate his losses in the event of the evacuation of the Peninsula.[16]

Kitchener must have suspected that Hamilton's answer would be more or less a foregone conclusion. On the one hand, in his reply on October 12 Sir Ian may have deliberately overestimated his casualties during an evacuation as fifty or more per cent of his total force (the official Australian military historian has charged Hamilton on this count) and, on the other, Hamilton made clear that he personally would have no part of any such action. Long subject to much criticism of Hamilton, both military and civilian, the Government immediately decided to relieve him. At the same time a general of what Hamilton later called "the most blameless, sealed pattern type" e.g. a Westerner, was sent from France to give the Government an independent report on the question of evacuation.[17] As with General Charles Gordon, almost to the end Hamilton's epitaph would remain honour, not honours.

With Hamilton's recall the Gallipoli dam finally broke. After Sir Edward Carson resigned somewhat prematurely in protest against a continuance of the Gallipoli rather than the Salonika operation, and, following Bonar Law's threat to do likewise, in a personal visit to London on October 17 Joffre induced Kitchener to reinforce Salonika with more British troops. Within two weeks a new government had been formed in France under the pro-Salonika Aristide Briand and, from the Dardanelles, Hamilton's sealed-type replacement, General Sir Charles Monro, reported on October 31 that in view of the lateness of the season, the exhaustion and continued wastage of the troops and the imminent arrival of fresh German munitions, he recommended the evacuation of the Gallipoli Peninsula. Two out of Monro's three Corps Commanders concurred. Monro's estimate of the casualties to be anticipated in evacuation ran between thirty and forty per cent, still a hardly encouraging figure to an uncertain Cabinet, let alone to the distraught Kitchener.[18]

To cover the increasingly anticipated failure at Gallipoli, at Balfour's apparent instigation and with Churchill's approval, the Government authorized on October 23 the overconfident General Sir J. E. Nixon to undertake a risky advance upon Baghdad in Mesopotamia, notwithstanding his inadequate strength and overextended lines of communication.[19] Nothing short of utter disaster, it would seem, could teach the Government the dangers, let alone the futility, of pursuing half-hearted political campaigns on the periphery so long as it might thereby avoid facing the implications of the deadlock in France. "How long," wrote D. H. Lawrence at this time to Lady Cynthia Asquith, "will the nations continue to empty the future?"[20] Even within the narrower military sense of Lawrence's question, the question was rhetorical, since the answer was becoming only too obvious—so long as they could get away with it.

15

The Rack of Choice

(October 31, 1915—January 8, 1916)

Carried away by one impulse, all [the Athenian army] with shrieks and groans . . . ran down, some to help the ships, others to guard what was left of their wall, while the remaining and most numerous part already began to consider how they should save themselves. Indeed the panic of the present moment had never been surpassed.[1]

THUCYDIDES

In politics you must never retreat, never retrace your steps, never admit a mistake—otherwise you are discredited. If you make a mistake, you must persevere—that will put you in the right.[2]

NAPOLEON

His words came smoking hot from his mind to his lips and I sometimes think that the power of his eloquence would carry on the pageantry of his conceptions even if the entire audience were to disappear.[3]

MARGOT ASQUITH
ON WINSTON CHURCHILL

A politician is just as much of a real fact as a Lyddite shell.[4]

WINSTON CHURCHILL

WITH his feline sense of timing, David Lloyd George seized the moment of the arrival of General Monro's report to present the Prime Minister with a new ultimatum. Alluding to Kitchener's alleged failure on the munitions question in order to get at the War Minister for refusing to abandon Gallipoli, on October 31 Lloyd George threatened to resign if Kitchener were not deposed. Having already discarded the proposal of the combined Army and Navy Staffs for the reinforcement of Gallipoli rather than Salonika as "insane", Lloyd George was now fully supported by Bonar Law in what really amounted to an ultimatum to Asquith to quit Gallipoli as well as Kitchener. Furthermore, Asquith was evidently well aware that on the morrow, in his delayed resignation speech to the House of Commons, Sir Edward Carson would savagely condemn, not merely the whole campaign in the Dardanelles, but also the futility of a poorly staffed Dardanelles Committee whose decisions were not binding upon the Cabinet.[5]

Consequently, to head off Carson's criticism, on November 2 Asquith announced the setting up of the new War Committee to be composed, at Lloyd George's canny suggestion, initially of only three to five members, and to be sustained with more adequate staffing and methods of informing the larger Cabinet of its decisions. Nevertheless, like all of its predecessors, the War Committee was ultimately responsible to an old-time Cabinet, a Cabinet which kept no agenda or records and which often reflected too little sense of responsibility in casually overturning the conclusions of the War Committee. Moreover, aside from the Prime Minister, the members of the soon rapidly expanding War Committee were already overburdened with their heavy duties as heads of the various Departments of State.[6]

To conciliate Lloyd George and Bonar Law on the matter of Kitchener, after a week-long struggle with Law, the Prime Minister worked out yet another of his provisional compromises; the still publicly popular Secretary of State for War was to be sent to the Near East on a tour of inspection to supplement Monro's report with his own conclusions. Meanwhile—and most of the Cabinet obviously wished it would be a long while—Asquith would assume Kitchener's functions in the latter's absence. Pending receipt of Kitchener's report, Law somewhat sourly consented to accept this Asquithian solution; yet, in practice, as the composition of the new War Committee would reveal on November 11, Lloyd George and Law had won their battle against the Dardanelles. Law was still on the Committee, while both Churchill and Curzon, the two strongest advocates of the operation, were off,[7] and Kitchener was supposed to be absent.

Even before this settlement on the composition of the War Committee, on November 3, the Prime Minister, Kitchener and Balfour had considered a revival of the early concept of an abrupt naval *coup de main* upon the Straits, on this occasion with some degree of Army support. This plan, now nourished with far ampler naval resources than were available earlier in the year, had been energetically pushed by Commodore Keyes in person in London over the course of the previous week. At Mudros Admiral Wemyss had come round to favouring it and, in fact, unknown to him, had already been selected by the Admiralty as commander of the assault in the event it went through.

Kitchener seized upon this purported naval solution to his difficulties with his usual alacrity. On November 3 he cabled his intimate on Gallipoli, General Birdwood, that the Army and Navy "must do it right this time". Most reluctant to accept evacuation with its certain loss of prestige in the East and apparently high casualties, Kitchener broached to Birdwood the influential journalist Ellis Ashmead-Bartlett's old idea of cutting off the neck of the Gallipoli Peninsula at Bulair. Like Hamilton before him, Birdwood promptly replied that Bulair was out of the question, since the Turks had always protected their logistical jugular vein with the utmost care. And the next day Kitchener gathered from the First Sea Lord, Admiral Sir Henry Jackson, that the Navy was counting upon a heavy Army attack simultaneous with their own assault. Lacking the Army resources for any such attack, a sorely disappointed Kitchener had to cable Birdwood on November 4: "I fear the Navy may not play up. . . . The more I look at the problem, the less I see my way through, so you had better very quietly and very secretly work out any scheme for getting the troops off [the Peninsula]."

In Paris the next day, on his way to the Straits, Kitchener's hopes of staving off evacuation were somewhat revived by French open-mindedness on Salonika, and at the same time Churchill's sole surviving friend on the War Committee, Arthur Balfour, cabled Admiral de Robeck, hinting broadly that he might well resign in favour of a more enthusiastic proponent of action in the Straits. Keyes had done his work well.[8]

But in Keyes' inadvertent absence, on November 10, after a day's consultation at Mudros with Monro, de Robeck and Birdwood, Kitchener lost no more time than had the much criticized Monro on his first tour of inspection in accepting the necessity for evacuation. Probably Birdwood's grudging recognition that only three or four more good divisions could seriously hope to aid a naval assault had served to discourage Kitchener most, although de Robeck's pessimism and Monro's tactful resurrection of the old plan for a compensatory attack on Alexandretta, as a cover for the abandonment of Gallipoli, no doubt helped to sway the War Minister's mind.

Notwithstanding further doubts, in his final report on November 22 Kitchener reiterated his conclusion in favour of the early evacuation of all of the Gallipoli Peninsula except its tip at Helles, which the Navy wished to retain. In London and Paris the Alexandretta cover plan was quickly slaughtered, for once the Cabinet and the General Staff having agreed against adding another Eastern campaign to the current plethora of such enterprises, while with good reason the French had never accepted the purity of Kitchener's military motives for invading Syria.[9] At least, in one of his most remarkable perceptions at the moment of his departure, the ageing War Minister had abruptly surmised that the dreaded evacuation would be pulled off without losing a man.[10] Unlike so many of his critics, in certain basic respects Kitchener was an inspired realist to the end.

The receipt of Kitchener's first report on November 10, combined with that of his own public exclusion from the new War Committee on November 11, precipitated Churchill's resignation from the Government. In a speech to the House of Commons on November 15—a speech which, when under criticism in February 1942, he would quote, in part, again to the House—Churchill said: "In this war the tendencies are far more important than the episodes. Without winning any sensational victories we may win this war. . . . It is not necessary for us in order to win the war to push the German lines back over all the territory they have absorbed, or to pierce them. . . . Germany may be defeated more fatally in the second or third year of the war than if the Allied Armies had entered Berlin in the first." Churchill denied that he had "foisted" a civilian plan for an unsupported naval assault upon "reluctant [naval] officers and experts".

In his peroration Churchill displayed more candour, crying: "Undertake no operation in the West which is more costly to us in life than to the enemy; in the East, take Constantinople. Take it by ships if you can. Take it by soldiers if you must. Take it by whichever plan, military or naval, commends itself to your military experts. But take it; take it soon; take it while time remains."[11] Mr Churchill then proceeded to the eventual command of a battalion in France, a sad diminution from the corps or even brigade which so recently he had aspired to lead in the field.

On November 22 on the same day on which Lord Kitchener advised the Government to evacuate Gallipoli, the General Staff of the Army in London reached the same conclusion in a memorandum to the War Committee. The General Staff admitted that withdrawal might cost 50,000 casualties, but such action would nevertheless provide 140,000 more men for France in 1916, a margin which it declared might lead to a "decisive success" in offensive operations in that year. Since the General Staff no longer believed that the Straits could be forced, the loss of British prestige resulting from evacuation would be far less than that resulting from being driven out by the Turks, now at last more adequately supported with German aid.[12]

On November 23 the War Committee unanimously reported in favour of a total evacuation of the Peninsula, rejecting alike the naval arguments on behalf of retaining Helles and the political disadvantages implicit in a total evacuation. In the Cabinet, however, Lord Curzon led the opposition to ratification of the War Committee decision to such effect that he gained several days' grace with which to develop arguments against evacuation. In two memoranda, the first on November 25, replete with a gruesome analogy from Thucydides, suggesting a British panic and disaster in the event of evacuation, Curzon warned of the loss of British prestige abroad and of morale at home as well as of Russian disappointment.

In a vein of similar romanticism, as Foreign Secretary in 1920, Curzon would again affirm that "the main object for which the war in the East was fought and the sacrifice of Gallipoli endured . . . [was] the liberation of Europe from the Ottoman Turks". Conceivably the motive may be included among the many others of that Hellenophile Tory, Arthur Balfour, but of Curzon's more dazzling and fickle ambivalence Lord Beaverbrook has written that he did not understand how the same man could be both a wit and a bore. Apparently such inconsistency was among the lesser accomplishments of Bonar Law's most serious rival for the leadership of the Conservative Party.[13]

At the request of the Prime Minister, Colonel Hankey also presented a memorandum which reinforced Curzon's arguments for hanging on to Gallipoli by stressing the dangers of the loss of prestige in the East and the fact that evacuation would free many Turkish divisions for operations elsewhere.[14] And on November 28 Admiral Wemyss, who had now replaced de Robeck in command of the Fleet off the Straits, informed the Admiralty of his plan for a naval assault, essentially that of Keyes.

From Paris, not surprisingly, General Robertson would write to Haig: "Things are still in a frightful jumble and it is very difficult to put them straight because the politicians keep the power in their hands and yet will not decide on anything."[15] Well might Sir Henry Wilson tell Churchill, also in France, what he thought of him, of Asquith, and of the "idiotic schemes" of what Wilson was now justly calling the "Cabinet of all the Indecisions". At this juncture Churchill's opinion of the Cabinet does not seem to have been very different.[16]

No doubt exhausted by the utter failure of mortals so far as the higher direction of war in Great Britain was concerned, the gods now decided to intervene in the Aegean. A series of mild storms over the first three weeks of November developed into a gale by the twenty-ninth of the month. Before November 30 the gale had turned into a blizzard, followed by bitter cold. So much damage was done to the British supply lines to Gallipoli that, for a time, even evacuation was out of the question. The British Army on the Peninsula suffered over 10,000 cases of frostbite or exposure in flooded trenches among troops not fully recovered from the diseases of the summer. As the dismayed Admiral Wemyss would would remark in retrospect: "Such a disaster . . . coming as it did, at this critical and decisive moment . . . was a catastrophe" for the Easterners as well as for the troops.[17]

Yet so determined were the frantic Easterners to save Galli-poli that divine intervention itself would have proved unavailing, had not Great Britain's allies acted. To be sure, the Turkish shelling of the British trenches was ominously increasing each day, German ammunition and Austrian howitzers having at last reached the Peninsula. Nevertheless, embarrassment over current British difficulties in Mesopotamia, as well as the hope of aban-doning Salonika, made the Cabinet still reluctant to face reality in the Straits either. Bonar Law had, however, reached the end of his patience. In a memorandum replying to Curzon on December 4, Law concluded:

It is the fact, therefore, that every military authority, without a single exception, whom we have consulted, has reported in favour of evacuation.

But this is not all. Some time ago the Cabinet unanimously came to the conclusion that the war could not be carried on by a body so large as the Cabinet. A War Committee was therefore appointed. The views of the military authorities came before this Committee, two of whose members, the Prime Minister and the First Lord of the Admiralty, were opposed in the strongest possible way to evacuation; yet this Committee reported unanimously in favour of acting upon the advice of our military advisers. Their recommendation was brought before the Cabinet, with the result that on a matter to which delay must be dangerous and may be fatal, no decision has been reached. I hope that my colleagues will agree with me that the war cannot be carried to a successful issue by methods such as these.[18]

Among the changes with respect to the conduct of the war already imposed by Law's pressure was the further curtailment of the powers, if no longer the position, of Lord Kitchener. Having rejected all inducements on the part of the Cabinet to tarry in the Levant, on November 30 Kitchener had returned to London. There he immediately offered his resignation to the Prime Minister whom, perhaps optimistically, he considered his only friend in the Cabinet. Asquith notified Kitchener of the supersession of his old *bête noire*, Sir John French, by Sir Douglas Haig in France, and informed him that he would no longer remain in charge of strategy at the War Office. Appealing successfully to Kitchener's sense of duty, the Prime Minister asked him to arrange a transfer of authority to Sir William Robertson as a new Chief of the Imperial General Staff with full power over strategic matters.

Without illusions concerning his role—in fact, he told Esher: "They want to use my name and deprive me of authority"—Kitchener, nevertheless, consented to a series of conditions demanded by the blunt and brutally effective Robertson. To the astonishment of many, the new arrangement worked out very well, the final proof of Robertson's tactless good sense.[19]

The Robertson memorandum, dated December 5, 1915, from British General Headquarters in France, goes so directly to the root of the causes for the Dardanelles failure that it deserves citation at length:

Dear Lord Kitchener

You were kind enough yesterday to express your willingness to receive some observations of mine regarding the conduct of the war, with special reference to the status and duties of the Chief of the Imperial General Staff.

For a long time past I have given careful and anxious consideration to this question. Both the history of past wars and our experience in the present war show that certain conditions are normally essential to the successful conduct of military operations, though there have, it is true, been isolated instances of commanders of genius who have triumphed in the absence of these conditions.

These conditions are:

(I) There should be a supreme directing authority whose function is to formulate policy, decide on the theatres in which military operations are to be conducted, and determine the relative importance of these theatres. This authority must also exercise a general supervision over the conduct of the war, and must select the men who are to execute the policy on which it has decided. Its constitution must be such that it is able to come to quick decisions, and therefore as regards the conduct of the war it must be absolute.

The War Council should be capable of performing the functions of this supreme authority, provided it is relieved of responsibility to the Cabinet as a whole as regards the conduct of military operations, and that it has real executive power and is not merely an advisory committee.

The War Council will frequently find itself in a position similar to that of a commander in the field—that is, it will have to come to a decision when the situation is obscure, when information is deficient, and when the wishes and the powers of our Allies are uncertain. Whatever these difficulties may be, if and when a decision is required, it must be made. If it is deferred success cannot be expected; the commander concerned will have a grossly unfair burden placed upon him; and in fact the absence of a decision may be little less than criminal because of the loss of life which may be entailed.

(II) In order that the War Council may be able to come to timely decisions on the questions with which it has to deal, it is essential that it should receive *all* advice on matters concerning military operations through one authoritative channel only. With us that channel must be the Chief of the Imperial General Staff. It is his function, so far as regards military operations, to present to the War Council his reasoned opinion as to the military effect of the policy which they propose, and as to the means of putting this approved policy into execution. The War Council are then free to accept or reject the reasoned advice so offered.

Advice regarding military operations emanating from members of the Cabinet, or of the War Council in their individual capacity, or from any other individual, should be sifted, examined, and presented, if necessary with reasoned conclusions, to the War Council by the Chief of the Imperial General Staff before it is accepted by the War Council.

Robertson's memorandum terminated with the injunction that "it is of paramount importance in war that there should be a definite plan of operations, and that that plan should be carried out with promptness and decision. It is impossible that this should be so if the War Council is itself compelled to listen to conflicting advice, and to decide between the merits of rival experts."[20] Of course, Robertson's strictures were effective in large measure because they transferred the real power of decision from a Coalition Cabinet, which was hopelessly split, to a single soldier who knew very well what he wanted, namely as great a concentration as possible upon the Western Front.

Before Robertson could assume control of strategy in late December, the matter of Gallipoli had to be finally settled within the Cabinet. Seeing the strength of the political pressure at home against evacuation, in a conference at Calais on December 5, Kitchener, Balfour and the Prime Minister endeavoured to talk the French Government out of Salonika, in order to return the weak garrison there to Gallipoli. Unfortunately the ostensible *raison d'être* for the new Briand Cabinet would be jeopardized by any such cold-blooded decision in favour of British political needs rather than French; so, by December 7, with Russian pressure supporting the French, the War Committee had thrown in the sponge. A message went out to Admiral Wemyss ordering the evacuation of most of the Peninsula as soon as possible.[21]

As a tardy but enthusiastic convert to an offensive in the Straits, Wemyss protested vigorously against this final decision, and his fellow Easterner in belated authority, Arthur Balfour, had to explain on December 10 that the Admiralty deemed naval success "most doubtful" in any resumption of an attack on the Straits. Presumably contributing to the pessimism in the Admiralty was the knowledge that the Army was no longer in condition for any type of simultaneous offensive.[22] The lack of additional delay was fortunate, indeed, since immediately upon the completion of the first evacuations on December 20 without any losses whatsoever, a fresh gale destroyed the landing piers on the beaches.

The relief of the Prime Minister was immense, Herbert Asquith describing it the "most wonderful retirement in war history, far surpassing even Sir John Moore's at Corunna". With Generals Monro at the Straits and Robertson taking over at home, the grateful War Committee now agreed without delay to the evacuation of the last Gallipoli beachhead at Helles. As usual, the Cabinet was less tractable, but by December 28 the masterful new Chief of Imperial General Staff was able to send out the order for the final evacuation of the Peninsula on January 8, 1916. The, at last, relatively efficient amphibious techniques of the two Services again functioned perfectly in reverse and the evacuation was again a complete success.[23]

A witness hardly less concerned than Asquith, General Liman von Sanders, was overcome with admiration for the professional skill with which the two evacuations were conducted and which he had been quite unable to disrupt. Sanders also thought the British wise in leaving when they did, since he already had twenty-one divisions on hand with fresh units and ammunition constantly arriving. And in London, stripped of most of his power by the jealous politicians, Kitchener suffered in health and spirit throughout this desperate final month. As Esher had put it in mid-December, "We teach prudence and we secretly dislike it. The generous error appeals to Lord K . . . and he possesses to an unusual degree the English virtue of tenacity. . . . He is uncertain of the effect of evacuation upon the eastern mind, and, above all, his temperament rebels against an admission of failure."[24]

N

16

Wully Redivivus

There is the question of high policy, and there is the question of strategy. In all preliminary examinations of the subject, these two should be kept absolutely separate. It is only when we come to the question of making a decision that they must be put together and their respective claims weighed and balanced.[1]

SIR HENRY WILSON

It is not my purpose to enlarge upon the evils which accompany the tendency to change from one plan to another—at bewilderingly short intervals and without sufficient reason. . . . The General Staff must expect to have the same experience in future wars, and they must try neither to despair nor to become impatient. . . . Much will depend on the personality of ministers and of their responsible professional advisers.[2]

SIR WILLIAM ROBERTSON

It is obvious that this purely rational treatment of warlike affairs allowed, under certain circumstances, of the worst atrocities, even in the absence of a strong political hatred . . .[3]

JACOB BURCKHARDT

War will be less popular when it is more democratic.[4]

OSCAR WILDE

I F at the end of 1914 the General Staffs of all the belligerents had essentially run out of ideas for winning the war, by the end of 1915, at least among the Entente, the advocates of an Eastern solution to the deadlock on the Western Front had similarly been thwarted in their hopes and expectations. In short, given the prevailing conditions of military technology and the approximate equality in strength of the contestants, a military solution to the war no longer appeared viable either by the policy in the East desired by so many Allied statesmen, or by the strategic means in the West favoured by the military.

This intellectual deadlock would continue over the remaining three years of the war, parallel to and reinforcing the military deadlock on the Western front. So late as July 30, 1918, less than four months from the unexpected victory in November of that year, Prime Minister David Lloyd George was complaining that his new nominee as Chief of the Imperial General Staff, Field-Marshal Sir Henry Wilson, was upholding none other than the Western outlook of his finally ousted predecessor, the indomitable Field-Marshal Sir William (or Wully) Robertson. In disgust Lloyd George described this normal inclination among the higher British generals in the First World War as "Wully redivivus", and told Hankey that, as far as he was concerned, Irish military whiskey was just as potent as Scotch.[1]

Oblivious to the effect upon the Western front of the hundreds of thousands of veteran British replacements recalled from the periphery by the great German attack of the spring of 1918, Lloyd George and his closest colleagues, Smuts and Milner, were pessimistic concerning the potential impact of the fresh hordes of American youth now pouring in France in ever larger numbers. Too many new British armies had been sacrificed, seemingly in vain, wearing down the German resistance in 1916 and 1917, for the British generals themselves, let alone their political superiors, any longer to entertain rash hopes of speedy victory in 1918. If in 1914 almost everyone, professional or amateur, believed that the war must end shortly, four appalling years later almost everyone felt that the war would go on indefinitely.

Thus on the eve of victory, Easterners and Westerners alike in Britain had achieved a tacit agreement on one issue at least, that is, while the war might be lost in the West, it evidently could not be won there in the near future. As in the Second World War, only the fresh American ally, both from ideological conviction and logistical necessity, laboured under the delusion that green manpower might achieve decisive results in the West, and even the naïve optimists from the New World were planning for a bitter campaign in the Rhineland for the years of their unfolding strength, 1919–20.

In an endeavour to explain such fundamental misconceptions in Great Britain regarding the First World War, it is necessary to examine the motives of the leading protagonists in their great strategic debate, especially since what amounted to the essence of the Eastern ideology would determine British strategy throughout most of the Second World War.

It will be recalled that in the First World War, even before Churchill had finally come over to their side in January 1915, the arguments of the Easterners had been officially unveiled in two papers, Hankey's so-called Boxing Day Memorandum in 1914 and Lloyd George's *de facto* ultimatum to the Prime Minister on December 31 of that year. What, then, were the probable motives for the well-known arguments of Colonel Hankey and Lloyd George on behalf of what the Easterners often professed was a way around the Western Front?

On the face of it, of course, the motives of so articulate a war leader and of so effective a war organizer as David Lloyd George were belligerent in the extreme. Much given to damning the war measures of Mr Asquith's Government as being too little and too late, on the level of policy Lloyd George effectively rode the whirlwind and directed the storm. But in strategy, what his fellow romantic, Curzon, has termed his "amazing faculty of confusing the issues, of a calculated and overpowering irrelevance in argument"[6] render insight into the true motives of the Welsh Wizard difficult. Nevertheless, certain facts are clear.

In the first place, Lloyd George had commenced his political career a pro-Boer Radical, and a *de facto* pacifist. His belated support of the Liberal Government in August 1914 had been anxiously awaited by Asquith and, in fact, was vital in bringing over much of the Liberal and Labour Left to accept the war. Although his language, thereafter, was bellicose enough, the actual strategy which he advocated from 1915 until 1918 was much less so. A constant proponent of striking the enemy at his weakest spot—a spot which with Churchill he would discover on the Mediterranean flank far from France—Lloyd George would write of campaigns in the Balkans or Near East that these were "essentially suited to the special abilities and experience of British generals. It was the kind of warfare in which our army excelled, and in which we could reasonably hope to deal smashing blows on our enemies and to knock away the props by which the German power was sustained."[7]

To be sure, in the First World War the majority of British general officers, at last somewhat indirectly imbued at Camberley with the doctrines of Clausewitz, did not believe that such large-scale colonial campaigns against peripheral enemies were in any serious measure related to the defeat of Germany, but there is no doubt that apparent victories would be easier to win against inferior opponents, and this generals desire almost as much as statesmen. Furthermore, although the Austrians and Turks might be sustained throughout the struggle with German aid rather than the other way around, this exceedingly expedient argument regarding the supposed German props in the Mediterranean would be heard again during the Second World War.[8]

On the level of logic, then, Lloyd George's arguments might not make much sense. Nevertheless, so far as their emotional impact was concerned, his desire and that of a growing sector of the British public to escape the casualties inherent in winning a war against the German Army would in time lend increasing appeal to the bellicose pacificism which he so passionately embodied.

If considerations of public opinion thus imposed what a soldier such as Kitchener would term "eye-wash" upon the meaning of Lloyd George's true position in strategy, so it also did to his policy. When, in November, 1916, Lord Lansdowne broached his honest and courageous proposal to make a mediated peace as such, publicly David Lloyd George would have none of it, although in private he may have regretted not trying to exploit such possibilities. In logic, Lloyd George's and Hankey's 1914–15 strategy of a limited means, that is of seizing bargaining counters on the periphery instead of attempting to defeat the principal force of the enemy, could lead only to a mediated peace. But if, like Hankey, Lloyd George had lost hope of winning a military victory very early in the war,[9] unlike the Tory soldiers, the Radical Lloyd George may have already suspected that the shadow of an imperialistic victory in the Mediterranean would prove more real for Great Britain than the substance of a military victory in France. In the long run the price in British casualties on the Western Front would come to be recognized as far higher than any commensurate victory for British national interests on the Continent.

Quite naturally the soldiers—although often less simpleminded than a *ci-devant* pacifist Radical would have them—could swallow little of this. They were, after all, the technicians of the means of war rather than the philosophers of its ends, and, as such, even so sophisticated a warrior as Field Marshal Wavell has justly criticized the irrelevance of Lloyd George's strategic means to his avowed ends. Like most of Lloyd George's critics, Wavell may not have grasped the real ends of this often too subtle statesman. Conversely, even as Prime Minister, Lloyd George would rail at Lord Riddell: "It is no use being Prime Minister unless you can do what you want to do. It is useless for me to say I can, because I can't. I have to make compromises all the time in order to conciliate different sections."[10] With Herbert Asquith before him, Lloyd George was discovering that the art of leading a Cabinet Government was almost entirely incompatible with what he liked to consider the essentially similar art of conducting a war.

Hankey's motives are easier to ascertain. As a Marine and originally Fisher's man on the Committee of Imperial Defence, Hankey opposed any large-scale Continental commitment and preferred an amphibious type of warfare in any event. Having little faith in the possibilities of amphibious operations against the efficient and well-armed Germans in the North Sea, let alone in the Baltic, by December 1914 Hankey felt it wiser to divert British nautical offensives towards a seemingly safer enterprise on the periphery, that is against Turkey. At first, not fully appreciating what this might mean both at the Dardanelles and in its influence on the Grand Fleet, Fisher eagerly grabbed at this way out from the ever less promising prospects for amphibious action nearer the United Kingdom. So long as the Navy was to carry the principal burden, Kitchener gladly followed suit. Such indecisive statesmen as Grey and Asquith went along from considerations of diplomatic policy or of domestic compromise, while Balfour was always an Easterner at heart.[11]

Although long an advocate of some form of offensive against Turkey, in January 1915 Churchill at first merely followed the current in favour of attacking the Straits. Large German armies now firmly held his former Flemish amphibious stamping grounds and Fisher's brief enthusiasm for the Dardanelles had unleashed a temperament always prone to action of a belligerent character. To be sure, like those of Kitchener, Churchill's initial motives for an offensive against Turkey included a strong desire for imperial gains *per se*. With these he might hope, in Lord Beaverbrook's view, first to lure the Russians and thereafter to recoup his lost position with the leaders of the Tory Opposition. But, once his emotions and political prestige were committed to success in the Dardanelles, Churchill's tough, stubborn, and aggressive temperament kept him pounding at the Straits long after most of the other original advocates of the operation had backed away from an obviously too well padlocked gate. The largely *ex post facto* argument that the operation had been designed primarily to bring relief to Russia recalls the same convenient rationalization for the North African campaign in 1942, and overlooks the painful fact that in 1915–16 Tsarist Russia required a far more fundamental reformation[12] than that afforded by the British munitions surplus of 1916–17 before she would be able and willing to wage large-scale modern warfare of any duration.

Had the British Government in the spring of 1915 been better organized for the higher direction of war and had the Cabinet confined its attentions to the legitimate domain of policy, in all probability the two professionals, Kitchener and Fisher, could have agreed upon some more limited but practical offensive against the really soft spots of the Turkish under-belly, such as that proposed against Haifa or Alexandretta. Such operations could, in fact, have constituted war on the cheap for Great Britain, if dear for Turkey. Moreover, unlike the Dardanelles, the professional military staffs could have supported such more limited operations wholeheartedly, since they would constitute no direct and immediate threat to the Western Front. As Hankey himself advised his fellow Easterner, David Lloyd George, in 1916: "It was better to have a second best plan and to conform your whole policy to further it, than to have a plan that your soldiers didn't believe in."[13]

The danger of allowing the personal engagement of Winston Churchill to predominate over the judgment of the professionals in matters of strategy or even of tactics would again be witnessed in a long series of dangerous and unnecessary offensives in and about the Mediterranean between 1940 and 1942, scratch and largely nugatory operations, which only through good fortune did not collectively amount to more than the 250,000 Allied casualties of the Dardanelles expedition. It was for excellent reason that Churchill's admirer, Lloyd George, in words evocative of Henry Stimson and Sir Alan Brooke in the future, would write that men of Churchill's "ardent temperament and powerful mentality need exceptionally strong brakes" to curb their "more erratic impulses . . . before plunging into action".[14]

Nevertheless the remarkable shift between 1915 and 1945 in British Conservative opinion regarding Winston Churchill must be accounted for by more than his triumphant war leadership during the Second World War; it was based upon a growing perception that, in advocating a limited war to spare British casualties, Churchill was really serving a basic national as well as Conservative Party interest. Popular journalists aside, following the embittered aftermath of the First World War and the renewed disaster of the Second, such serious students of war as Lord Ismay or Captain Stephen Roskill have written that Churchill's strategic opinions in the First War were now vindicated. Similarly the Labour Deputy Prime Minister in the Second World War, Clement Attlee, has said that Gallipoli was "an immortal gamble that did not come off. . . . Sir Winston . . . had the one strategic idea in the war. He did not believe in throwing away masses of people to be massacred."[15]

Here Attlee left to the generals the invidious role of throwing away British lives in their grim war of attrition in the West. Unfortunately, without any allies still capable of paying the piper with offensive operations after 1916, if the British armies did not attack the Germans, nobody else could, and a military victory would have to be postponed indefinitely, perhaps for ever. But in postwar eras in which a military victory is taken for granted and, thus, is no longer particularly valued, the price paid for such a victory is naturally criticized as too high, although it is rarely stated outright that it would have been better to have let some ally carry a larger share of the butcher's bill.

The case in strategy for the Westerners has been well stated by the Director of Military Operations, Major-General Charles Callwell. Subsequent to the war Callwell wrote:

Some statesmen are ever, unconsciously perhaps, but none the less instinctively, gravitating towards the line of least resistance, or towards what they imagine to be the line of least resistance. . . . That theory was founded on the fallacy that the Western Front represented the enemy's strongest point. It was, on the contrary, the enemy's weakest point, because this front was from its geographical position the one where British and French troops could most easily be assembled, and it was the one on which a serious defeat to the enemy necessarily threatened that enemy with a grave, if not an irretrievable, disaster.[16]

What the Easterners could never concede in strategy was, in fact, demonstrated by the exploits of Churchill's heroic tandem, Hindenburg and Ludendorff, in the German conduct of the war. Here, notwithstanding Falkenhayn's opposition, Hindenburg and Ludendorff accomplished all of the fondest dreams of the British Easterner in defeating Serbia, Roumania and finally Russia herself—the equivalent of an Allied defeat of Turkey, Bulgaria, and Austria-Hungary. Yet these successive and popular victories in the East simply dissipated Germany's resources, so that when, like the Allies, she had to return in 1918 to seek a decision in the West as opposed to simply more victories elsewhere, she lacked the power to destroy the new British conscript armies, at last fully trained and equipped for war.[17]

From the First World War, through their debates with Winston Churchill in the Second World War, the American position on strategy was Western, as may be seen in Colonel Repington's classic diatribe on "Churchillian Strategy". In 1924 Repington observed: "When the Americans came along they at once displayed a healthy and rooted contempt for the sideshow and all its works. They went for the gloves, sought the centre of gravity of the principal enemy, found it, and by attracting to themselves 47 German divisions between September 26 and November 11, 1918, contributed greatly to the final victory."[18]

What Ismay, Roskill, and Attlee, not to mention Sir Winston's multitude of other admirers today, really have had in mind was that Churchill's *policy* rather than his *strategy* in the First World War has been vindicated by events. In this realm, the realm of the statesman rather than that of the soldier, a very good case can be made for Churchill's foresight and rectitude in both general wars when so many others have been shown to be mistaken. But, as Churchill, if not all of his sympathizers, well knew in both wars, during the actual struggle a policy of sparing casualties for your own country at the expense of some hard-pressed ally cannot be admitted, even in private. In fact, in postwar memoirs, such a policy frequently needs to pass under the purportedly more patriotic uniform of strategy.[19]

As a deeply conservative nation in each of her two general and absolute wars in the twentieth century, rather than changing the essential bases of her society to meet the demands of modern war, as had Germany and Russia, in effect Great Britain attempted to change the nature of contemporary war to meet the desires of her society. Of course this is more easily done through retrospective rationalization than in reality; and in some small particulars it could not be realized at all.

The fatal weakness of the Easterners was that, like Winston Churchill in both wars, they were trying to gain the political benefits of a military victory without first winning that victory. Like the Americans in 1945, the deadly fault of the Westerners in the First World War lay in their passion for obtaining a military victory without reference to the subsequent political terms which alone could justify the enormous sacrifices then implicit in the only available strategic means for a military decision over Germany. War, in short, was more complex than either Easterners or Westerners, with their grasp of only certain facets of its nature, could admit. Indeed, this was why Clausewitz had defined war as an art, as an aspect of man's social life. As in any art, a successful War Council or war policy has to reconcile inherently incompatible ends and means.

Thus the happy belief that through organizational devices the means of strategy can thereby be reconciled with the incorrigibly antagonistic ends of policy might at first glance appear to smack of a peculiarly innocent German or American fantasy. Nevertheless, following the failure at Gallipoli, Great Britain, too, accentuated her efforts to improve her mechanism for the higher direction of war. Lloyd George's War Cabinet in 1917 and 1918, the Chiefs of Staff Committee in 1923, Churchill's War Cabinet from 1940, in which he served as Minister of Defence with the Service Ministers excluded, and, finally, the establishment of the long-sought Ministry of Defence in 1946, all would seem to involve major advances in the modernization of British methods of making war.

Yet the consequences of so much patient endeavour do not appear to have changed very much—perhaps it was the men who were lacking, perhaps the alterations were not of a sufficiently radical character to obtain serious improvement, and, most probably, the issues continued to outpace the growth of the methods designed to cope with them. In any event, 1917–18 witnessed Lloyd George's inability to control his generals, generals who went ahead and won their military victory in spite of the best efforts of Lloyd George's more efficient War Cabinet to place other considerations of policy to the fore instead. It is for this, among other reasons, that many Westerners still question Lord Balfour's conclusion that, under the leadership of Lloyd George rather than that of Asquith, the Dardanelles campaign would have been won.[20]

Of the conduct of the Norwegian campaign in the spring of 1940, Hankey's lineal heir as Secretary of the Committee of Imperial Defence in its incarnation of the future, Lord Ismay, has written: "The worst shortcomings of the First World War, as exemplified by the conduct of the Dardanelles campaign, were faithfully repeated. The Chief of Naval Staff and the Chief of the Imperial General Staff acted with sturdy independence. They appointed their respective commanders without consultation with each other; and, worse still, they gave directives to these commanders without harmonizing them. Thereafter they continued to issue separate orders to them."[21]

So late as 1961, an anonymous reviewer in *The Economist* would conclude: "Everyone agrees that the Suez fiasco of 1956 was ill-organized to the point of absurdity, but the fiasco sprang directly from the doctrine that ministers, not generals, must decide; and many of the ministers rule us yet. Have any useful steps been taken since to revise and improve the machinery both for mounting combined operations, and for ensuring they are not undertaken at all in circumstances of such desperate folly?"[22]

The appalling inadequacies of the Cabinet, or for that matter of the Cabinet form of government, as an instrument for the effective direction of long-range and decisive war strategy have been revealed in all of Great Britain's modern wars: inadequacies of an order, indeed, leading to grave doubts regarding the capacity for survival of a political structure so incorrigibly dedicated to the need for constant short-range military successes at the expense of less immediate or appealing, but more fundamental, war planning. Only to a degree has the development of the Chiefs of Staff Committee and small War Cabinet, based upon a Coalition Government, met this problem.

Similarly, in what an innocent outsider might be forgiven for imagining would be the *spécialité de la maison anglaise*, that is, amphibious warfare, the picture is equally uneven. To be sure, on St George's Day—or, more accurately, night—of 1918 Roger Keyes pulled off the beautifully planned, if still largely ineffectual, raid on Zeebrugge. Yet with the outbreak of war in 1939 the only Amphibious Training School in the United Kingdom was discontinued by the Chiefs of Staff on the grounds that there would be no combined operations in the forthcoming war. As a consequence, Captain Roskill, the official British naval historian, has written of several premature amphibious ventures unsuccessfully urged by Mr Churchill in 1939–41 that it was most fortunate they never took place.[23]

In the larger sense of changing war, or at least of rewriting military history, to meet the needs of British society, in recent years success has unquestionably crowned the efforts of Sir Winston Churchill and his supporters. What the despairing and largely neglected former Commandant of the Imperial Defence College, Admiral Sir Herbert Richmond, termed in 1943 the new "continental" school of military doctrinaires had advanced the view that the Royal Air Force should strike directly at the civilian population of an enemy in the hope of destroying its morale through bombing.[24] This new prescription for victory without heavy British military casualties had seen its birth in a memorandum by Hugh Trenchard, presented to Parliament by Winston Churchill as a White Paper in December 1919. With the Foreign Secretary Anthony Eden, from 1942 until 1945, Mr Churchill advocated bombing aimed essentially at enemy civilians, although other pretexts were to be adduced to stave off criticism on moral grounds.[25]

Unfortunately others, too, would discover the relatively facile joys of slaughtering enemy civilians, however irrelevant, or even domestic scapegoats, in preference to heavy sacrifices of their own soldiers in rational campaigns leading to a bona fide military victory. In fact, it was during the campaign in the Dardanelles that at the expense of the Armenians the Turks pioneered the revival of genocide as a popular modern compensation for anticipated military impotence.

Thereafter, among the democracies the development of nuclear weapons in the last stages of the Second World War was a logical culmination of an ever more desperate determination to evade facing the brutal reality that is war. If the great error of the First World War was the divorce of policy from strategy under the aegis of the military, the Second World War saw the rapid accentuation of this divorce, notwithstanding its domination in large measure by civilians. In the most fundamental sense for the post-Christian men of contemporary society, means have, in fact, become ends, and the means are at last mortal on an absolutely democratic scale.

Bibliography

Aga Khan. *Memoirs: World Enough and Time.* Cassell, 1954.

Amery, L. S. *My Political Life.* Vol. II. London, Hutchinson, 1953.

Ansel, Lt. Walter C. "Naval Gunfire in Support of Landings, Lessons from Gallipoli", *U.S. Naval Institute Proceedings.* Annapolis, July, 1932.

Armstrong, H. C. *Grey Wolf, the Life of Kemal Ataturk.* Arthur Barker, 1932.

Arthur, Sir George. "Kitchener", *Famous British Generals.* Edited by B. Parker. London, Nicholson and Watson, 1951.

——. *Life of Lord Kitchener.* Vols. I–III. London, Macmillan, 1920.

Ashmead-Bartlett, E. *The Uncensored Dardanelles.* London, Hutchinson, 1928.

Aspinall-Oglander, Brig.-Gen. C. F. *History of the Great War; Military Operations, Gallipoli.* Vols. I–II. London, Heinemann, 1929.

——. *Roger Keyes.* London, Hogarth, 1951.

Asquith, Herbert. *The Earl of Oxford and Asquith: Memories and Reflections, 1852–1927.* Vols. I–II. Cassell, 1928.

——. *Papers.* The Bodleian Library, Oxford.

Asquith, Margot, Countess of Oxford and Asquith. *Autobiography.* Vols. I–II. Thornton Butterworth, 1920–2.

——. *More Memories.* Cassell, 1933.

Aston, Brig.-Gen., G. G. *Letters on Amphibious Wars.* London, John Murray, 1911.

Atkins, J. B. *Incidents and Reflections.* London, Christophers, 1947.

Bacon, Admiral Sir Reginald. *The Life of John Rushworth, Earl Jellicoe*. London, Cassell, 1936.

——. *The Life of Lord Fisher of Kilverstone*. Vols. I–II. London, Hodder and Stoughton, 1929.

Barrow, Gen. Sir George. *The Life of Sir Charles Monro*. London, Hutchinson, 1931.

Bean, C. E. W. *The Story of Anzac*. Vols. I–II. Sydney, Angus and Robertson, 1921–4; and London, Australian Book Co., 1925.

Beaverbrook, Lord. *Politicians and the War, 1914–1916*. Thornton Butterworth, 1928.

——. *The Decline and Fall of Lloyd George*. London, Collins, 1963.

Bennett, Geoffrey. *Coronel and the Falklands*. London, Batsford, 1962.

Bertie, Lord. *The Diary of Lord Bertie of Thame, 1914–1918*. London, Hodder and Stoughton, 1924.

Birkenhead, Viscount. *Points of View*. Vols. I–II. London, Hodder and Stoughton, 1922.

Blake, Robert. "Great Britain: The Crimean War to the First World War", *Soldiers and Governments*. Edited by M. Howard. London, Eyre and Spottiswoode, 1957.

——. *The Unknown Prime Minister; The Life and Times of Andrew Bonar Law, 1852–1923*. London, Eyre and Spottiswoode, 1953.

Blunt, W. S. *My Diaries; Being a Personal Narrative of Events, 1888–1914*. Parts I–II. London, Martin Secker, 1920.

"Book Review", *The Economist*. London, January 21, 1961.

Bradford, Admiral Sir Edward, *Life of the Admiral of the Fleet Sir Arthur Knyvet Wilson*. London, John Murray, 1923.

British Documents on the Origins of the War. Edited by H. Temperley and G. P. Gooch. Vols. V, VI, IX and X. London, H. M. Stationery Office, 1928–38.

Bryant, Sir Arthur. Vol. I, *The Turn of the Tide, 1939–1943*. Vol. II, *Triumph in the West, 1943–1946. Based on the Diaries and*

Autobiographical Notes of Field Marshal The Viscount Alanbroke. London, Collins, 1957–9.

Bunbury, Lt.-Gen. Sir H. *Narratives of Some Passages in the Great War with France, 1799–1810.* London, R. Bentley, 1854.

Butler, Sir J. R. M. *History of the Second World War, United Kingdom Military Series, Grand Strategy.* Vol. II, *September 1939–June 1941.* London, H.M. Stationery Office, 1957.

Cabinet Papers (to 1912) Public Record Office, London.

Callwell, Maj.-Gen. Sir C. E. *Experiences of a Dug-out, 1914–1918.* London, Constable, 1920.

——. *Field Marshal Sir Henry Wilson, His Life and Diaries.* Vols. I–III. Cassell, 1927.

——. *The Dardanelles.* London, Constable, 1919.

Cecil, Lady Gwendolen. *Robert, Marquis of Salisbury.* Vols. I–IV. London, Hodder and Stoughton, 1921–32.

Chalmers, Rear-Admiral W. S. *The Life and Letters of David, Earl Beatty.* London, Hodder and Stoughton, 1951.

Chamberlain, Sir Austen. *Politics from Inside, An Epistolary Chronicle, 1906–1914.* London, Cassell, 1936.

Chatterton, E. K. *Dardanelles Dilemma; the Story of the Naval Operations.* London, Rich and Cowan, 1935.

Churchill, Sir Winston. *Thoughts and Adventures.* Thornton Butterworth, 1932.

——. *My Early Life.* Thornton Butterworth, 1930.

——. *Great Contemporaries.* London, Thornton Butterworth, 1937.

——. *Ian Hamilton's March.* London, Longmans, Green, 1920.

——. *Lord Randolph Churchill.* Vol. II. London, Macmillan, 1906.

——. *Marlborough, His Life and Times.* Vol. III. Harrap, 1936.

——. *The Second World War.* Cassell, 1948–54.

——. Vol. II, *Their Finest Hour.*

——. Vol. V, *Closing the Ring.*

193

o

Churchill, Sir Winston. *The World Crisis: the Eastern Front.* Thornton Butterworth, 1931.

——. *The World Crisis, 1911–1918.* (One volume edition, with an additional chapter.) Thornton Butterworth, 1931: reprinted Four Square Books, 1960.

——. *The World Crisis, 1911–1918.* Vols. I–V. Macmillan, 1923–1929.

Clark, Alan. *The Donkeys.* London, Hutchinson, 1961.

Collier, Basil. *Brasshat; A Biography of Field-Marshal Sir Henry Wilson.* London, Secker and Warburg, 1961.
"Control of the Sword", *The Times Literary Supplement.* London, December 16, 1960.

Cooper, Duff. *Haig.* 2 vols. Faber, 1935–6.

Corbett, Sir Julian. *History of the Great War: Naval Operations.* Vols. I–III. London, Longmans, Green, 1920–3.

——. *Some Principles of Maritime Strategy.* London, Longmans, Green, 1911.

Cowles, Virginia. *Winston Churchill, The Era and the Man.* Hamish Hamilton, 1953.

Crossman, R. H. S. "Western Defence in the 1960's", *Journal of the Royal United Service Institution.* London, August, 1961.

Cruttwell, C. R. M. *The Role of British Strategy in the Great War.* Cambridge, Cambridge University Press, 1936.

Dardanelles Commission, First Report and Supplement. London, H.M. Stationery Office, 1917.

Dardanelles Commission, The Final Report. Parts I and II. London, H.M. Stationery Office, 1917.

Dawson, R. M. *Winston Churchill at The Admiralty. 1911–1915.* Toronto, University of Toronto Press, 1940; and Oxford University Press.

Derry, T. K. *History of the Second World War. The Campaign in Norway.* London, H.M. Stationery Office, 1952.

Dewar, Vice-Admiral K. G. B. *The Navy from Within.* London, Gollancz, 1939.

Die Grosse Politik der Europäischen Kabinette, 1871–1914. Edited by J. Lepsius, A. M. Bartholdy and F. Thimme. Vol. XXXVIII. Berlin, Deutsche Verlagsgesellschaft für Politik und Geschichte, 1924.

Djemal, Ahmad Pasha. *Memories of a Turkish Statesman, 1913–1919.* Hutchinson, 1922.

Dugdale, Blanche. *Arthur James Balfour, 1906–1930.* Vols. I–II. London, Hutchinson, 1936.

Dunlop, Col. John. *The Development of the British Army, 1899–1914.* London, Methuen, 1938.

Egerton, Mrs Frederick. *Admiral of the Fleet Sir Geoffrey Phipps Hornby.* London, 1886.

Edmonds, Brig.-Gen. Sir J. E. *Military Operations: France and Belgium, 1914.* Vols. I–II. London, Macmillan, 1922–5.

Ehrman, John. *Cabinet Government and War, 1890–1940.* Cambridge, Cambridge University Press, 1958.

Einstein, Lewis. *Inside Constantinople; A Diplomatist's Diary During the Dardanelles Expedition, April–September, 1915.* London, John Murray, 1917.

Ellison, Lt.-Gen. Sir Gerald. *The Perils of Amateur Strategy.* London, Longmans, Green, 1926.

Elton, Lord. *General Gordon.* Collins, 1954.

Esher, Viscount. *Journals and Letters.* Edited by Oliver, Viscount Esher and M. V. Brett. Vols. I–IV. London, Nicholson and Watson, 1934–8.

——. *The Tragedy of Lord Kitchener.* London, John Murray, 1921.

Falkenhayn, Gen. Erich von. *General Headquarters, 1914–1916, and Its Critical Decisions.* London, Hutchinson, 1919.

Falls, Cyril. *The First World War.* Longmans, 1960.

Ferguson, Brig. Bernard. *The Watery Maze, the Story of Combined Operations.* London, Collins, 1961.

Fisher, Admiral of the Fleet Lord. *Fear God and Dread Nought; The Correspondence of Admiral of the Fleet Lord Fisher of Kilverstone.* Vols. I–III. Edited by Arthur J. Marder. London, Jonathan Cape, 1952–9.

Fisher, Admiral of the Fleet. *Memories.* London, Hodder and Stoughton, 1919.

——. *Papers.* The Duke of Hamilton Collection. Lennoxlove, East Lothian.

——. *Records.* London, Hodder and Stoughton, 1919.

Flag Officer. "Lest We Forget—The Tragedy of the Dardanelles", *The National Review.* London, October, 1925.

Fortescue, Sir John. *Following the Drum.* Edinburgh, Blackwood and Sons, 1931.

Foundations of British Foreign Policy from Pitt (1792) to Salisbury (1902). Edited by H. Temperley and L. Penson. Cambridge, Cambridge University Press, 1938.

French, Field-Marshal Viscount of Ypres. *1914.* London, Constable, 1919.

French, Maj. Gerald. *The Life of Field Marshal Sir John French, First Earl of Ypres.* Cassell, London, 1931.

Gardiner, A. G. *Pillars of Society.* Nisbet, 1913.

George, Earl David Lloyd. *Papers.* Lord Beaverbrook Collection. London.

——. *War Memories.* Vols. I–II. London, Odhams, 1938.

George, Earl Lloyd. *Lloyd George.* London, Frederick Muller, 1960.

Germains, Victor, *The Tragedy of Winston Churchill.* London, Hurst and Blackett, 1931.

G.G.A.E. "Gallipoli Viewed from the Turkish Side", *Journal of the Royal United Service Institution.* London, February–November, 1923.

Gibbs, Norman. *The Origins of Imperial Defence.* Oxford, Clarendon Press, 1955.

——. "Winston Churchill and the British War Cabinet", *Total War and Cold War.* Edited by H. C. Coles. Columbus, Ohio State University Press, 1962.

Gibbs, Peter. *Crimean Blunder.* Frederick Muller, 1960.

Goelitz, Walter. *History of the German General Staff, 1657–1945.* New York, Praeger, 1953.

Gollin, A. M. *The Observer and J. L. Garvin, 1908–1914.* London, Oxford University Press, 1961.

Goodwin-Austen, Brevet-Major A. *The Staff and the Staff College.* London, Constable, 1927.

Gottlieb, W. W. *Studies in Secret Diplomacy During the First World War.* London, Allen and Unwin, 1957.

Grew, E. S. *Field Marshal Lord Kitchener.* Vols. I–III. London, Gresham Publishing Co., 1916.

Grey of Fallodon, Viscount. *Twenty Five Years, 1892–1916.* Vols. I–II. Hodder and Stoughton, 1925.

Haig of Bemersyde, Field-Marshal Earl. *The Private Papers of Douglas Haig, 1914–1919.* Edited by Robert Blake. London, Eyre and Spottiswoode, 1952.

Haldane, Richard Burdon. *An Autobiography.* Hodder and Stoughton, 1929.

——. *Before the War.* Cassell, 1920.

Hamilton, Lt.-Gen. Sir Ian. *A Staff Officer's Scrapbook During the Russo-Japanese War.* Vols. I–II. London, Edward Arnold, 1907.

——. *Compulsory Service.* London, John Murray, 1911.

——. *Gallipoli Diary.* Vols. I–II. New York and London, George Doran and Edward Arnold, 1920.

——. *Listening for the Drums.* London, Faber and Faber, 1944.

——. *The Commander, A Study of His Art.* London, Hollis and Carter, 1957.

——. *The Soul and Body of an Army.* London, Edward Arnold, 1921.

Hammond, J. L. *C. P. Scott of the Manchester Guardian.* London, G. Bell and Sons, 1934.

Hankey, Lord. *Government Control in War.* Cambridge, Cambridge University Press, 1945.

——. *Politics, Trials and Errors.* Oxford, Pen-In-Hand, 1950.

——. *The Supreme Command, 1914–1918.* Vols. I–II. London, Allen and Unwin, 1961.

Hart, Capt. Liddell. *The Real War, 1914–1918.* Faber and Faber, 1930.

——. *Through the Fog of War.* London, Faber and Faber, 1938.

Hassell, Christopher. *Edward Marsh, Patron of the Arts.* London, Longmans, Green, 1959.

Henderson, Col. G. F. R. *The Science of War. A Collection of Essays and Lectures, 1892–1903.* London, Longmans, Green, 1905.

Hibbert, Christopher. *The Destruction of Lord Raglan, A Tragedy of the Crimean War, 1854–1855.* London, Longmans, Green, 1961.

Higgins, Trumbull. *Winston Churchill and the Second Front, 1940–1943.* New York, Oxford University Press, 1957.

Holt, Edgar. *The Boer War.* London, Putnam, 1958.

House of Commons Debates. 1903–1917. London, Hansard.

Huguet, General. *Britain and the War.* London, Cassell, 1928.

"In the Heyday of Imperialism", *The Times Literary Supplement.* London, February 27, 1959.

Ironside, Field-Marshal Sir Edmund. *Diaries 1937–1940.* Edited by Colonel Roderick MacLeod and Denis Kelly. London, Constable, 1962.

Ismay, Lord. *Memoirs.* Heinemann, 1960.

James, Admiral Sir William. *The Eyes of the Navy, A Biographical Study of Admiral Sir Reginald Hall.* London, Methuen, 1955.

Jerrold, Douglas. *The Royal Naval Division.* London, Hutchinson, 1923.

Johnson, F. A. *Defence by Committee, The British Committee of Imperial Defence, 1885–1959.* London, Oxford University Press, 1960.

——. "The British Committee of Imperial Defence: Prototype of U.S. Security Organization", *Journal of Politics*, November, 1961.

Kannengeisser, Hans. *The Campaign in Gallipoli.* London, Hutchinson, 1928.

——. "The Landing of the British Forces in Gallipoli 1915", *Wissen und Wehr*. Berlin, December, 1940.

Kearsey, A. H. *Notes and Comments on the Dardanelles Campaign* Aldershot, Gale and Polden, 1934.

Kennedy, Maj.-Gen. Sir John. *The Business of War*. London, Hutchinson, 1957.

Kerr, Admiral Mark. *Prince Louis of Battenberg, Admiral of the Fleet*. London, Longmans, Green, 1934.

Keyes, Admiral of the Fleet Sir Roger. *Naval Memoirs: The Narrow Seas to the Dardanelles, 1910–1915*. Thornton Butterworth, 1934.

——. *Papers*. Tingewick House, Bucks.

Keynes, John Maynard. *Essays in Biography*. Macmillan, 1933; and Heinemann (Mercury Books), 1961.

King, J. C. *Generals and Politicians; Conflict Between France's High Command, Parliament and Government, 1914–1918*. Berkeley, University of California Press, 1951.

King-Hall, Commander Stephen. *My Naval Life, 1906–1929*. London, Faber and Faber, 1942.

——. "Defence in the Nuclear Age, 1961", *Journal of the Royal United Service Institution*. London, May, 1961.

Kingston-McCloughry, Air Vice-Marshal E. J. *The Direction of War; A Critique of the Political Direction and High Command in War*. New York, Praeger, 1955.

Kitchener, Field-Marshal Lord. *Papers* (to 1912). London, Public Record Office.

Langer, William L. *The Diplomacy of Imperialism*. New York, Knopf. Revised edition, 1951.

Law, Andrew Bonar. *Papers*. Bonar Law-Bennett Library. Fredericton, New Brunswick.

Lawrence, T. E. *Seven Pillars of Wisdom, A Triumph*. Jonathan Cape, 1935.

Lee, Sir Sidney. *King Edward VII; A Biography*. Vols. I–II. London, Macmillan, 1925–7.

Les Armées Françaises Dans La Grande Guerre. Vol. VIII, *La Campagne D'Orient.* Paris, Ministry of War, 1923.

"Lloyd George and Curzon", *The Times Literary Supplement.* London, October 28, 1960.

Ludendorff, Gen. Erich. *My War Memories, 1914–1918.* Vols. I and II. Hutchinson, 1919.

Mackenzie, Sir Compton. *Gallipoli Memories.* Cassell, 1929.

Mackesy, Piers. *The War in the Mediterranean.* London, Longmans, Green, 1957.

Magnus, Sir Philip. *Kitchener; Portrait of an Imperialist.* London, John Murray, 1958.

Mahan, Capt. A. T. *The Life of Nelson, The Embodiment of the Sea Power of Great Britain.* London, Sampson Low, 1899.

———. *The Major Operations of the Navies in the War of American Independence.* London, Low, Marston and Co., 1913.

Marder, Arthur J. *From the Dreadnought to Scapa Flow; The Royal Navy in the Fisher Era, 1904–1919.* Vol. I, *The Road to War.* London, Oxford University Press, 1961.

———. *Portrait of an Admiral; The Life and Papers of Admiral Sir Herbert Richmond.* Jonathan Cape, 1952.

———. *The Anatomy of British Sea Power; A History of British Naval Policy in the Pre-Dreadnought Era, 1880–1905.* New York, Knopf, 1940.

———. *Fear God and Dread Nought.* Jonathan Cape, 1956.

Masterman, Lucy. *C. F. G. Masterman; A Biography.* London, Nicholson and Watson, 1939.

Maund, Rear-Admiral L. E. *Assault From the Sea.* London, Methuen, 1949.

Maurice, Maj.-Gen. Sir Frederick. *Haldane 1856–1928, The Life of Viscount Haldane of Cloan,* Vols. I–II. London, Faber and Faber, 1942.

———. *Lessons of Allied Co-operation: Naval, Military and Air, 1914–1918.* London, Oxford University Press, 1942.

Maurois, André. *Disraeli; A Picture of the Victorian Age.* John Lane (The Bodley Head), 1927.

Maurois, André. *King Edward and his Times*. Cassell, 1933.

McKenna, Stephen. *Reginald McKenna, 1863–1943, A Memoir*. London, Eyre and Spottiswoode, 1948.

Mendelssohn, Peter de. *The Age of Churchill: Heritage and Adventure, 1874–1911*. London, Thames and Hudson, 1961.

Miles. Maj.-Gen. Sherman. "Notes on the Dardanelles Campaign of 1915", *Coast Artillery Journal*. Washington, March 9, 1938.

Monks, Noel. *That Day at Gibraltar*. London, Frederick Muller, 1957.

Montgomery, Field-Marshal The Viscount. *The Path to Leadership*. Collins, 1961.

Moorehead, Alan. *Gallipoli*. London, Hamish Hamilton, 1956.

Morgenthau, Henry. *Ambassador Morgenthau's Story*. Hodder and Stoughton, 1918.

Morley, Lord. *Memorandum on Resignation, August 1914*. Macmillan, 1928.

——. *Recollections*. Vols I–II. Macmillan, 1917.

Morison, Samuel Eliot. *Strategy and Compromise*. Boston, Little, Brown, 1958.

Nicolson, Sir Harold. *Curzon: The Last Phase, 1919–1925*. Constable, 1934.

——. *King George the Fifth, His Life and Reign*. London, Constable, 1952.

North, John. *Gallipoli, The Fading Vision*. London, Faber and Faber, 1936.

Official Historical Account of the Dardanelles. The Turkish General Staff. Washington, U.S. Army War College, November, 1925.

Oman, Sir Charles. "The German Losses on the Somme", *The World Crisis, A Criticism*. London, Hutchinson, undated.

Oxford, Margot, Countess of. See Asquith.

Owen, Frank. *Tempestuous Journey: Lloyd George, His Life and Times*. Hutchinson, 1954.

Paléologue, Maurice. *An Ambassador's Memoirs.* Vols I–II. London, Hutchinson, 1922–3.

Playfair, Maj.-Gen. I.S.O., and Others. *History of the Second World War; United Kingdom Military Series.* Edited by J. R. M. Butler. *The Mediterranean and Middle East,* Vol. I. London, H.M. Stationery Office, 1954.

Poincaré, Raymond. *Memoirs.* Heinemann, 1930.

Pound, R. and G. Harmsworth. *Northcliffe.* London, Cassell, 1959.

Puleston, Capt. W. D. *High Command in the World War.* London, Scribner, 1934.

——. *The Dardanelles Expedition.* Annapolis, Md., U.S. Naval Institute, 1927.

Repington, Lt.-Col. C. à Court. *Policy and Arms.* London, Hutchinson, 1924.

——. *The First World War, 1914–1918: personal experiences.* Vols. I–II. Constable, 1920.

Richmond, Admiral Sir Herbert. *Statesmen and Sea Power,* Oxford, Clarendon Press, 1946.

Riddell, Lord. *More Pages from My Diary.* London, Nicholson and Watson, 1934.

——. *War Diary, 1914–1918.* London, Nicholson and Watson, 1933.

Ritter, Gerhard. *The Schlieffen Plan; Critique of a Myth.* London, Oswald Wolff, 1958.

Robertson, Field-Marshal Sir William. *From Private to Field Marshal.* London, Constable, 1921.

——. "Policy and Strategy", *The Army Quarterly.* London, October, 1921, January, 1922.

——. *Soldiers and Statesmen, 1914–1918.* Vols. I–II. London, Cassell, 1926.

Rodd, Sir James Rennell. *Social and Diplomatic Memories, 1902–1919.* London, Edward Arnold, 1925.

Roskill, Capt. S. W. *The War at Sea, 1939–1945.* Vol. III. London, H.M. Stationery Office, 1961.

——. *The Strategy of Sea Power.* London, Collins, 1962.

Sanders, Gen. Liman von. *Five Years in Turkey.* Annapolis, Md., 1927.

Sazonov, Serge. *Fateful Years, 1909–1916.* London, Jonathan Cape, 1928.

Scott, A. M. *Winston Churchill in Peace and War.* London, G. Newnes, 1916.

Scott, Admiral Sir Percy. *Fifty Years in the Royal Navy.* London, J. Murray, 1919.

Sitwell, Sir Osbert. *Great Morning!* Macmillan, 1948.

Sommer, Dudley. *Haldane of Cloan; His Life and Times, 1856–1928.* London, Allen and Unwin, 1960.

Spender, J. A. and Cyril Asquith. *Life of Herbert Henry Asquith, Lord Oxford and Asquith.* Vols. I–II. London, Hutchinson, 1932.

Storrs, Sir Ronald. *Orientations.* London, Nicholson and Watson, 1937.

Sydenham of Combe, Lord. *My Working Life.* London, John Murray, 1927.

Sydenham, Lord, and Others. *The World Crisis by Winston Churchill, A Criticism.* Hutchinson, London, undated.

Taylor, A. J. P. *Lloyd George, Rise and Fall.* Cambridge, Cambridge University Press, 1961.

Temperley, Harold. *England and the Near East, The Crisis.* London, Longmans, Green, 1936.

Terraine, John. "Armistice: November 11, 1918", *History Today.* London, November, 1958.

——. *Mons, The Retreat to Victory.* London, Batsford, 1960.

——. "The Genesis of the Western Front", *History Today,* London, July, 1960.

The Anvil of War, Letters Between F. S. Oliver and His Brother, 1914–1918. Edited by S. Grognan, Macmillan, 1936.

The Mind of Napoleon. A selection of his written and spoken words, edited by C. Herold. New York, Columbia University Press, and Oxford University Press, 1955.

The Turkish War in the World War. The Turkish General Staff.

Translated by Maj. M. Larcher. Washington, U.S. Army War College, January 1931.

Tirpitz, Grand Admiral Alfred von. *My Memoirs*. London, Hurst and Blackett, 1919.

Trask, David F. *The United States in the Supreme War Council; American War Aims and Inter-Allied Strategy, 1917–1918.* Middletown, Conn., Wesleyan University Press, 1961.

Trumpener, Ulrich. "German Military Aid to Turkey in 1914: An Historical Re-Evaluation", *The Journal of Modern History*. Chicago, June, 1960.

Tuchman, Barbara. *August, 1914*. Constable, 1962.

Tyler, J. E. *The British Army and the Continent. 1904–1914.* London, Edward Arnold, 1938.

Wavell, Field-Marshal Earl. *Soldiers and Soldiering*. London, Jonathan Cape, 1953.

Webb, Beatrice. *Our Partnership*. London, Longmans, Green, 1948.

Webster, Sir Charles, and Noble Frankland. *The Strategic Air Offensive Against Germany, 1939–1945.* Vols I–III. London, H.M. Stationery Office, 1961.

Wester-Wemyss, Admiral of the Fleet Lord. *The Navy in the Dardanelles Campaign*. London, Hodder and Stoughton, 1924.

Wilkinson, Spenser. *Government and the War*. London, Constable, 1918.

——, and Sir Charles Dilke. *Imperial Defence*. London, Macmillan, 1898.

——. *The Brain of the Navy*. London, Constable, 1895.

Williams, Major O. "The Evacuation", *The National Review*. London, 1920.

Woodward, David. "Antwerp, 1914", *History Today*. London, December 1960.

Woodward, E. L. *Great Britain and the German Navy*. Oxford, Clarendon Press, 1935.

Notes

PREFACE

1 See below, footnote 3.
2 *Journals and Letters of Reginald Viscount Esher*. Edited by Oliver, Viscount Esher, and M. V. Brett, Vol. III (London, 1938), 221.
3 Julian Corbett, *Some Principles of Maritime Strategy* (London, 1911), 42–43.
4 Guglielmo Ferrero, *The Gamble; Bonaparte in Italy 1796–1797* (New York, 1961; and London, 1939, reprinted 1961).
5 Lord Riddell, *More Pages From My Diary* (London, 1934), 181.
6 Field-Marshal Sir William Robertson, *Soldiers and Statesmen 1914–1918* (London, 1926), Vol. I, XV; cf. Captain S. W. Roskill, *The Strategy of Sea Power, Its Development and Application* (London, 1962), 241–2.

CHAPTER 1

THE KINGFISHER

1 Winston Churchill, *Lord Randolph Churchill* (London, 1906), Vol. II, 160–2.
2 William L. Langer, *The Diplomacy of Imperialism* (New York, 1951), 328; cf. *Foundations of British Foreign Policy*. Edited by H. Temperley and L. Penson (Cambridge, 1938), 495.
3 Esher, *op. cit.*, Vol. II, 1903–10 (London, 1934), 249.
4 R. M. Dawson, *Winston Churchill at the Admiralty, 1911–1915* (Toronto, 1940), 6.
5 Piers Mackesy, *The War in the Mediterranean* (London, 1957), 160–1.
6 Admiral of the Fleet Sir Roger Keyes, *The Narrow Seas to the Dardanelles, 1910–1915* (New York and London, 1934), 174.
7 Mackesy, *op. cit.*, 169.
8 *Ibid.*, 176–7.
9 E. Keble Chatterton, *Dardanelles Dilemma; The Story of the Naval Operations* (London, 1935), 114; cf. Mackesy, *op. cit.*, 196–7.
10 General Sir H. Bunbury, *Narratives of Some Passages in the Great War with France, 1799–1810* (London, 1854), 283. For Castlereagh's criticisms of Fox in this connection, see Harold Temperley, *England and the Near East: The Crisis* (London, 1936), 45–46.
11 Mackesy, *op. cit.*, 198–9.
12 Brigadier-General C. F. Aspinall-Oglander, *History of the Great War; Military Operations, Gallipoli* (London, 1929), Vol. I, 26.

13 *Ibid.*, 26–27; cf. *Foundations of British Foreign Policy*, 361; Peter
    Gibbs, *Crimean Blunder* (New York and London, 1960), 70–71; Mrs
    Frederick Egerton, *Admiral of the Fleet Sir Geoffrey Phipps Hornby*
    (London, 1886), 217ff.

14 Arthur J. Marder, *The Anatomy of British Sea Power; A History of
    British Naval Policy in the Pre-Dreadnought Era, 1880–1905.* Cited
    hereafter as *Anatomy* (New York, 1940), 154–6.

15 Langer, *op. cit.*, 196–207.

16 Marder, *Anatomy*, 159ff., 246ff.

17 *Ibid.*, 578–9.

18 *Ibid.*, 268–70. Such military pessimism does not seem to have
    seriously abated Lord Salisbury's appetite for the seizure of the Dar-
    danelles. *British Documents on the Origin of the War.* Edited by H.
    Temperley and G. P. Gooch, Vol. IX, *The Balkan Wars* (London,
    1933), Part I, 776. See below Chap. III.

19 Marder, *Anatomy*, 402–3.

20 *Dardanelles Commission*, First Report. Cited hereafter as D.C., I. By
    authority, London, 1917, 48; cf. Admiral of the Fleet Lord Fisher,
    Memories (London, 1919), 65, 94; *Fear God and Dread Nought, The
    Correspondence of Admiral of the Fleet Lord Fisher of Kilverstone.*
    Edited by Arthur J. Marder, Vol. II, *Years of Power, 1904–1914*
    (London, 1956), 84–85.

21 *D.C.*, I, 13; Aspinall-Oglander, *op. cit.*, Vol. I, 28.

22 Aspinall-Oglander, *op. cit.*, Vol. I, 28–29; *The Final Report of the
    Dardanelles Commission.* By authority (London, 1917), Part II, 7–8.

23 John Terraine, "Armistice: November 11, 1918", *History Today*
    (London, November 1958), 759; Aspinall-Oglander, *op. cit.*, Vol. I,
    29; cf. Major-General Sir C. E. Callwell, *Experiences of a Dug-out,
    1914–1918* (London, 1920), 87–96 for Campbell-Bannerman's all-
    too-successful suppression of this General Staff conclusion on security
    grounds.

24 *The Turkish in the World War.* Translated by Major M. Larcher
    (U.S. Army War College: January 1931), 6; W. S. Blunt, *My Diaries,
    Being a Personal Narrative of Events, 1888–1914* (London, 1920), Part
    II, 403; Letter of Major Reginald Hargreaves, September 12, 1962.

25 Spenser Wilkinson, *The Brain of the Navy* (London, 1895), 51–52.

26 F. A. Johnson, *Defence by Committee, The British Committee of Im-
    perial Defence, 1885–1959* (London, 1960), 16–29; cf. Robert Blake,
    "Great Britain: The Crimean War to the First World War" in *Sol-
    diers and Governments*, edited by Michael Howard (London, 1957)
    28–36; "In the Heyday of Imperialism", *The Times Literary Supple-
    ment* (London, February 27, 1959), 108; Colonel Lord Sydenham of
    Combe, *My Working Life* (London, 1927), 101ff.; Norman Gibbs,
    The Origins of Imperial Defence (Oxford, 1955), 13ff.

27 Johnson, *op. cit.*, 36ff.; Robertson, *op. cit.*, Vol. I, 12; *Public Record
    Office* (London) file CAB 1–1–733B; Sir Charles Dilke and Spenser
    Wilkinson, *Imperial Defence* (London, 1898).

28 Lord Hankey, *The Supreme Command 1914–1918* (London, 1961),
    Vol. I, Chap. V; cf. Johnson, *op. cit.*, Chap. II; Sydenham, *op. cit.*,
    Chap. XIV; *Public Record Office* file CAB 1–37, 287, 420; Gibbs, *op.
    cit.*, 18ff.

29 Esher, *op. cit.*, Vol. II, 428–30; cf. Arthur J. Marder, *From the Dread-*

nought to Scapa Flow, The Royal Navy in the Fisher Era, 1904–1919,
Vol. I, *The Road to War, 1904–1914* (London, 1961), 341–3.

30 Colonel G. F. R. Henderson, *The Science of War. A Collection of Essays and Lectures 1892–1903* (London, 1905); cf. Major-General Sir Charles Callwell, *Field Marshal Sir Henry Wilson, His Life and Diaries* (New York and London, 1927), Vol. I, 56–65; Basil Collier, *Brasshat; A Biography of Field Marshal Sir Henry Wilson* (London, 1961), 88–92; Blake, *loc. cit.,* 33–34; Richard Burdon Haldane, *Before the War* (New York and London, 1920), 22, 193–4; Elie Halévy, *The Rule of Democracy 1905–1914* (New York, 1961; London, 1952), 172–4; *Public Record Office,* file CAB 1–15–743.

31 Hankey, *op. cit.,* 61–65; Johnson, *op. cit.,* 79–81; Marder, *The Road to War,* 117–19.

32 Marder, *The Road to War,* 118–19; cf. Marder, *Anatomy,* 503–8.

33 Robertson, *op. cit.,* Vol. I, 28–29; cf. Johnson, *op. cit.,* 83–85.

34 Lt.-Colonel C. à Court Repington, *The First World War, 1914–1918,* Vol. I (Boston and London, 1920), 11–12; cf. J. E. Tyler, *The British Army and the Continent* (London, 1938), 21ff.; Michael Howard, *The Franco-Prussian War; The German Invasion of France, 1870–1871* (London, 1961), 455; Johnson, *op. cit.,* 115–16; Marder, *The Road to War,* 385–6.

35 Admiral Sir Reginald Bacon, *The Life of Lord Fisher of Kilverstone,* Vol. II (London, 1929), 182–3; Marder, *The Road to War,* 387–8; cf. Fisher, *Correspondence,* Vol. II, 215.

36 Fisher, *Correspondence* Vol. II, 214–16; Marder, *The Road to War,* 186–206; Johnson, *op. cit.,* 96–97; Hankey, *op. cit.,* Vol. I, 71–74; Stephen McKenna, *Reginald McKenna, 1863–1943, A Memoir* (London, 1948), 87ff.; *Public Record Office,* file CAB 16–9A; 17–7.

37 Winston S. Churchill, *The World Crisis,* in one volume (New York, 1949; London, 1931 and 1960), 65-66.

CHAPTER 2

LORD OF THE ASCENDANT

1 J. B. Atkins, *Incidents and Reflections* (London, 1947), 131; cf. Major-General Sir John Kennedy, *The Business of War* (London, 1957), 61, 106, 156–7, 173, 209, 225.

2 Margot Asquith, *Autobiography* (London, 1936), Vol. II, 99.

3 Marder, *The Road to War,* 253; cf. Lucy Masterman, *C. F. G. Masterman; A Biography* (London, 1939), 98, 234.

4 *The Moffat Papers 1919–1943.* Edited by N. Hooker (Cambridge, Mass., 1956), 203.

5 Sir Sidney Lee, *King Edward VII, A Biography* (London, 1927), Vol. II, 534; cf. Fisher, *Correspondence,* Vol. II, 114.

6 Esher, *op. cit.,* Vol. II, 326–44; cf. Blunt, Part II, 77 and 163; Lord Morley, *Recollections* (New York and London, 1917), 255.

7 Masterman, *op. cit.,* 128.

8 Beatrice Webb, *Our Partnership* (London, 1948), 404.

9 Frank Owen, *Tempestuous Journey: Lloyd George, His Life and Times* (New York, 1955; London, 1954), 193.

10 Peter de Mendelssohn, *The Age of Churchill: Heritage and Adventure 1874–1911* (London, 1961), 335, 401–2; cf. Fisher, *Correspondence*, Vol. II, 171.

11 *House of Commons Debates*, Fifth Series, Vol. XIV, 149ff.; Vol. LXXXII, 2023; cf. Fourth Series, Vol. XCIII, 1523; Vol. CIV, 3; Colonel John Dunlop, *The Development of the British Army, 1899–1914* (London, 1938), 123–37.

12 Fisher, *Correspondence*, Vol. II, 221–7; Mendelssohn, *op. cit.*, 406–415.

13 Owen, *op. cit.*, 161–2; Mendelssohn, *op. cit.*, 402–5; Esher, *op. cit.*, Vol. II, 323–6.

14 Fisher, *Memories*, 196.

15 Fisher, *Correspondence*, Vol. II, 332.

16 *Ibid.*, Vol. II, 409.

17 Masterman, *op. cit.*, 173; cf. Riddell, *More Pages From My Diary*, 18–19; Blunt, *op. cit.*, Part II, 335–6. (After the Boer War Churchill had deserted the Tories to join the new Liberal Government. The bitter Conservatives would take long before restoring him to their full confidence and respect, a process not really completed until the Second World War.)

18 *The World Crisis*, 49; cf. Collier, *op. cit.*, 116–19. Sir Austen Chamberlain, *Politics from Inside, An Epistolary Chronicle, 1906–1914* (London, 1936), 127.

19 See Collier, *op. cit.*, 118 for the fuller account, as opposed to Callwell, Vol. I, 98–99.

20 Callwell, *op. cit.*, Vol. I, 99; cf. "Control of the Sword", *The Times Literary Supplement* (London, December 16, 1960), 806.

21 Callwell, *op. cit.*, Vol. I, 99; Blunt, *op. cit.*, Part II, 280–7 and 310.

22 *The World Crisis*, 57–59; cf. Tyler, *op. cit.*, 51, 84, 122; Dunlop, *op. cit.*, 242; Esher, *op. cit.*, Vol. II, 358; Gerhard Ritter, *The Schlieffen Plan; Critique of a Myth* (London, 1958), 71–85, 162; Collier, *op. cit.*, 124; Marder, *The Road to War*, 394. Mendelssohn, *op. cit.*, 540, notes the inverted chronology of Churchill's account here, the only apparent motive for which may be a desire to gloss over the lack of impact of his memorandum of August 13 upon the C.I.D. meeting of August 23, 1911.

23 General Huguet, *Britain and The War* (London, 1928), 8–9.

24 Johnson, *op. cit.*, 114–15.

25 Ritter, *op. cit.*, 81–82; Robertson, *op. cit.*, Vol. 1, 24–25.

26 Hankey, *op. cit.*, Vol. I, 79–80; *The World Crisis*, 52–53; Callwell, *op. cit.*, Vol. I, 100.

27 Hankey, *op. cit.*, Vol. I, 81; cf. Fisher's *Correspondence*, Vol. II, 330, N2 for the identity of views between Fisher and Sir Arthur Wilson; Marder, *The Road to War*, 204–14, 389ff.; Johnson, *op. cit.*, 115.

28 Marder, *The Road to War*, 389–93; Hankey, *op. cit.*, Vol. I, 81–82; Richard Burdon Haldane, *An Autobiography* (New York and London, 1929), 241–2; J. A. Spender and Cyril Asquith, *Life of Herbert Henry Asquith, Lord Oxford and Asquith*, Vol. I (London, 1932), 346; Ritter, *op. cit.*, 71; Johnson, *op. cit.*, 115–16; *The World Crisis*, 53–54; *Public Record Office* file CAB 17–8.

NOTES

29 Major-General Sir Frederick Maurice, *Haldane 1856–1928, The Life of Viscount Haldane of Cloan*, Vol. I (London, 1939), 281–4; cf. Hankey, *op. cit.*, Vol. I, 83; Haldane, *op. cit.*, 227–8.
30 Owen, *op. cit.*, 212–13; cf. Viscount Grey of Fallodon, *Twenty Five Years, 1892–1916* (New York and London, 1925), Vol. I, 242–3, Callwell, *op. cit.*, Vol. I, 102–3.
31 Esher, *op. cit.*, Vol. III, 61; Tyler, *op. cit.*, Chaps. VII and X.
32 Margot Asquith, Countess of Oxford and Asquith, *More or Less About Myself* (New York, 1934; and as *More Memories*, London, 1933), 60.
33 Dudley Sommer, *Haldane of Cloan; His Life and Times, 1856–1928* (London, 1960), 246–8; cf. Spender and Asquith, Vol. I, 347; Mendelssohn, *op. cit.*, 546ff.; Marder, *The Road to War*, 248–9.
34 Fisher, *Correspondence*, Vol. II, 505; cf. Christopher Hassell, *Edward Marsh, Patron of the Arts* (London, 1959), 175.
35 Maurice, *op. cit.*, Vol. I, 285–6; cf. Peter Gibbs, *op. cit.*, 13ff.; Haldane, *op. cit.*, 245–6.
36 Johnson, *op. cit.*, 138; Maurice, *op. cit.*, Vol. 273–5 and 287.
37 Blunt, *op. cit.*, Part II, 383–4; cf. Masterman, *op. cit.*, 234; Marder, *The Road to War*, 249–51; *Lord Riddell's War Diary 1914–1918* (London, 1933), 13; McKenna, *op. cit.*, 113–15.
38 Chamberlain, *op. cit.*, 366–7.
39 Marder, *The Road to War*, 255–8 and 406–7; Esher, *op. cit.*, Vol. III, 61; Fisher, *Correspondence*, Vol. II, 459, N1; Callwell, *op. cit.*, Vol. I, 118; *The World Crisis*, 71–75; Admiral Sir Edward Bradford, *Life of Admiral of the Fleet Sir Arthur Knyvet Wilson* (London, 1923), 227ff.
40 Marder, *The Road to War*, 258–9.
41 *The World Crisis*, 74; Rear-Admiral W. S. Chalmers, *The Life and Letters of David, Earl Beatty* (London, 1951), 108–10; R. C. K. Ensor, *England 1870–1914* (Oxford, 1936), 436.
42 Admiral Sir R. H. Bacon, *The Life of John Rushworth, Earl Jellicoe* (London, 1936), 181–3.
43 Esher, *op. cit.*, Vol. III, 110–11.
44 Stephen King-Hall, *My Naval Life, 1906–1929* (London, 1942), 76; Keyes, *op. cit.*, 45; Chalmers, *op. cit.*, 109–12; Flag Officer, "Lest We Forget—The Tragedy of the Dardanelles", *The National Review* (London, October, 1925), 265–6.
45 Winston Churchill, *Amid These Storms; Thoughts and Adventures* (New York and London, 1932), 130–1.
46 *The World Crisis*, First Edition (New York and London, 1923), Vol. I, 138; cf. Fisher, *Memories*, 209–14.
47 Fisher, *Correspondence*, Vol. II, 459–62.
48 *Ibid.*, 443; cf. Owen, *op. cit.*, 254–8.
49 Hankey, *op. cit.*, Vol. I, 84–87 and 140; cf. Fisher, *Correspondence*, Vol. II, 434, especially N3.
50 Marder, *The Road to War*, 277–8; cf. E. L. Woodward, *Great Britain and The German Navy* (Oxford, 1935), 325; Sommer, *op. cit.*, 255–8; *British Documents*, Vol. VI, *Anglo-German Tension, 1907–1912* (London, 1930), 666–7, 676ff.
51 Fisher, *Correspondence*, Vol. II, 437 and 469.
52 Marder, *op. cit.*, 279–90.

P

53 Marder, *The Road to War*, 290–2; cf. Callwell, *op. cit.*, Vol. I, 112–13; Esher, *op. cit.*, Vol. II, 95ff.
54 Marder, *The Road to War*, 292–3; Sir George Arthur, *Life of Lord Kitchener* (London, 1920), Vol. II, 336; Philip Magnus, *Kitchener; Portrait of an Imperialist* (London, 1958), 118–25, 248–50; Chalmers, *op. cit.*, 112–15; Hassell, *op. cit.*, 223; Blunt, *op. cit.*, Part II, 405–6; Public Record Office, *Kitchener Papers*, 30–57–38.
55 Marder, *The Road to War*, 293–4; cf. Callwell, *op. cit.*, Vol. I, 115.
56 Esher, *op. cit.*, Vol. III, 100; cf. Marder, *The Road to War*, 294–8.
57 *The World Crisis*, 82.

CHAPTER 3

KNAVISH TRICKS

1 Captain A. T. Mahan, *The Life of Nelson, The Embodiment of the Sea Power of Great Britain* (London, 1899), 463–6.
2 Fisher, *Correspondence*, Vol. II, 385.
3 A. G. Gardiner, *Pillars of Society* (New York, 1914; and London, 1913), 57.
4 Sir John Fortescue, *Following the Drum* (Edinburgh, 1931), 187.
5 Marder, *The Road to War*, 299–303; Djemal Pasha, *Memories of a Turkish Statesman* (New York and London, 1922), 73–74; *The Turkish War in the World War; British Documents*, Vol. IX, Part I, 779–780.
6 Liman von Sanders, *Five Years in Turkey* (Annapolis, 1927), 1–9. For the fullest appraisal of the Sanders mission, see *Die Grosse Politik der Europäischen Kabinette*, 1871–1914. Edited by J. Lepsius, A. M. Bartholdy, and F. Thimme (Berlin, 1924), Vol. XXXVIII, 193–312; and also W. W. Gottlieb, *Studies in Secret Diplomacy During the First World War* (London, 1957), 24–33.
7 Gottlieb, *op. cit.*, 39–42; Djemal, *op. cit.*, 123ff; Marder, *The Road to War*, 202–3; Aspinall-Oglander, *op. cit.*, Vol. I, 41–46; *British Documents*, Vol. X, Part I, *The Near and Middle East on the Eve of War* (London, 1936), 347ff., 401–2; Henry Morgenthau, *Ambassador Morgenthau's Story* (Garden City and London, 1918), 46; Fisher, *Correspondence*, Vol. II, 385–9.
8 Morgenthau, *op. cit.*, 28ff.; Alan Moorehead, *Gallipoli* (London, 1956), 20–21; Grey, *op. cit.*, Vol. II, 174–6. For an unusually candid portrait, see Felix Frankfurter, *Felix Frankfurter Reminisces* (New York and London, 1960, 1961).
9 Harold Nicolson, *Curzon: The Last Phase, 1919–1925* (Boston and London, 1934), 199.
10 *The World Crisis*, 121–2; Hankey, *op. cit.*, Vol. I, 153–8; Marder, *The Road to War*, 432–3; Grey, *op. cit.*, Vol. II, 62–63; Callwell, *op. cit.*, Vol. I, 152; Spender and Asquith, Vol. II, 84–101; Djemal, *op. cit.*, 116–17; *The Diary of Lord Bertie of Thame, 1914–1918* (New York and London, 1924), Vol. II, 6; Mark Kerr, *Prince Louis of Battenberg, Admiral of the Fleet* (London, 1934), 242–3.
11 John Morley, *Memorandum on Resignation, August 1914* (New York and London, 1928), 24.

12 Herbert Asquith, *The Earl of Oxford and Asquith: Memories and Reflections, 1852–1927* (Boston and London, 1928), Vol. II, 26.

13 *The World Crisis*, 130–6; Sir Julian Corbett, *History of the Great War: Naval Operations* (London, 1920), Vol. I, Chap. III; Aspinall-Oglander, *op. cit.*, Vol. I, 9ff.; Gottlieb, *op. cit.*, 43–46; Grand Admiral von Tirpitz, *My Memoirs* (London, 1919), Vol. II, 80–82; Roskill, *The Strategy of Sea Power*, 113.

14 Hans Kannengiesser, *The Campaign in Gallipoli* (London, 1927), 25–26; Aspinall-Oglander, *op. cit.*, Vol. I, 9–14; Djemal, *op. cit.*, 118–22; *The World Crisis*, 278–9; Admiral Sir William James, *The Eyes of the Navy, A Biographical Study of Admiral Sir Reginald Hall* (London, 1955), 60–61.

15 Noel Monks, *That Day at Gibraltar* (London, 1957), 93; cf. Asquith, *op. cit.*, Vol. II, 56; Corbett, *op. cit.*, Vol. I, 70; Bertie *op. cit.*, Vol. II, 6; and particularly, Admiral Sir Herbert Richmond, *Statesmen and Sea Power* (Oxford, 1947), 359–61; Kerr, *op. cit.*, 246ff.

16 Fisher, *Correspondence*, Vol. III, 52–53, N4; cf. *ibid.*, Vol. II, 418, 447, 451, 458. For a more detailed recent account, see Barbara Tuchman, *The Guns of August* (New York, 1962), Chap. X; (*August, 1914*, London, 1962).

17 *The World Crisis*, 283–4; Aspinall-Oglander, Vol. I, 15.

18 Asquith, *op. cit.*, Vol. II, 32–34.

19 Magnus, *op. cit.*, Chap. XIII; Aga Khan, *Memoirs: World Enough and Time* (New York and London, 1954), 164–6.

20 Morgenthau, *op. cit.*, 93–94; cf. Ulrich Trumpener, "German Military Aid to Turkey in 1914: An Historical Re-Evaluation", *The Journal of Modern History* (Chicago, June 1960), 145–9.

21 Winston Churchill, *A Roving Commission, The Story of My Early Life* (New York, 1945; London, 1930), 154.

22 Asquith, *op. cit.*, Vol. II, 34; cf. Aga Khan, *op. cit.*, 120.

23 *Supplement to the Dardanelles Commission, First Report* (London, 1917), 2; cf. Aspinall-Oglander, *op. cit.*, Vol. I, 41; Callwell, *Experiences*, 89; Lloyd George *Papers*, Lord Beaverbrook Collection (London), E8–1–7.

24 Grey, *op. cit.*, Vol. II, 172ff; cf. *The World Crisis*, 282–3; Asquith *Papers*, Printed Government Papers, *April–May Box* (The Bodleian Library, Oxford) for May 28, 1915.

25 Grey, *op. cit.*, Vol. II, 178–9; cf. David Lloyd George, *War Memoirs* (London, 1938), Vol. I, 59.

26 Aspinall-Oglander, *op. cit.*, Vol. I, 42–43. For a well balanced defence by a British Conservative of the often slandered King Constantine, see L. S. Amery, *My Political Life* (London, 1953), Vol. II, *War and Peace 1914–1929*, 51ff.

CHAPTER 4

WAR BY SANHEDRIN

1 Spenser Wilkinson, *Government and the War* (London, 1918), 208.

2 *The Private Papers of Douglas Haig, 1914–1918*. Edited by Robert Blake (London, 1952), 35; cf. Callwell, *Experiences*, 68.

3 T. E. Lawrence, *Seven Pillars of Wisdom, A Triumph* (New York, 1938; and London, 1935), 564; cf. *ibid.*, 190.

4 *Samson Agonistes.*

5 *House of Commons Debates*, Fifth Series, Second Session, 1917, Vol. XLI, 1755–6; Lord Hankey, *Government Control in War* (Cambridge, 1945), 33–34; Blake, *loc. cit.*, 35–36; Johnson, *op. cit.*, 149–53; *The Memoirs of General Lord Ismay* (New York and London, 1960), 48–49; Air Vice-Marshal E. J. Kingston-McCloughry, *The Direction of War; A Critique of the Political Direction and High Command in War* (New York, 1955), 50–51; *D.C.* I, 4–7.

6 Johnson, *op. cit.*, 139–160; cf. his "The British Committee of Imperial Defense: Prototype of U.S. Security Organization", *Journal of Politics* (November, 1961), 231–61; Lieutenant-General Sir Gerald Ellison, *The Perils of Amateur Strategy* (London, 1926), Chaps. X–XII.

7 Hankey, *op. cit.*, Vol. I, 176–8.

8 *D.C.*, I, 12–13; cf. Johnson, *op. cit.*, 155–8; Ellison, *op. cit.*, IX.

9 Asquith, *op. cit.*, Vol. II, 55.

10 *D.C.*, I, 13; cf. Ellison, *op. cit.*, VII–VIII; Hankey, *op. cit.*, Vol. I, 168.

11 Sommer, *op. cit.*, 307; Arthur, *op. cit.*, Vol. III, 3; Magnus, *op. cit.*, 285–6; R. Pound and G. Harmsworth, *Northcliffe* (London, 1959), 464–82.

12 Sir Osbert Sitwell, *Great Morning!* (Boston and London, 1947, 1948), 289–90.

13 Lloyd George, *op. cit.*, Vol. I, 51; cf. *ibid.*, 450; Lord Beaverbrook, *Politicians and The War, 1914–1916* (New York and London, 1928), Vol. I, 178–87; Magnus, *op. cit.*, 278; Callwell, *Experiences*, 47ff.

14 Asquith, *op. cit.*, Vol. II, 30; Beaverbrook, *op. cit.*, Vol. I, 176; *D.C.*, I, 41; Magnus, *op. cit.*, 174ff.; Ronald Storrs, *Orientations* (London, 1937), 146.

15 Blake, *loc. cit.*, 39–41.

16 General Sir Ian Hamilton, *The Commander, A Study of His Art* London, 1957), 99–100; cf. Reginald Viscount Esher, *The Tragedy of Lord Kitchener* (London, 1921), 27 ff., 66.

17 E. S. Grew, *Field Marshal Lord Kitchener* (London, 1916), 15; cf. Arthur, *op. cit.*, Vol. II, 174ff.; Brevet-Major A. Goodwin-Austen, *The Staff and the Staff College* (London, 1927), 249.

18 *D.C.*, I, 43, cf. *ibid.*, 6–13; Beaverbrook, *op. cit.*, Vol. I, 182; Hamilton, *The Commander*, 135; Asquith, *op. cit.*, Vol. II, 97–98; *House of Commons Debates*, Fifth Series, Vol. XCI, 1759.

19 Hamilton, *The Commander*, 137; cf. *The Soul and Body of an Army* (London, 1921), 38–51; Field-Marshal Sir William Robertson, *From Private to Field Marshal* (London, 1921), 236–42, 287–8; Magnus, *op. cit.*, 302–3; Collier, *op. cit.*, 162.

20 Esher, *op. cit.*, Vol. III, 177.

21 *The World Crisis*, 140; cf. Magnus, *op. cit.*, 284–6; Edgar Holt, *The Boer War* ((London, 1958), 164; Captain W. D. Puleston, *High Command in World War* (London, 1934), 57; Viscount Birkenhead, *Points of View*, Vol. I (London, 1922), 22.

22 *War and Peace*, edited by G. Crothers for the Carnegie Endowment (New York, 1960), 67; cf. Alan Clark, *The Donkeys* (London, 1961), 27–28; see above, Chap. II and Grey, *op. cit.*, Vol. II, 68–69, 239–40.

NOTES

23 Esher, *The Tragedy of Lord Kitchener*, 32ff.; cf. Sir George Arthur, "Kitchener", *Famous British Generals*. Edited by B. Parker (London, 1951), 103.
24 Callwell, *op. cit.*, Vol. I, 158–9.
25 Esher, *The Tragedy of Lord Kitchener*, 24.
26 Esher, *Journals and Letters*, Vol. III, 180–1; cf. Callwell, *op. cit.*, Vol. I, 178.
27 Blanche Dugdale, *Arthur James Balfour*, 1906–30 (London, 1936), Vol. II, 119; Beaverbrook, *op. cit.*, Vol. I, 42–45. For a greater stress on the importance of Haldane's role on this occasion, see Grey, *op. cit.*, Vol. II, 64–65.
28 Collier, *op. cit.*, 165; cf. Callwell, *op. cit.*, Vol. I, 159, 165; *The World Crisis*, 137.
29 Callwell, *op. cit.*, Vol. I, 158; cf. *The World Crisis*, 137.
30 Haig *Papers*, 68–69; cf. John Terraine, "The Genesis of the Western Front", *History Today* (London, July 1960), 475; Duff Cooper, *Haig* (New York and London, 1936), Vol I, 131.
31 Field-Marshal Viscount French of Ypres, *1914* (London, 1919), 3–7; cf. Lloyd George, *op. cit.*, Vol. I, 50; Esher, *op. cit.*, Vol. III, 176–95; Hankey, *op. cit.*, 169–71; Terraine, *op. cit.*, 32–38, 58; Winston Churchill, *Great Contemporaries* (London, 1957), 81–83.
32 Collier, *op. cit.*, 163–4; Callwell, *op. cit.*, Vol. I, 162–3; Arthur, *op cit.*, Vol. III, 21–22; Magnus, *op. cit.*, 8–9, 124; Repington, *op. cit.*, Vol. I, 24–25.
33 John Terraine, *Mons, The Retreat to Victory* (London, 1960), 43–44; Callwell, *op. cit.*, Vol. I, 161–3; Arthur, op. cit., Vol. III, 21–23; Robertson, *Soldiers and Statesmen*, Vol. I, 55.
34 Tyler, *op. cit.*, 181–2.

CHAPTER 5

RESURRECTED

1 Fisher, *Correspondence*, Vol. II, 201.
2 General Sir Ian Hamilton, *Compulsory Service* (London, 1911), 20.
3 Fisher, *Correspondence*, Vol. II, 457. The "Vosages" (Vosges) Mountains were the then French-German frontier in Alsace.
4 Riddell, *More Pages From My Diary*, 139–40.
5 Asquith, *op. cit.*, Vol. II, 35ff.; *The World Crisis*, 196; Hankey, *op. cit.*, Vol. I, 193–8; Hassell, *op. cit.*, 295, 107–8; Corbett, *op. cit.*, Vol. I, Chap. VI; Arthur J. Marder, *Portrait of an Admiral; The Life and Papers of Admiral Sir Herbert Richmond* (Cambridge, Mass. and London, 1952), 92.
6 French, *op. cit.*, Chap. VIII; Corbett, *op. cit.*, Vol. I, 189–90; *The World Crisis*, 201–4. Callwell, *op. cit.*, Vol. I, 180–1; Brig.-Gen. Sir J. E. Edmonds, *Military Operations: France and Belgium, 1914–1915* (London, 1922), Vol. II, 28–37.
7 Grey, *op. cit.*, Vol. II, 78–80; Edmonds, *op. cit.*, Vol. II, 39ff.; *The World Crisis*, 204ff.; Douglas Jerrold, *The Royal Naval Division* (London, 1923), 20ff.; David Woodward, "Antwerp, 1914" *History*

Today (London, December 1960), 842ff.; Hankey, *op. cit.*, Vol. I, 199–210.

8 Asquith, *op. cit.*, Vol. II, 49–55; Magnus, *op. cit.*, 287–304; *The World Crisis*, 205–16; Virginia Cowles, *Winston Churchill, The Era and The Man* (New York and London, 1953), 179–81.

9 Callwell, *op. cit.*, Vol. I, 181–2; cf. Jerrold, *op. cit.*, 39; Scott, *op. cit.*, Chap. IX; French, *op. cit.*, 183; and, especially, Callwell, *Experiences*, 38–41, 65.

10 Robert Blake, *The Unknown Prime Minister; The Life and Times of Andrew Bonar Law, 1858–1923* (London, 1955), 234–5.

11 Collier, *op. cit.*, 130.

12 Marder, *Richmond*, 111–12. For favourable, but much later views on Churchill's role at Antwerp, see Corbett, *op. cit.*, Vol. I, 207–8; C. R. M. Cruttwell, *The Role of British Strategy in the Great War* (Cambridge, 1936), 28–29; Major-General Sir Frederick Maurice, *Lessons of Allied Co-operation: Naval, Military and Air, 1914–1918* (London, 1942), 13; Liddell Hart, *Through the Fog of War* (London, 1938), 188.

13 Asquith, *op. cit.*, Vol. II, 53.

14 Owen, *op. cit.*, 278; cf. *The World Crisis*, 227; Marder, *The Road to War*, 371–7; Corbett, *op. cit.*, Vol. I, 177–83.

15 Marder, *Richmond*, 96–110.

16 *The World Crisis*, 221–6; cf. Chalmers, *op. cit.*, 156–7. Hankey, *op. cit.*, Vol. I, 180–1; Corbett, *op. cit.*, Vol. I, 217ff., 249ff.

17 Riddell, *War Diary*, 199.

18 Marder, *Richmond*, 203, 254.

19 Bacon, *op. cit.*, Vol. II, 162–3; cf. *The Anvil of War, Letters Between F. S. Oliver and His Brothers, 1914–18*. Edited by S. Grognan (London, 1936), 45; Admiral of the Fleet Lord Wester-Wemyss, *The Navy in the Dardanelles Campaign* (London, 1924), 272ff.; King-Hall, *op. cit.*, 76, 96, 266; Repington, *op. cit.*, Vol. I, 47; Fisher, *Correspondence*, Vol. III, 55–61; *D.C.*, I, 12, 37; Ellison, *op. cit.*, 47–55.

20 A. M. Scott, *Winston Churchill in Peace and War* (London, 1916), 93.

21 *The World Crisis*, 227–8; Beaverbrook, *op. cit.*, Vol I, 67ff.

22 Harold Nicolson, *King George the Fifth, His Life and Reign* (London, 1952), 251–2; *The World Crisis*, 229; Blake, *op. cit.*, 236; Fisher, *Correspondence*, Vol. III, 59–65, 100–3; Chalmers, *op. cit.*, 179; Asquith, *op. cit.*, Vol. II, 56; comment of Arthur J. Marder, October 22, 1962.

23 With the permission of Admiral Chalmers and of Hodder and Stoughton. Chalmers, *op. cit.*, 160–1; cf. Keyes, *op. cit.*, 133; Riddell, *War Diary*, 199; Corbett, *op. cit.*, Vol. I, Chap. XXV; Beaverbrook, *op. cit.*, Vol I, 103–4.

24 Fisher, *Correspondence*, Vol. III, 39–57.

CHAPTER 6

SPECIAL FUN

1 Fisher, *Correspondence*, Vol. II, 425.
2 Asquith, *op. cit.*, Vol. II, 60.

3 Arthur Bryant, *Triumph in the West, 1943–1946. Based on the Diaries and Autobiographical Notes of Field Marshal, the Viscount Alanbroke* (London, 1959), 170, N1; cf. *ibid.*, 137.
4 Kennedy, *The Business of War*, 336.
5 Bacon, *op. cit.*, Vol. II, 164–71; Cowles, *op. cit.*, 162; John Ehrman, *Cabinet Government and War, 1890–1940* (Cambridge, 1958), 45–48.
6 Fisher, *Correspondence*, Vol. III, 99–100; cf. Hankey, *op. cit.*, Vol. I, 224. For a recent well-informed account of Fisher's antipathy to Sturdee, see Geoffrey Bennett, *Coronel and the Falklands* (London, 1962), 81–101, and Chapter VI.
7 Bacon, *op. cit.*, Vol. II, 172–9; cf. Fisher, *Correspondence*, Vol. III, 43–44; Corbett, *op. cit.*, Vol. I, 379ff.; Kerr, *op. cit.*, 244–5.
8 Bennett, *op. cit.*, 117–32; Fisher, *Correspondence*, Vol. III, 71–72.
9 Spender and Asquith, *op. cit.*, Vol. II, 129; cf. Hankey, *Government Control in War*, 34; Lloyd George, *op. cit.*, Vol. I, 481.
10 General Erich von Falkenhayn, *General Headquarters, 1914–1916, and Its Critical Decisions* (London, 1919), 49–50; cf. Trumbull Higgins, *Winston Churchill and the Second Front, 1940–1943* (New York, 1957), 16; Walter Goelitz, *History of the German General Staff, 1657–1945* (New York, 1953), 168.
11 Aspinall-Oglander, *op. cit.*, Vol. I, 42–43; Grey, *op. cit.*, Vol. II, 165; Callwell, *Experiences*, 89–91.
12 Conversation with Lord Hankey, May 28, 1962; Hankey, *The Supreme Command*, Vol. I, 181, 223–4; and his *Politics, Trials and Errors* (Oxford, 1950), Chap. IV; Robertson, *op. cit.*, Vol. I, 80; Corbett, *op. cit.*, Vol. I, 372–8; Bacon, *op. cit.*, Vol. II, 205; *The World Crisis*, 285; see below Chap. XVI.
13 Aspinall-Oglander, *op. cit.*, Vol. I, 32–37.
14 *D.C.*, I, 10; Hankey, *Government Control in War*, 36–37; Hankey, *The Supreme Command*, Vol. I, 208–39; Asquith, *op. cit.*, Vol. II, 104–5; Ismay, *op. cit.*, 48–49; Ellison, *op. cit.*, 109–18; Johnson, *op. cit.*, 149–62.
15 Hankey, *The Supreme Command*, Vol. I, 242–3; Arthur, *op. cit.*, Vol. III, 98–99; Djemal, *op. cit.*, 57ff.; Temperley, *op. cit.*, 91; *British Documents*, Vol. V, *The Near East 1903–1909* (London, 1928), 39; Vol. X, Part II, *The Last Years of Peace* (London, 1938), 824ff.; Lawrence, *op. cit.*, 7, 59, 74; Gottlieb, *op. cit.*, 67–74; Grey, *op. cit.*, Vol. II, Chap. XXVI; *Public Record Office*, CAB 1–7–658 and 17–71.
16 *D.C.*, I, 14; cf. Hankey, *op. cit.*, Vol. III, 242–3; Aga Khan, *op. cit.*, 90; Robertson, *op. cit.*, Vol. I, 80; Aspinall-Oglander, *op. cit.*, Vol. I, 44; *The World Crisis*, 286; Major-General Sir Charles Callwell, *The Dardanelles* (London, 1919), 8–11.
17 Oliver Warner, *The Battle of The Nile* (New York and London, 1960), 27; cf. Mendelssohn, *op. cit.*, 325; Thucydides, *The Peloponnesian War*, Book VI, Chap. XVIII, "Speech of Niceas"; *D.C.*, I, 14.
18 Bacon, *op. cit.*, Vol. II, 206, N1; Hankey, *op. cit.*, Vol. I, 242–3; Aspinall-Oglander, *op. cit.*, Vol. I, 44; Robertson, *op. cit.*, Vol. I, 58–59.
19 Marder, *Richmond*, 127; cf. French, *op. cit.*, 309–14; Arthur, *op. cit.*, Vol. III, 87–90; Fisher, *Correspondence*, Vol. III, 77, N1.
20 Fisher, *Correspondence*, Vol. III, 91; cf. Huguet, *op. cit.*, 158–60; Asquith, *op. cit.*, Vol. II, 58; Callwell, *Wilson*, Vol. I, 186–7; Hart,

op. cit., 108; Maurice, *Lessons of Allied Co-operation*, 36. Like Churchill in this period, Kitchener also tended to overestimate the impact of naval artillery upon land forts as a consequence of misunderstanding the German capture of the Antwerp fortresses. Lloyd George *Papers*, C16–3–2.
21 Callwell, *op. cit.*, Vol. I, 193; cf. Magnus, *op. cit.*, 305–8; Asquith, *op. cit.*, Vol. II, 60.
22 *The World Crisis*, 268–73; Marder, *Richmond*, 121ff.; Hankey, *op. cit.*, Vol. I, 240–2.
23 *The World Crisis*, 232–3; Fisher, *Correspondence*, Vol. III, 41–42; Fisher, *Memories*, 55, and *Records* ((London, 1919), Chap. XV; Victor Germains, *The Tragedy of Winston Churchill* (London, 1931), 104ff.

CHAPTER 7

NINEPINS

1 Spender and Asquith, *op. cit.*, Vol. II, 230.
2 Repington, *op. cit.*, Vol. I, 420.
3 Kennedy, *The Business of War*, 265.
4 Esher, *op. cit.*, Vol. IV, 74.
5 Asquith, *op. cit.*, Vol. II, 61–62; cf. *The World Crisis* in four volume edition (New York and London, 1923–9), Vol. II, *1915*, 30.
6 Esher, *op. cit.*, Vol. III, 200.
7 *House of Commons Debates*, Fifth Series, Vol. LXXV, 1507; Lloyd George, *op. cit.*, Vol. I, 87; Terraine, *op. cit.*, 478; Edwards, *op. cit.*, Vol. II, 379ff.; Spender and Asquith, Vol. II, 136ff.; Johnson, *op. cit.*, 137.
8 Puleston, *op. cit.*, 105–6.
9 Hankey, *op. cit.*, Vol. I, 244–50; cf. conversation with Lord Hankey May 28, 1962; Asquith *Papers* "Printed Government Papers, October–December, 1914"; Fisher, *Memories*, 78–79; Aspinall-Oglander, *op. cit.*, Vol. I, 49–50. In mid-January in a memorandum to the Cabinet, Lord Selborne would also allude to the bargaining assets of Turkey as a method of regaining Belgium in a mediated settlement. Lloyd George *Papers*, D23–4.
10 Puleston, *op. cit.*, 119; cf. *The World Crisis* (one volume edition), 269ff.; Asquith, *op. cit.*, Vol. II, 62.
11 Owen, *op. cit.*, 280; *The World Crisis*, 320–1; Gottlieb, *op. cit.*, 78; Hankey, *op. cit.*, Vol. I, 253.
12 Hart, *op. cit.*, 159ff.; *The World Crisis*, Chap. XXVIII.
13 Lloyd George, *op. cit.*, Vol. I, 219–26.
14 Robertson, *op. cit.*, Vol. I, 84; Hankey, *op. cit.*, Vol. I, 253.
15 *The World Crisis*, 322.
16 Arthur, *op. cit.*, Vol. III, 85–87; cf. Aspinall-Oglander, *op. cit.*, Vol. I, 50–51: French, *op. cit.*, 323; Hankey, *op. cit.*, Vol. I, 261–2.
17 Magnus, *op. cit.*, 312; French, *op. cit.*, 314–18.
18 Fisher, *Correspondence*, Vol. III, 117–18; cf. *D.C.*, I, 20; *The World Crisis*, 323. Perhaps suspecting Fisher's hostile motives regarding this offer of command, Sturdee may have refused to accept the

Dardanelles post on the grounds of the unpracticability of the operation. Flag Officer, *loc. cit.*, 268; Bennett, *op. cit.*, Chaps. IV and V.

19 *The World Crisis*, 324; Ellison, *op. cit.*, 47–48; Germains, *op. cit.*, 47.
20 Dugdale, *op. cit.*, Vol. II, 128–9.
21 *The World Crisis*, 325.
22 *The World Crisis*, 325–6; cf. *D.C.*, I, 12, 17, 37, 49; cf. Flag Officer,
    loc. cit., 265ff.; Bacon, *op. cit.*, Vol. II, 203–8; Fisher, *Memories*, 111.
23 *D.C.*, I, 17–18; cf. *ibid.*, 41–42, 60, 88; Aspinall-Oglander, *op. cit.*,
    Vol. I, 57, N1; Keyes, *op. cit.*, 181; *House of Commons Debates*, Fifth
    Series, Vol. XCI, 1789–92. For an interesting description of Admirals
    Jackson and Oliver, see Bennett, *op. cit.*, 103–4.
24 *D.C.*, I, 21, 50; cf. *The World Crisis*, 324.
25 *D.C.*, I, 21; cf. Bacon, *op. cit.*, Vol. II, 204–8.
26 Riddell, *War Diary*, 198–9; cf. Callwell, *The Dardanelles*, 11; Major
    the Honourable Gerald French, *The Life of Field Marshal Sir John
    French* (London, 1931), 273; Asquith, *op. cit.*, Vol. II, 65.
27 *The World Crisis*, 355–6; cf. *House of Commons Debates*, Fifth Series,
    Vol. XCI, 1801–2.
28 Riddell, *War Diary*, 204–5; *D.C.*, *Final Report*, Part II, 7; Bacon, *op.
    cit.*, Vol. I, 154.
29 Within a fortnight Churchill would employ this old Alexandretta
    scheme as a new gambit with which to win over Kitchener. He wrote
    the latter on January 20 that an operation against Alexandretta
    should be simultaneous with the fleet action against the Straits in
    order to cover a possible failure of the latter. Lloyd George *Papers*
    C16–16.
30 *D.C.*, *Final Report*, Part II, 6; Hankey, *op. cit.*, Vol. I, 262; Aspinall-
    Oglander, *op. cit.*, Vol. I, 56; Spender and Asquith, *op. cit.*, Vol. II,
    154–5; Magnus, *op. cit.*, 312–15; Corbett, *op. cit.*, Vol. II, 65–66.
31 Arthur, *op. cit.*, Vol. III, 90–94; *D.C.*, *Final Report*, Part II, 6.
32 Aspinall-Oglander, Vol. I, 57–60; *The World Crisis*, 326–7.
33 *D.C.*, I, 16–21; Magnus, *op. cit.*, 316; Arthur, *op. cit.*, 105; *The World
    Crisis*, 328; Aspinall-Oglander, Vol. I, 58; Flag Officer, *loc. cit.*, 271–
    272.
34 Marder, *Richmond*, 136.
35 Hankey, *op. cit.*, Vol. I, 263–5; *D.C.*, I, 19–24; Grey, *op. cit.*, Vol. II,
    183ff.; Magnus, *op. cit.*, 319; Lloyd George *Papers*, E8–1–42 and 5.
36 Hankey, *op. cit.*, Vol. I, 265–6.
37 *D.C.*, I, 19–20; cf. Spender and Asquith, *op. cit.*, Vol. II, 155–6; *The
    World Crisis*, 328–31; Bacon, *op. cit.*, Vol. II, 208; and, especially,
    Admiral Sir Percy Scott, *Fifty Years in the Royal Navy* (London,
    1919), 328–31.
38 *D.C.*, I, 21; cf. Bradford, *op. cit.*, 243.
39 Wester-Wemyss, *op. cit.*, 259–61. Fisher admitted as much in his
    letter of May 11, 1915 to Churchill. Asquith *Papers*, "Miscellaneous",
    Box 27.
40 Hankey, *op. cit.*, Vol. I, 266–7; *D.C. Final Report*, Part II, 6.
41 *D.C.*, I, 22ff.; cf. *D.C.*, *Final Report*, Part II, 6, and Hankey, *op. cit.*,
    Vol. I, 267, N1.
42 *The World Crisis*, 331; C. E. W. Bean, *The Story of Anzac* (The
    Official Australian History of the War) (Sydney, 1921), Vol. I, 201.
43 See, for example, Churchill's characteristic conclusion that free will

and predestination are identical and that both are apparently decided by what in the Second World War he would enjoy calling "strategic natural selection", *A Roving Commission*, 28; Higgins, *op. cit.*, 233, N1.

CHAPTER 8

FRUITS DE MER

1 Alexander Kinglake, *The Invasion of the Crimea: Its Origin and an Account of its Progress Down to the Death of Lord Raglan* (New York, 1864; and London, 1863).
2 Fisher, *Memories*, 61; cf. Hankey, *The Supreme Command*, Vol. I, 325–6.
3 Lady Gwendolen Cecil, *Robert, Marquis of Salisbury* (London, 1921–1932), Vol. II, 153.
4 Kennedy, *The Business of War*, 295.
5 Lloyd George, *op. cit.*, Vol. II, 1175; cf. *ibid.*, Vol. I, 228–9; Corbett, *op. cit.*, Vol. II, 121ff.; J. C. King, *Generals and Politicians; Conflict Between France's High Command, Parliament and Government, 1914–1918* (Berkeley, 1951), 41–42; French, *op. cit.*, 324; Gottlieb, *op. cit.*, 78ff.
6 *The Memoirs of Raymond Poincaré, 1915* (New York, 1931; and London, 1930), 21–2.
7 Esher, *The Tragedy of Lord Kitchener*, 101.
8 *D.C.*, I, 21; cf. Aspinall-Oglander, *op. cit.*, Vol. I, 63–64; Corbett, *op. cit.*, Vol. II, 103–4.
9 Fisher, *Correspondence*, Vol. III, 129–30.
10 Marder, *Richmond*, 139ff.; cf. *The United States and World Sea Power*. Edited by E. B. Potter and J. R. Freidland (Englewood Cliffs, N.J., 1955), 498–9.
11 Marder, *Richmond*, 137–8.
12 Fisher, *Correspondence*, Vol. III, 132–3.
13 Asquith, *op. cit.*, Vol. II, 67–68; cf. Hankey, *op. cit.*, Vol. I, 269.
14 *The World Crisis*, 348–9; cf. Lloyd George *Papers*, D 23–5–3; Fisher, *Correspondence*, Vol. III, 147, N1; *D.C.*, I, 25–27.
15 *The World Crisis*, 349–52.
16 Marder, *The Road to War*, 384–404; Keyes, *op. cit.*, 162; Corbett, *op. cit.*, Vol. II, 105–6.
17 Fisher, *Correspondence*, Vol. III, 147, N1; cf. Hankey, *op. cit.*, Vol. I, 270, for the implication that Asquith rather than Churchill thwarted the circulation of the Fisher memorandum.
18 Fisher, *Correspondence*, Vol. III, 147–8; cf. *The World Crisis*, 352; Bacon, *op. cit.*, Vol. II, 208–9; *D.C.*, I, 27.
19 Fisher, *Memories*, 60–61.
20 *D.C.*, I, 20–26; cf. *The World Crisis*, 352.
21 Asquith, *op. cit.*, Vol. II, 70; cf. *The World Crisis*, 352; Bacon, *op. cit.*, Vol. II, 209.
22 Fisher, *Correspondence*, Vol. III, 149–50; cf. Fisher, *Memories*, 80.
23 Gottlieb, *op. cit.*, 89–90; especially no. N2; cf. Serge Sazonov, *Fateful Years, 1909–1916* (London, 1928), 255–6; *House of Commons Debates*, Fifth Series, Vol. XLI, 1762–3, 1793; Lloyd George *Papers*,

E8–1–T; *Les Armées Françaises Dans La Grande Guerre*, Vol. VIII, *La Campagne D'Orient*, Ministry of War (Paris, 1923), Chap. 19.
24 *D.C.*, I, 26; cf. *The World Crisis*, 352–3; cf. Lloyd George, *op. cit.*, Vol. I, 234–5; Dugdale, *op. cit.*, Vol. II, 130–1; Lloyd George *Papers*, E8–1–5.
25 Hankey, *op. cit.*, Vol. I, 271; *The World Crisis*, 353.
26 Fisher, *Memories*, 80; cf. *D.C.*, I, 27; Bacon, *op. cit.*, Vol. II, 210–13; Magnus, *op. cit.*, 320; Ellison, *op. cit.*, 62 and Gottlieb, *op. cit.*, 86ff., for his discussion of Churchill's supposed desire to anticipate the Russians in Constantinople. See also *House of Commons Debates*, Fifth Series, Vol. XCI, 1800–7.
27 Bacon, *op. cit.*, Vol. II, 214–17; cf. *D.C.*, I, 28; Robertson, *op. cit.*, Vol. I, 97; *House of Commons Debates*, Fifth Series, Vol. XCI, 1763; Bradford, *op. cit.*, 243.
28 *D.C.*, I, 29.
29 *House of Commons Debates*, Fifth Series, Vol. XCI, 1762–3; cf. Wester-Wemyss, *op. cit.*, 279–80; Bacon, *op. cit.*, Vol. II, 219.
30 *The World Crisis*, 354–5.
31 Hankey, *op. cit.*, Vol. I, 272–5; Corbett, *op. cit.*, Vol. II, 107–9.
32 Lloyd George, *op. cit.*, Vol. I, 240; Law *Papers* (Bonar Law-Bennett Library, Fredericton, New Brunswick), 36–2–57.
33 Blake, *op. cit.*, 236–7.

CHAPTER 9

MIASMA-ED

1 Atkins, *op. cit.*, 124–6.
2 Christopher Hibbert, *The Destruction of Lord Raglan, A Tragedy of the Crimean War, 1854–1855* (London, 1961), 35.
3 Field-Marshal Sir Edmund Ironside *Diaries 1937–1940*. Edited by Colonel Roderick MacLeod and Denis Kelly (London, 1962), 191–2; cf. *ibid.*, 257ff.
4 Francis Williams, *A Prime Minister Remembers: The War and Post-War Memoirs of the Right Honourable Earl Attlee* (London, 1961), 46.
5 Major Gerald French, *op. cit.*, 276–7; cf. *D.C.*, I, 30; Aspinall-Oglander, Vol. I, 64–65; Lt.-Colonel C. à Court Repington, *Policy and Arms* (London, 1924), 203.
6 Asquith, *op. cit.*, Vol. II, 72.
7 Marder, *Richmond*, 140; cf. Lloyd George, *op. cit.*, Vol. I, 242–4; Corbett, *op. cit.*, Vol. II, 124–5; Lloyd George *Papers*, C16–16.
8 Aspinall-Oglander, *op. cit.*, Vol. I, 66–67.
9 *D.C.*, I, 30; cf. Hankey, *op. cit.*, Vol. I, 277–8.
10 Hankey, *op. cit.*, Vol. I, 277; see above, Chap. I, and Asquith *Papers* "Printed Government Papers, February–March 1915", Letter of February 5, 1915.
11 Lloyd George *Papers*, C4–11–5 and 6.
12 Asquith, *op. cit.*, Vol. II, 75. For the confusion in motives characteristic of the whole operation, see the opposite implication in Hankey's statement on March 1 to the effect that the ultimate aim in the Dardanelles was for a successful operation to bring in the Balkan States.

Asquith *Papers*, "Printed Government Papers, February–March 1915," March 1, 1915. Conversation with Lord Hankey, May 28, 1962, in London.

13 Marder, *Richmond*, 141–5; cf. Corbett, *op. cit.*, Vol. II, 125–6.
14 *D.C.*, I, 30; Aspinall-Oglander, *op. cit.*, Vol. I, 67, N2; cf. Corbett, *op. cit.*, Vol. II, 124; for orthodox Marine opinion see, especially, Brigadier-General G. G. Aston, *Letters on Amphibious Wars* (London, 1911), 104ff., 358ff.; for Churchill's criticisms of the memorandum, see *The World Crisis*, 362.
15 Hankey, *op. cit.*, Vol. I, 280–1; the prewar C.I.D. paper was not read out to the full War Council until February 19, when it was held that the increasing power of naval ordnance and the declining strength of Turkey had altered conditions in favour of the operation. *D.C.*, *Final Report*, Part II, 7–8; Lloyd George *Papers*, E8–1–5.
16 *D.C.*, I, 30; cf. Aspinall-Oglander, *op. cit.*, Vol. I, 68–69; Hankey, *op. cit.*, Vol. I, 278–81; *The World Crisis*, 363–4 and see above, Chap. I.
17 Fisher, *Memories*, 50–58; cf. Aspinall-Oglander, *op. cit.*, Vol. I, 68; Corbett, *op. cit.*, Vol. II, 126ff.
18 *The World Crisis*, 362–3.
19 Major-General Sherman Miles, "Notes on the Dardanelles Campaign of 1915," *Coast Artillery Journal* (Washington, March 9, 1938), 5, especially for Hamilton's remark on this conclusion of General Miles: "This hits the bull's eye"; cf. Bacon, *op. cit.*, Vol. II, 220; *The World Crisis*, 364ff.
20 Aspinall-Oglander, *op. cit.*, Vol. I, 71–72; *The World Crisis*, 364; Corbett, *op. cit.*, Vol. II, 143ff.; Hankey, *op. cit.*, Vol. I, 282; Lloyd George, *op. cit.*, Vol. I, 247–8.
21 Arthur, *op. cit.*, Vol. III, 113–15; Ellison, *op. cit.*, 29ff.; 72ff.
22 Sir Arthur Bryant, *The Turn of the Tide*, Vol. I of the *Diaries and Autobiographical Notes of Field Marshal the Viscount Alanbrooke* (London, 1957), 627; cf. *ibid.*, 415–24; Callwell, *Wilson*, Vol. II, 239; *The World Crisis*, 364; Corbett, *op. cit.*, Vol. II, 151–2.
23 Magnus, *op. cit.*, 321; Fisher had already heard that 70,000 men were going to Gallipoli, Fisher, *Correspondence*, Vol. III, 158.
24 Aspinall-Oglander, *op. cit.*, Vol. I, 73–75; Corbett, *op. cit.*, Vol. III, 152–3; Keyes, *op. cit.*, 193–4.
25 *D.C.*, I, 32; cf. *D.C.*, *Final Report*, Part II, 8–9; Aspinall-Oglander, Vol. I, 76.
26 Ellison, *op. cit.*, 84–86; cf. Grey, *op. cit.*, Vol. II, 75–77.
27 Higgins, *op. cit.*, 152–3.
28 Hankey, *op. cit.*, Vol. I, 283; *D.C.*, I, 31–32; *D.C.*, *Final Report*, Part II, 7. Balfour, too, had now come to favour the employment of an ample number of troops in the Straits. Asquith *Papers*, "Printed Government Papers, February–March 1915". Letter, February 24, 1915.
29 Aspinall-Oglander, *op. cit.*, Vol. I, 75; *D.C.*, I, 56.
30 *The World Crisis*, 365–9; cf. Asquith, *op. cit.*, Vol. II, 158; *D.C.*, I, 32; Hankey, *op. cit.*, Vol. I, 283; Spender and Asquith, *op. cit.*, Vol. II, 158.
31 Aspinall-Oglander, *op. cit.*, Vol. I, 76–77; cf. *D.C.*, *Final Report*, Part II, 8–9; Arthur, *op. cit.*, Vol. III, 118–19. The Maxwell estimate of Turkish strength at the Straits was about the same as that of Hankey

NOTES

at this date. Asquith *Papers*, "Printed Government Papers, February–March 1915", March 1, 1915.

32 Fisher, *Correspondence*, Vol. III, 165–6; cf. *The World Crisis*, 370ff; Keyes, *op. cit.*, 202ff.; Flag Officer, *loc. cit.*, 274.

33 Magnus, *op. cit.*, 322–3.

34 Aspinall-Oglander, *op. cit.*, Vol. I, 84–85; cf. Arthur, *op. cit.*, Vol. III, 121; *D.C.*, I, 33. The pessimistic Director of Naval Intelligence, Captain Reginald Hall, at this juncture suggested bribing the Turks as a means of passing the Straits. Fisher turned him down. James, *op. cit.*, 62–63.

35 *D.C.*, *Final Report*, Part II, 10; cf. *D.C.* I, 34; Aspinall-Oglander, 72 N1, 86, 93 N2; *The World Crisis*, 363–5, 373–4; Corbett, *op. cit.*, Vol. II, 202–3.

36 Winston Churchill, *The Second World War*, Vol. II, *Their Finest Hour* (Boston and London, 1949), 14–15; cf. Hankey, *op. cit.*, Vol. I, 297.

CHAPTER 10

MOMENT OF TRUTH

1 Bernard Ferguson, *The Watery Maze, The Story of Combined Operations* (London, 1961), 222.

2 *The Mind of Napoleon*. A selection edited by C. Herold (New York, 1955), 216.

3 C. P. Snow, *Science and Government* (Cambridge, Mass. and Oxford, 1961).

4 Lieutenant-General Sir Ian Hamilton, *A Staff Officer's Scrapbook During the Russo-Japanese War* (London, 1907), Vol. I, V.

5 *The World Crisis*, 378–9; cf. Hankey, *op. cit.*, Vol. I, 284–6; Gottlieb, *op. cit.*, 95–96, 305ff.; Djemal, *op. cit.*, 166; Maurice Paléologue, *An Ambassador's Memoirs* (London, 1922), Vol. I, 294.

6 Lloyd George *Papers*, C3–3–1. With permission of Lord Balfour.

7 Paléologue, *op. cit.*, Vol. I, 294; cf. Liddell Hart, *The Real War* (Boston and London, 1930), 150.

8 Hankey, *op. cit.*, Vol. I, 286–7; cf. *The World Crisis*, 379; Grey, *op. cit.*, Vol. II, 183ff; Asquith, *op. cit.*, Vol. II, 77.

9 Law *Papers*, 36–6–23; Blake, *op. cit.*, 240; Sazonov, *op. cit.*, 256–60; Gottlieb, *op. cit.*, 97–101.

10 *The World Crisis*, 388–9; Asquith, *op. cit.*, Vol. II, 78; Captain W. D. Puleston, *The Dardanelles Expedition* (Annapolis, 1927), 45; Keyes, *op. cit.*, 216–21; Wester-Wemyss, *op. cit.*, 39–40; *D.C.*, I, 35, 57–58.

11 See above Chap. II; Magnus, *op. cit.*, 323; Hamilton, *A Staff Officer's Scrapbook*, Vol. I, 282, and *The Commander*, 122–7; Jerrold, *op. cit.*, Aspinall-Oglander, *op. cit.*, Vol. I, 86; Public Record Office, Kitchener *Papers*, 30–57–37.

12 General Sir Ian Hamilton, *Gallipoli Diary* (London, 1920), Vol. I, 2–15; cf. Aspinall-Oglander, *op. cit.*, Vol. I, 88–89; *D.C.*, *Final Report*, Part II, 10.

13 *D.C.*, *Final Report*, Part II, 10; cf. *The World Crisis*, 384; Hankey, *op. cit.*, Vol. I, 290.

14 *D.C.*, *Final Report*, Part II, 10–11; cf. Wester-Wemyss, *op. cit.*, 40–41; and *The Turkish War In the First World War*, 24; and Major-General Hans Kannengiesser, "The Landing of the British Forces in Gallipoli 1915", *Wissen und Wehr* (Berlin, December, 1940), for the Gallipoli Peninsula as an irrational theatre for an army as opposed to a naval concept of war.

15 Hamilton, *op. cit.*, Vol. I, 16; cf. Winston Churchill, *Ian Hamilton's March* (London, 1920), 134–6; Hamilton, *The Commander*, 129; and, especially, his *Listening for the Drums* (London, 1944), Chap. XIV, for his close early friendship with Churchill.

16 Aspinall-Oglander, *op. cit.*, Vol. I, 89–90; Magnus, *op. cit.*, 325–6; Hamilton, *Gallipoli Diary*, Vol. I, 16–17; Robertson, *op. cit.*, Vol. I, 113; Arthur, *op. cit.*, Vol. II, 77 N1; Bean, *op. cit.*, Vol. I, 202–3.

17 *D.C.*, I, 36–37; cf. *The World Crisis*, 388–9 and 401–3.

18 E. Ashmead-Bartlett, *The Uncensored Dardanelles* (London, 1928), 27; Fisher *Papers* (Lennoxlove, East Lothian), Box 38–9.

19 *D.C.*, *Final Report*, Part II, 11–12; cf. Aspinall-Oglander, *op. cit.*, Vol. I, 94–96; Hamilton, *op. cit.*, Vol. I, 21–29; Lt. Walter C. Ansel "Naval Gunfire in Support of Landings, Lesson From Gallipoli", *U.S. Naval Institute Proceedings* (Annapolis, July 1932), 1001ff.

20 Fisher, *Memories*, 56, 75, 83; cf. *D.C.*, I, 38; Hankey, *op. cit.*, Vol. I, 292–3; *The World Crisis*, 395; Keyes, *op. cit.*, 248; Wester-Wemyss, *op. cit.*, 41; Corbett, *op. cit.*, Vol. II, 223ff.; Puleston, *The Dardanelles Expedition*, 54–56.

21 See especially, Fisher, *Memories*, 84–85, 97; Morgenthau, *op. cit.*, 225–7; *The World Crisis*, 406–7; Bacon, *op. cit.*, Vol. II, 228ff.; Keyes, *op. cit.*, 245–8; Aspinall-Oglander, *op. cit.*, Vol. I, 105–6; Callwell, *The Dardanelles*, 23ff.; Callwell, *Experiences*, 93–94; Sanders, *op. cit.*, 55ff.; Corbett, *op. cit.*, Vol. II, Chap. XIII; Vice-Admiral K. G. B. Dewar, *The Navy from Within* (London, 1939), 1–84, 197ff.; *Official Historical Account of the Dardanelles*. Turkish General Staff (U.S. Army War College, Washington, November 1925), 6–8.

22 *D.C.*, *Final Report*, Part II, 12; cf. Hamilton, *op. cit.*, Vol. I, 37–39.

23 Hankey, *op. cit.*, Vol. I, 293–300; Lloyd George *Papers*, C4–19–4.

24 Hamilton, *op. cit.*, Vol. I, 41ff.; *The World Crisis*, 401–2; Bean, *op. cit.*, Vol. I, 208–9; Keyes, *op. cit.*, 256ff.; Magnus, *op. cit.*, 327.

25 *D.C.*, *Final Report*, Part II, 13; cf. *The World Crisis*, 395–6; *D.C.*, I, 38–43.

26 Asquith, *op. cit.*, Vol. II, 80–82; cf. *The World Crisis*, 396–7; *D.C.*, I, 38; Spender and Asquith, Vol. II, 162–3.

27 *D.C.*, *Final Report*, Part II, 13–14. As Lord Sydenham had warned over thirty years before. Sydenham, *op. cit.*, 34–35, 174.

CHAPTER 11

THE CRUELLEST MONTH

1 Garrett Mattingly, *The Armada* (Boston and London, 1959).

2 Field-Marshal the Viscount Montgomery, *The Path to Leadership* (New York and London, 1961).

NOTES

3 Wynford Vaughan-Thomas, *Anzio* (New York and London, 1961)
cf. J. R. M. Butler, *History of the Second World War, United
Kingdom Military Series, Grand Strategy*, Vol. II, September 1939–
June 1941 (London, 1957), 531–2.
4 Winston Churchill, *The Second World War*, Vol. V, *Closing the Ring*
(Boston and London, 1951), 385.
5 Marder, *Richmond*, 148; cf. Hassell, *op. cit.*, 330; Hankey, *op. cit.*,
Vol. I, 300.
6 Wester-Wemyss, *op. cit.*, 45–51.
7 Germains, *op. cit.*, 190.
8 Fisher, *Correspondence*, Vol. III, 178–81; cf. Bacon, *op. cit.*, Vol. II,
227.
9 Fisher, *Correspondence*, Vol. III, 185, N2 and 186.
10 *Ibid.*, 190–1; cf. *The World Crisis*, 418–19.
11 Hankey, *op. cit.*, Vol. II, 301.
12 Blake, *op. cit.*, 241.
13 Callwell, *Wilson*, Vol. I, 215–16.
14 Marder, *Richmond*, 149–51; Hankey, *op. cit.*, Vol. I, 301.
15 Hamilton, *Gallipoli Diary*, Vol. I, 62–94; cf. *D.C.*, *Final Report*, Part
II, 15; Hankey, *op. cit.*, Vol. I, 301; Gottlieb, *op. cit.*, 114; Callwell,
Wilson, Vol. I, 221–2.
16 Hankey, *op. cit.*, Vol. I, 301–2.
17 Sanders, op. cit., 56–64; *The Turkish War in the World War*, Chap.
II, 19–20; Corbett, *op. cit.*, Vol. II, 298–9; H. L. Armstrong, *Grey
Wolf, The Life of Kemal Ataturk* (New York, 1961), 38; Aspinall-
Oglander, *op. cit.*, Vol. I, Chap. VIII. British intelligence estimates
for this period were close to accurate. Lloyd George *Papers*, C. 16–4.
18 Fisher, *Correspondence*, Vol. III, 199–201; cf. Hankey, *op. cit.*, Vol. I,
302–3; Hamilton, *op. cit.*, Vol. I, Chap. IV; Miles, *loc. cit.*, 25–30;
Aspinall-Oglander, *op. cit.*, Vol. I, 138ff.
19 Hamilton, *The Commander*, 117.
20 *War Poets, 1914–1918*. Edited by E. Blunden (London, 1958), 16–17;
cf. Diana Cooper, *The Rainbow Comes and Goes* (London, 1958), 160;
Hassell, *op. cit.*, 326–9; Winston Churchill, *The Unknown War, The
Eastern Front* (New York and London, 1931), 306ff.; Jerrold, *op. cit.*,
78.

CHAPTER 12

THE FALL OF ICARUS

1 *Agamemnon.*
2 Esher, *op. cit.*, Vol. II, 199.
3 Lord Elton, *Gordon of Khartoum; The Life of General Charles Gordon*
(New York, 1955; London, 1954), 339.
4 *Great Contemporaries*, 141–8.
5 Fred Majdalany, *The Battle of Cassino* (Boston, 1957), 84ff.; cf.
Aspinall-Oglander, *op. cit.*, Vol. I, Chaps. X–XIII; Armstrong, *op.
cit.*, Chap. XII; Rupert Furneaux, *The Breakfast War* (New York,
1958), 323. Discussion with Major Reginald Hargreaves, May 16,
1962. Hargreaves, a participant in the landings, has stressed the unnecessary weakness of the British forces engaged, in opposition to
the view of Captain Liddell Hart on this score.

223

6   Wester-Wemyss, *op. cit.*, 70–106; cf. Hankey, *op. cit.*, Vol. 1, 303; Callwell, *Experiences*, 99–100; for Churchill's public line at this moment, see his unusually misleading remarks to Riddell, *War Diary*, 82–83.

7   Hamilton, *Gallipoli Diary*, Vol. I, 161.

8   D.C., *Final Report*, Part II, 21–22.

9   Aspinall-Oglander, *op. cit.*, Vol. I, 349 and N2.

10 Asquith, *op. cit.*, Vol. II, 94ff.; cf. Hankey, *op. cit.*, Vol. I, 315; Magnus, *op. cit.*, 331–7; French, *op. cit.*, Chap. XVIII; Beaverbrook, *op. cit.*, Vol. I, Chaps. V and VII; Esher, *The Tragedy of Lord Kitchener*, 116–23.

11 Aspinall-Oglander, *op. cit.*, Vol. I, 354.

12 Fisher, *Correspondence*, Vol. III, 215–21; cf. Keyes, 189, 335ff.; Asquith, *op. cit.*, Vol. II, 108; Asquith *Papers*, "Miscellaneous", Box 27, letters of May 11 and May 12.

13 Hankey, *op. cit.*, Vol. I, 314; Fisher, *Correspondence*, Vol. III, 221–2; Keyes, *op. cit.*, 337ff.; Aspinall-Oglander, *op. cit.*, Vol. I, 359–60; Corbett, *op. cit.*, Vol. II, 404–8; Vol. III, 24ff.; D.C., *Final Report*, Part II, 23; Bacon, *op. cit.*, Vol. II, 241–2.

14 Magnus, *op. cit.*, 338–9; cf. Aspinall-Oglander, *op. cit.*, Vol. I, 363–4; Callwell, *Experiences*, 65–68.

15 Bacon, *op. cit.*, Vol. II, 244–6; cf. Hankey, *op. cit.*, Vol. I, 314–15.

16 Aspinall-Oglander, *op. cit.*, Vol. I, 363; Falkenhayn, *op. cit.*, 90ff.; *Ludendorff's Own Story* (New York and London, 1919), Vol. I, 166ff.

17 Aspinall-Oglander, *op. cit.*, Vol. I, 364–5; *ibid.*, Vol. II, 4–5; *The World Crisis*, 446–8.

18 *The World Crisis*, 449; cf. Asquith *Papers*, "May 1915", Letters of May 13 *et al.*

19 Bacon, *op. cit.*, Vol. II, 251–4.

20 Bacon, *op. cit.*, Vol. II, 256; *The World Crisis*, 451; cf. Corbett, *op. cit.*, Vol. II, 408–11; Fisher, *Correspondence*, Vol. III, 222–4, especially N1; Asquith, *op. cit.*, Vol. II, 108–9 and Asquith *Papers*, "Miscellaneous", Box 27, correspondence for May 11.

21 Fisher, *Correspondence*, Vol. III, 228–9; cf. *ibid.*, 213; Hassell, *op. cit.*, 331; J. L. Hammond, *C. P. Scott of the Manchester Guardian* (London, 1934), 195–6; *The World Crisis*, 452; Asquith *Papers*, "Miscellaneous", Box 27, May 19, 1915.

22 Fisher, *Correspondence*, Vol. III, 230–4; Bacon, *op. cit.*, Vol. II, 257–258.

23 Asquith, *op. cit.*, Vol. II, 110–11; cf. Chap. XI, above, for the apparent discrepancy in the position of the junior Sea Lords from April 7–8; Bacon, *op. cit.*, Vol. II, 261–3; *The World Crisis*, 452–3; Hankey, *op. cit.*, Vol. I, 315; Blake, *op. cit.*, 255; see James, *op. cit.*, 83–85, for the junior Lords' distrust of Fisher by this period.

24 Fisher, *Correspondence*, Vol. III, 236–8; Law *Papers*, 37-2-34; cf. especially, Hankey, *op. cit.*, Vol. I, 316–19; and Lloyd George, *op. cit.*, Vol. I, 135–7; Earl Lloyd George, *Lloyd George* (London, 1960), 133; Blake, *op. cit.*, 243–7; Beaverbrook, *op. cit.*, Vol. I, 100–9; Spender and Asquith, *op. cit.*, Vol. II, 164ff.; Asquith *Papers*, "Miscellaneous", Box 27.

25 Magnus, *op. cit.*, 340; Fisher, *Correspondence*, Vol. I, *The Making of An Admiral, 1854–1904* (London, 1952), 154; A. M. Gollin, *The*

Observer and J. L. Garvin, 1908–1914 (London, 1961), Chap. III; Riddell, *War Diary*, 111. Conversation of the author with the Duke of Hamilton, May 25, 1962.

26 Hankey, *op. cit.*, Vol. I, 316; Bryant, *The Turn of the Tide*, 173–4, 230–1, 269–74, 298–302, 320, 336–40, 415; Kennedy, *op. cit.*, 60, 75, 173–4, 239; Higgins, *op. cit.*, 142–3.
27 *The World Crisis*, 453–8; Blake, *op. cit.*, 246, N1; Lloyd George, *op. cit.*, Vol. I, 139–40; Riddell, *War Diary*, 89–94; Beaverbrook, *op. cit.*, 120–33; Asquith, *op. cit.*, Vol. II, 125–6.
28 *The World Crisis*, 457; Magnus, *op. cit.*, 341; Keyes, *op. cit.*, 342.
29 Asquith, *op. cit.*, Vol. II, 111–13; Bacon, *op. cit.*, Vol. II, 268–75; and, especially, Law *Papers*, 50–3–1.
30 Beaverbrook, *op. cit.*, 128; Law *Papers*, 37–2–37, 50–3–20, and 26; cf. Blake, *op. cit.*, 252–3; Riddell, *More Pages From My Diary*, 27–29; John Maynard Keynes, *Essays and Sketches in Biography* (New York, 1956), 181–4; Lloyd George, *op. cit.*, Vol. I, 636ff.
31 Hankey, *op. cit.*, Vol. I, 317–18; Asquith, *op. cit.*, Vol. II, 125; Keyes, *op. cit.*, 352–4; Fisher, *Correspondence*, Vol. III, 214–15, 246–7, both footnotes and Fisher *Papers*, Box 38–5, Letter of February 19, 1917. Law *Papers*, 50–3–31. Comment of Arthur J. Marder, October 22, 1962.
32 Fisher, *Memories*, 57; cf. Riddell, *War Diary*, 111–12, 205; Marder, *The Road to War*, 21; Hankey, *op. cit.*, Vol. I, 335.
33 Riddell, *op. cit.*, 89–97; cf. Blunt, *op. cit.*, Part II, 289.
34 Esher, *op. cit.*, Vol. III, 242.
35 *The World Crisis*, 460.
36 Lloyd George, *op. cit.*, Vol. I, 638; cf. Riddell, *War Diary*, 94–118.

CHAPTER 13

FAILURE IN COMMAND

1 André Maurois, *Disraeli, A Picture of the Victorian Age* (New York, 1935; and London, 1927).
2 *Wellington at War; 1794–1815.* Letters Edited by A. Brett-James (London, 1961), XXXIII.
3 Winston Churchill, *Marlborough, His Life and Times*, Vol. III, 1702–1704 (New York, 1960; and London, 1936).
4 Anthony Nutting, *Lawrence of Arabia; The Man and the Motive* (New York and London, 1961), 246.
5 Hamilton, *Gallipoli Diary*, Vol. I, 235–40; cf. *D.C., Final Report*, Part II, 24.
6 Hankey, *op. cit.*, Vol. I, 333–7; and his *Government Control in War*, 37–38; Johnson, *op. cit.*, 148ff.; Blake, *op. cit.*, 261–2.
7 *D.C., Final Report*, Part II, 25; cf. Hankey, *The Supreme Command*, Vol. I, 336; Magnus, *op. cit.*, 342–3; Asquith *Papers*, "May 1915", Letter of May 28, 1916.
8 A. Kearsey, *Notes and Comments on the Dardanelles Campaign* (Aldershot, 1934), 3–4; cf. Sanders, *op. cit.*, 79; Aspinall-Oglander, *op. cit.*, Vol. II, 159; Hamilton, *op. cit.*, Vol. I, 263–5; Kannengeisser, *op. cit.*, 263; *D.C., Final Report*, Part II, 25.

Q

9 *D.C., Final Report*, Part II, 25–26; Hankey, *op. cit.*, Vol. I, 339–41; *The World Crisis*, 466–8; Magnus, *op. cit.*, 343; Lloyd George *Papers*, E8–1–13.

10 Callwell, *op. cit.*, Vol. I, 231; cf. Collier, *op. cit.*, 220; Hamilton, *op. cit.*, Vol. I, 278–84.

11 Riddell, *War Diary*, 105–6.

12 Aspinall-Oglander, *op. cit.*, Vol. II, 60–61; cf. Hankey, *op. cit.*, Vol. I, 342–3; Spender and Asquith, *op. cit.*, Vol. II, 180–2; Higgins, *op. cit.*, 125.

13 Aspinall-Oglander, *op. cit.*, Vol. II, 62–63; *D.C., Final Report*, Part II, 27.

14 Collier, *op. cit.*, 220–1; Callwell, *op. cit.*, Vol. I, 236–8; Lloyd George and Kitchener were likewise pessimistic regarding the prospects for Suvla, but still favoured reinforcements for it in this period. Lloyd George *Papers*, E8–1–3.

15 Hamilton, *Gallipoli Diary*, Vol. II (New York and London, 1920), 12–14; cf. *The World Crisis*, 502; Aspinall-Oglander, *op. cit.*, Vol. II, 63–64; Robertson, *op. cit.*, Vol. I, 127; Magnus, *op. cit.*, 343–5; Hankey, *op. cit.*, Vol. I, 348–51; Bacon, *op. cit.*, Vol. II, 766.

16 Callwell, *op. cit.*, Vol. I, 243–4; Blake, *op. cit.*, 265; Aspinall-Oglander, *op. cit.*, Vol. II, 64–66.

17 Magnus, *op. cit.*, 346–7.

18 Hankey, *op. cit.*, Vol. I, Chaps, XXXVI and XXXVII; Asquith *Papers*, Box 28, letters of July 28, August 12, August 14; Hamilton, *op. cit.*, Vol. II, 35–118; Bacon, *op. cit.*, Vol. II, 3, 366–429; Aspinall-Oglander, *op. cit.*, Vol. II, 71–76, 115–32, 168ff.; *D.C. Final Report*, 28–50; Miles, *loc. cit.*, 67–79; Corbett, *op. cit.*, Vol. III, Chaps. IV and V; Wester-Wemyss, *op. cit.*, 167ff.

19 *Official Historical Account*, Part III, 14–17; Miles, *loc. cit.*, 8; Aspinall-Oglander, *op. cit.*, Vol. II, Chap. XII; *The World War 1914–1918, Military Operations on Land*, Vol. IX, *Operations 1915*. German Government Archives, U.S. Army War College (Washington, 1934), 41ff.; Lewis Einstein, *Inside Constantinople; A Diplomatist's Diary During the Dardanelles Expedition, April–September, 1915* (London, 1917), 203ff.

20 Asquith *Papers*, "September 1915" letter of September 8, 1915; Ashmead-Bartlett, *op. cit.*, Chaps. X and XI; Lloyd George *Papers*, E8–1–3.

21 Compton Mackenzie, *Gallipoli Memories* (New York, 1930; and London, 1929), 361–2; and conversation with the author May 25, 1962; cf. Aspinall-Oglander, *op. cit.*, Vol. II, Chaps. XIII–XXIII; *The World Crisis*, Chap. XXXIV; Hankey, *op. cit.*, Vol. I, Chap. XXXVIII; *D.C., Final Report*, Part II, 28–51; Corbett, *op. cit.*, Vol. III, Chap. VI; Sanders, *op. cit.*, 87ff.; Armstrong, *op. cit.*, 57ff.; Moorehead, *op. cit.*, Chaps. XIII–XIV; Bean, *op. cit.*, Vol. II, 715ff.; G. G. A. E. "Gallipoli Viewed From the Turkish Side", Part II, "Suvla and The Evacuation", *Journal of the Royal United Service Institution*, Vol. 68 (London, February–November, 1923), 3–6; Cyril Falls, *The Great War* (New York, 1959; and London, 1960), 134–5; Hart, *Through the Fog of War*, 292–5; Miles, *loc. cit.*, 69–80; Keyes, *op. cit.*, Chaps. XXII–XXIII; Kannengeisser, *op. cit.*, 266ff.

NOTES

CHAPTER 14

WAR AS WE MUST

1   Bryant, *op. cit.*, Vol. I, 76.
2   Alan, Valentine, Lord George Germain (Oxford, 1962), 255.
3   André Maurois, *King Edward and His Times* (New York and London, 1933), 257.
4   Erich Eyck, *Pitt versus Fox, Father and Son* (London, 1950), 311–12.
5   Aspinall-Oglander, *op. cit.*, Vol. II, 336–7; cf. Hamilton, *op. cit.*, Vol. II, 110–18; Asquith *Papers*, Box 28, letter of August 17, 1915.
6   Magnus, *op. cit.*, 347; Spender and Asquith, *op. cit.*, Vol. II, 181–2; Asquith *Papers*, Box 28, letter of August 14, 1915.
7   Aspinall-Oglander, *op. cit.*, Vol. II, 337–8; Keyes, *op. cit.*, 421–6; Hamilton, *op. cit.*, Vol. II, 124–5; Asquith *Papers*, Box 28, letter of August 14, 1915.
8   *The World Crisis*, 502–4; Lloyd George *Papers*, X23–4–8, E8–1–3; Asquith *Papers*, "August 1915", letter August 30; cf. Aspinall-Oglander, *op. cit.*, Vol. II, 364–6; Grey, *op. cit.*, Vol. II, 208–10; *D.C.*, *Final Report*, 51–52; Haig *Papers*, 101–2; Magnus, *op. cit.*, 347–9; Hankey, *op. cit.*, Vol. I, 406–8; Paléologue, *op. cit.*, Vol. II, 11, 85–86.
9   Poincaré, *op. cit.*, 181–204; King, *op. cit.*, 75–79; cf. Hankey, *op. cit.*, Vol. I, 410–11; Callwell, *op. cit.*, Vol. I, 247–51; Hamilton, *op. cit.*, Vol. II, 163–80; Corbett, *op. cit.*, Vol. III, 110–12; Aspinall-Oglander, *op. cit.*, Vol. II, 369–74; *D.C.*, *Final Report*, Part II, 52; Magnus, *op. cit.*, 355–6.
10 Magnus, *op. cit.*, 350–4; Hankey, *op. cit.*, Vol. I, Chap. XL; Asquith *Papers*, Box 28, Balfour letter of September 23 to the Prime Minister.
11 Falkenhayn, *op. cit.*, 133–60; cf. Morgenthau, *op. cit.*, 262–71; Bean, *op. cit.*, Vol. II, 773–4; Aspinall-Oglander, *op. cit.*, Vol. II, 375; *The World Crisis*, 506–7.
12 Aspinall–Oglander, *op. cit.*, Vol. II, 376; Hamilton, *op. cit.*, Vol. II, 209–48; Bean, *op. cit.*, Vol. II, 775; Beaverbrook, *op. cit.*, Vol. I, 157–61; Blake, *op. cit.*, 266–7; Hankey, *op. cit.*, Vol. I, 411–21; Corbett, *op. cit.*, Vol. III, 155ff.; Spender and Asquith, *op. cit.*, Vol. II, 184–5; Poincaré, *op. cit.*, 1915, 225–37; Law *Papers*, 51–3–6 and 21.
13 King, *op. cit.*, 80–82; cf. Hankey, *op. cit.*, Vol. I, 422–3; Grey, *op. cit.*, Vol. II, 215ff; Corbett, *op. cit.*, Vol. II, 161–4.
14 Aspinall-Oglander, *op. cit.*, Vol. II, 378–82; *The World Crisis*, 509–10; Blake, *op. cit.*, 267; Falkenhayn, *op. cit.*, 191; Lloyd George *Papers*, D23–4–16.
15 Aspinall-Oglander, *op. cit.*, Vol. II, 384; Spender and Asquith, *op. cit.*, 197 N2; Major-General I. S. O. Playfair and others, *History of the Second World War; United Kingdom Military Series.* Edited by J. R. M. Butler. *The Mediterranean and Middle East* (London, 1954), Vol. I, *The Early Successes against Italy* (to May 1941), 371–96; Bean, *op. cit.*, Vol. II, 780; Lloyd George *Papers*, D23–4–13, E8–1–3.
16 Lloyd George, *op. cit.*, Vol. I, 294ff.; Hankey, *op. cit.*, Vol. I, 428–30; King, *op. cit.*, Chap. IV; Poincaré, *op. cit.*, 1915, 257ff.; Magnus, *op. cit.*, 356–7; Blake, *op. cit.*, 267–8; Callwell, *op. cit.*, Vol. I, 257–8.

17 Hamilton, *The Commander*, 16–18; cf. Hamilton, *Gallipoli Diary*, Vol. II, 249–73; *The World Crisis*, 531; Bean, *op. cit.*, Vol. II, 767–784; Aspinall-Oglander, *op. cit.*, Vol. II, 383–6; Corbett, *op. cit.*, Vol. III, 170–1; Hankey, *op. cit.*, Vol. I, 430; Keyes, *op. cit.*, 440; Ashmead-Bartlett, *op. cit.*, 241–52; Lloyd George *Papers*, D20–2–30, D23–4–18, E8–1–3.
18 *D.C.*, *Final Report*, Part II, 53–55; *The World Crisis*, 514–15; Beaverbrook, *op. cit.*, Vol. I, 161–2; Aspinall-Oglander, *op. cit.*, Vol. II, 386–407; Magnus, *op. cit.*, 358; Corbett, *op. cit.*, Vol. III, 179–201; Blake, *op. cit.*, 268; Haig *Papers*, 108; Robertson, *op. cit.*, Vol. I, 131–7; Bean, *op. cit.*, Vol. II, 784–6; Moorehead, *op. cit.*, 314 N1; General Sir George Barrow, *The Life of General Sir Charles Monro* (London, 1931), 64ff. Law *Papers*, 51–4–14 and 26, 56–6–44.
19 Corbett, *op. cit.*, Vol. III, Chap. X; Bean, *op. cit.*, Vol. II, 780; Fisher, *Correspondence*, Vol. III, 361; Repington, *op. cit.*, Vol. I, 287–8, and his letter to Law, November 20, 1915. Law *Papers*, 51–5–44; Falls, *op. cit.*, 165.
20 D. H. Lawrence, *Selected Letters* (London, 1950), 87.

CHAPTER 15

THE RACK OF CHOICE

1 *The Peloponnesian War*, Box VII.
2 *The Mind of Napoleon*, 165.
3 Asquith and Oxford, *op. cit.*, 64
4 Esher, *op. cit.*, Vol. III, 92.
5 Blake, *op. cit.*, 268; cf. Lloyd George *Papers*, D23–4–17; Lloyd George, *op. cit.*, Vol. I, 306–11; Aspinall-Oglander, *op. cit.*, Vol. II, 384 N1, 385 N1; Law *Papers*, 53–6–47 and 48; Spender and Asquith, *op. cit.*, Vol. II, 187–98; *House of Commons Debates*, Vol. LXXV, 533–534.
6 Hankey, *Government Control in War*, 39; and *The Supreme Command*, Vol. II, 439–44.
7 Law *Papers*, 51–5–7, 14, 117–1–24, and 32; Blake, *op. cit.*, 270–2; Beaverbrook, *op. cit.*, Vol. I, 160–7; Callwell, *op. cit.*, Vol. I, 260–4; Lloyd George *Papers*, D18–2–12; Asquith *Papers*, Box 28, letters of September 23 and October 15.
8 Aspinall-Oglander, *op. cit.*, Vol. II, 408–12; cf. *D.C.*, *Final Report*, Part II, 55–56; Keyes, *op. cit.*, 448–58; Corbett, *op. cit.*, Vol. III, 202–205; Wester-Wemyss, *op. cit.*, 208ff.; *The World Crisis*, 517–19; Ashmead-Bartlett, *op. cit.*, 257ff.; Lloyd George *Papers*, D17–2–2.
9 In March 1915 Kitchener had hoped to annex Alexandretta, hardly a new idea with him. Asquith *Papers*, "Printed Government Papers, February–March 1915", March 16, 1915; Lloyd George *Papers*, D23–5–5; Major O. Williams, "The Evacuation of the Dardanelles", *The National Review* (London, 1920); Aspinall-Oglander, *op. cit.*, Vol. II, 414–22; Bean, *op. cit.*, Vol. II, 790–4; Corbett, *op. cit.*, Vol. III, 206–11; *D.C.*, *Final Report*, 56–57; Hankey, *op. cit.*, Vol. II, 450; Keyes, *op. cit.*, 457–70; Keyes *Papers*, Files A and B; Law *Papers*, 51–5–24 and 29; Magnus, *op. cit.*, 361–6; Wester-Wemyss,

op. cit., 209–14; Poincaré, *op. cit.*, 1915, 286–9; Barrow, *op. cit.*, 81–82. For an understanding appraisal of Kitchener's position at this time, see Sir James Rennell Rodd, *Social and Diplomatic Memories, 1902–1919* (London, 1925), 279–80.

10 Cecil Aspinall-Oglander, *Roger Keyes* (London, 1951), 194–7; Lloyd George *Papers*, C23–5–5.

11 *House of Commons Debates*, Fifth Series, Vol. 378, 48ff.; cf. Cowles, *op. cit.*, 205–6; *The World Crisis*, 522.

12 Aspinall-Oglander, *Military Operations: Gallipoli*, Vol. II, 427; cf. Lloyd George *Papers*, D23–5–5; Law *Papers*, 51–5–24, 38, 42–45.

13 Nicolson, *op. cit.*, 113–14; cf. *D.C., Final Report*, Part II, 57; Aspinall-Oglander, *op. cit.*, Vol. II, 427–31; Blake, *op. cit.*, 272–3; Beaverbrook, *op. cit.*, Vol. I, 171–4; Lloyd George *Papers*, D23–5–8; Lord Beaverbrook, *The Decline and Fall of Lloyd George* (London, 1963), 153–67.

14 Hankey, *op. cit.*, Vol. II, 460–2. On November 6, with Balfour's support, Hankey had written Law urging his reconsideration of Gallipoli before taking any irrevocable step in opposition. Law *Papers*, 51–5–14 and 15.

15 Haig *Papers*, 114.

16 Callwell, *op. cit.*, Vol. I, 266–7; cf. Corbett, *op. cit.*, Vol. III, 213–14; Wester-Wemyss, *op. cit.*, 218ff.; Haig *Papers*, 113–15; Aspinall-Oglander, *op. cit.*, Vol. II, 431; Law *Papers*, 51–5–45.

17 Wester-Wemyss, *op. cit.*, 218; cf. Corbett, *op. cit.*, Vol. III, 214–15; Aspinall-Oglander, *op. cit.*, Vol. II, 432–4.

18 *D.C., Final Report*, Part II, 57–58; cf. Sanders, *op. cit.*, 96–97; Aspinall-Oglander, *op. cit.*, Vol. II, 434–6; Blake, *op. cit.*, 273; Hankey, *op. cit.*, Vol. II, 463–4; Lloyd George *Papers*, D23–5–9; Law *Papers*, 52–1–11.

19 Esher, *op. cit.*, Vol. III, 276–96; cf. Esher, *The Tragedy of Lord Kitchener*, 179–90; Hankey, *op. cit.*, Vol. II, 444–6; Beaverbrook, *op. cit.*, Vol. I, 196–205; Magnus, *op. cit.*, 366–7; Goodwin-Austen, *op.cit.*, 221, 256.

20 Robertson, *op. cit.*, Vol. I, 164–72; cf. *ibid.*, 193–245.

21 Aspinall-Oglander, *op. cit.*, Vol. II, 435–9; Hankey, *op. cit.*, Vol. II, 452–5; Poincaré, *1915*, 305–14; Lloyd George, *op. cit.*, Vol. I, 314–316; Robertson, *op. cit.*, Vol. I, 245–7; Corbett, *op. cit.*, Vol. III, 217–23; Callwell, *op. cit.*, Vol. I, 268–70; Bacon, *op. cit.*, Vol. II, 794–6; Grey, *op. cit.*, Vol. II, 223–6; Paléologue, *op. cit.*, Vol. II, 118–19.

22 *D.C., Final Report*, Part II, 59; cf. Wester-Wemyss, *op. cit.*, 224ff.; Bacon, *op. cit.*, Vol. II, 796–7, 907–8; Aspinall-Oglander, *Roger Keyes*, 201–2; Lloyd George *Papers*, D24–5–4.

23 Spender and Asquith, *op. cit.*, Vol. II, 201. Thanks particularly to the planning of Colonel Aspinall (Oglander), statement of Capt. Liddell Hart, May 28, 1962; cf. *D.C., Final Report*, Part II, 59–60; Hankey, *op. cit.*, Vol. II, 463; Robertson, *From Private to Field Marshal*, 270–274; Aspinall-Oglander, *Military Operations: Gallipoli*, Vol II, Chaps. XXXI, XXXII. At least the Prime Minister had a more accurate conception of Corunna than did Churchill in this period. See Barrow, *op. cit.*, 62.

24 Esher, *op. cit.*, Vol. III, 297; cf. Sanders, *op. cit.*, 97–99; Callwell, *The Dardanelles*, 359; *The World Crisis*, 531–3; Magnus, *op. cit.*, 367ff.

CHAPTER 16
WULLY REDIVIVUS

1 Callwell, *Wilson*, Vol. I, 215.
2 Field-Marshal Sir William Robertson, "Policy and Strategy", *The Army Quarterly* (London, October 1921, January 1922), 366.
3 Jacob Burckhardt, "War as a Work of Art", Part I, *Civilization of the Renaissance in Italy*.
4 Hesketh Pearson, *Oscar Wilde, His Life and Wit* (New York and London, 1946).
5 Hankey, *op. cit.*, Vol. II, 829–31.
6 "Lloyd George and Curzon", *The Times Literary Supplement* (London, October 28, 1960), 692; cf. Lloyd George, *War Memoirs*, Vol. I, 316.
7 Lloyd George, *op. cit.*, Vol. II, 1080–1; cf. Vol. I, 860–6; Earl Lloyd George, *op. cit.*, 141–3. Captain Liddell Hart has stressed Lloyd George's faith in flank attacks, *per se*, regardless of any subsequent motives in policy. Conversation, May 28, 1962.
8 Higgins, *op. cit.*, 246, N74.
9 Esher, *The Tragedy of Lord Kitchener*, 206; cf. Lloyd George, *War Memoirs*, Vol. II, 2034–7; Hankey, *op. cit.*, Vol. II, 556–7; Commander Sir Stephen King-Hall, "Defence in the Nuclear Age, 1961", *Journal of Royal United Service Institution* (London, May 1961), 167; A. J. P. Taylor, *Lloyd George, Rise and Fall* (Cambridge, 1961), 33–34.
10 Ehrman, *op. cit.*, 77ff.; cf. Callwell, *op. cit.*, Vol. II, 119; Field-Marshal Earl Wavell, *Soldiers and Soldiering* (London, 1953), 40–41; Lloyd George, *op. cit.*, Vol. II, 2037.
11 Hankey, *op. cit.*, Vol. I, Chaps. XXIII and XXIV; Spender and Asquith, *op. cit.*, Vol. II, 191–3; Grey, *op. cit.*, Vol. II, 75–80.
12 Paléologue, *op. cit.*, Vol. I, 349–50, Vol. II, 40ff.; Beaverbrook, *Politicians and the War*, Vol. I, 59.
13 Hankey, *op. cit.*, Vol. II, 555; cf. Callwell, *Experiences*, 61–63, 92–93; *House of Commons Debates*, Fifth Series, Vol. XCI, 1806–7.
14 Lloyd George, *op. cit.*, Vol. I, 635–6; cf. Beaverbrook, *op. cit.*, Vol. I, 58–60; Dugdale, *op. cit.*, Vol. II, 184–5; Higgins, *op. cit.*, 87ff., 137ff.; Huguet, *op. cit.*, 208–9.
15 *Time* (New York, November 18, 1957), 43; cf. Samuel Eliot Morison, *Strategy and Compromise* (Boston, 1958), 27; Roskill, *op. cit.*, 125–6; Ismay, *op. cit.*, 322.
16 Callwell, *Experiences*, 154–5.
17 *The Unknown War*, Chaps, XVII–XXIV.
18 Repington, *Policy and Arms*, 204; cf. David Trask, *The United States in the Supreme War Council; American War Aims and Inter-Allied Strategy, 1917–1918* (Middletown, Conn., 1962), 14–15; and the similar eventual conclusion of Sir Edward Grey, *op. cit.*, Vol. II, 74–76, as opposed to his initial position, *ibid.*, 195ff.
19 Riddell, *War Diary*, 303; Bertie, *op. cit.*, Vol. II, 185, 269–70, 302; Sir Charles Oman, "The German Losses on the Somme", in *The World Crisis, A Criticism* (London, undated), 40ff. See, for example,

the title of Senator John F. Kennedy's recent pre-election best seller, *A Strategy of Peace* (New York and London, 1960), when, by definition, peace is an objective of policy, not of strategy. For the contrast between the philosophies of war of Churchill and Clausewitz, see Chap. X of the author's previously cited work.

20 Dugdale, *op. cit.*, Vol. II, 184–5.

21 Ismay, *op. cit.*, 110ff.; cf. Johnson, *op. cit.*, 162; Kingston-McCloughry, *op. cit.*, 238; *Their Finest Hour*, Book I, Chap. I; T. K. Derry, *History of the Second World War. The Campaign in Norway* (London, 1952), 59–60, 236–42.

22 "Book Review", *The Economist* (London, January 21, 1961), 264; cf. Ferguson, *op. cit.*, 402–3.

23 Captain S. W. Roskill, *The War at Sea, 1939–1945*, Vol. III, *The Offensive, Part II* (London, 1961), 391, and his *The Strategy of Sea Power*, 105–6, 133–4, 157–8, 242–3; Ferguson, *op. cit.*, 35–43, 60ff.; Rear-Admiral L. E. Maund, *Assault From the Sea* (London, 1949), 19–21; *Public Record Office*, file CAB 1–3–288, p. 9.

24 Richmond, *op. cit.*, 315–16.

25 Sir Charles Webster and Noble Frankland, *The Strategic Air Offensive Against Germany, 1939–1945*, Vol. III, *Victory*, Part 5 (London, 1961), 6, 79–80, 115ff.; R. H. S. Crossman, "Western Defence in the 1960's", *Journal of the Royal United Service Institution* (London, August 1961), 334–5; Andrew Boyle, *Trenchard* (London, 1962), 351–3, 717–28.

Index

Admiralty War Staff, x, 13, 29, 30, 33, 35, 36, 38, 40, 49, 61, 71, 80, 82, 84, 90, 91, 93, 105, 106, 107, 108, 118, 125, 164
Adrianople, 115
Adriatic Sea, 86, 138
Aegean Sea, 6, 38, 41, 42, 79, 103, 108, 112, 117, 118, 120, 121, 129, 134, 135, 136, 137, 138, 140, 161, 172
Aeschylus, 135
Aga Khan, 42
Air Force, Royal, 189
Alexandretta, 45, 70, 83, 170, 184
Alexandria, 3, 122, 139
Amiens, 55
Ammunition, 38, 43, 70, 74, 77, 84, 89, 96, 99, 111, 123, 125, 129, 131, 132, 136, 137, 153, 156, 158, 163, 165, 173, 177, 183, 187
Amphibious Warfare: see Combined Operations
Anatolia, 46, 120
Antwerp, 12, 22, 26, 27, 54, 57, 58, 59, 60, 68, 103, 106
Anzacs, 70, 107, 108, 111
Anzio, 127, 136
Arabs, 70
Archangel, 44
Armenians, 189
Ashmead-Bartlett, Ellis, 169
Aspinall-Oglander, Brig.-Gen. C. F., x, 3, 121, 137
Asquith, Lady Cynthia, 166
Asquith, Herbert, x, 10, 12, 13, 15, 17, 18, 21, 25, 27, 28, 30, 35, 36, 39, 40, 42, 43, 47, 48, 50, 52, 55, 58, 59, 64, 68, 69, 72, 73, 75, 78, 80, 81, 82, 87, 91, 93, 94, 98, 102, 104, 124, 125, 129, 130, 131, 132, 135, 138, 139, 140, 141, 143, 144, 146, 147, 148, 149, 150, 152, 153, 155, 157, 160, 161, 162, 163,
168, 172, 174, 176, 177, 180, 182, 183, 188
Asquith, Margot, 140, 167
Attlee, Clement, 101, 185, 186
Augagneur, Victor, 89, 95, 138
Australia, x, 42, 52, 107
Austria-Hungary, 36, 41, 76, 89, 115, 157, 163, 173, 181, 185

Bacon, Admiral Sir Reginald, 12, 66, 71, 142
Baghdad, 166
Balfour, Lord, 10, 16, 18, 79, 80, 85, 96, 116, 125, 131, 137, 146, 147, 148, 152, 166, 169, 172, 176, 183
Baltic Sea, 11, 12, 24, 72, 75, 97, 158, 182
Battenburg, Prince Louis of, 29, 30, 32, 39, 40, 42, 53, 62, 64, 65
Bean, C. E. W., x, 87, 165
Beatty, Admiral Sir David, 30, 32, 60, 61, 62, 63, 66, 94
Beaverbrook, Lord, xi, 172, 183
Belgium, 21, 22, 26, 54, 55, 57, 58, 59, 60, 71, 72, 82, 183
Beresford, Admiral Lord Charles, 13, 15, 18, 19, 30, 63
Birdwood, Lt.-Gen. Sir William, 107, 108, 111, 112, 118, 125, 169, 170
Black Sea, 6, 41, 67, 84, 106, 114
Blunt, Wilfred, 16, 19, 29
Board of Admiralty (and Sea Lords), 28, 29, 31, 62, 65, 80, 128, 129, 140, 145, 146, 147
Boer War, 10, 14, 20, 50, 51, 118, 121, 180
Bonham-Carter, Mark, xi
Borkum, 72, 75, 78, 92
Bosphorus, 6, 43, 45, 70, 84
Braithwaite, Maj.-Gen. W. P., 119, 161

233

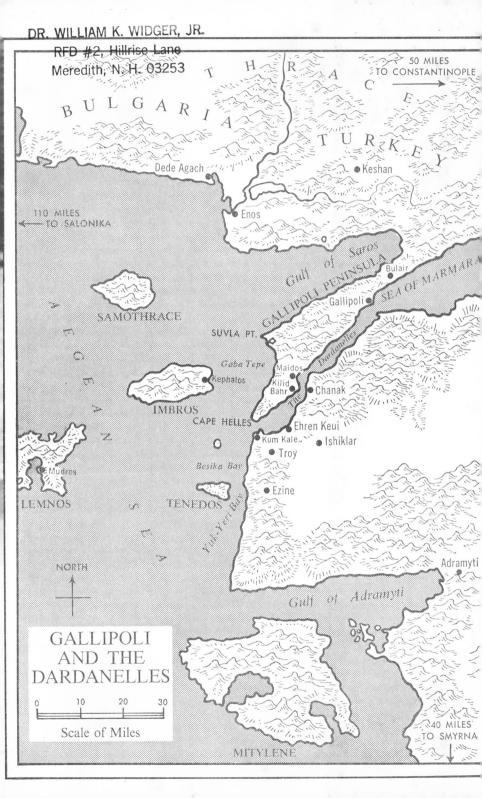

THRACE

BULGARIA

50 MILES
TO CONSTANTINOPLE

TURKEY

Dede Agach

Keshan

110 MILES
TO SALONIKA

Enos

Gulf of Saros

GALLIPOLI PENINSULA

Bulair

SEA OF MARMARA

SAMOTHRACE

Gallipoli

SUVLA PT.

Dardanelles

AEGEAN

Gaba Tepe

Maidos

Kephalos

Kilid
Bahr

Chanak

IMBROS

Tire

CAPE HELLES

Ehren Keui

Kum Kale

Ishiklar

SEA

Troy

Besika Bay

Ezine

Mudros

TENEDOS

Yuk-Yeri Bay

LEMNOS

Adramyti

NORTH

Gulf of Adramyti

GALLIPOLI
AND THE
DARDANELLES

0   10   20   30

Scale of Miles

40 MILES
TO SMYRNA

MITYLENE